Saving America, Chinese Style

By Xiaofeng "Frank" Li, Ph.D.

Dean,

This book is for you to enjoy & keep!

Frank Li
6/19/2013

Text copyright © 2012 Frank Li
All Rights Reserved

Some kind words from a fan ...

"I am 84 years old and I have been in the scale business since 1949. My tie with China goes way back to 1945, when I, serving in the U.S. Navy, stationed in China for a few months. It's amazing for me to see the changes in China in recent years. It's even more amazing for me to know Frank Li, a Chinese-American, who writes so well about American politics that I print out all his writings, save them in a folder, and read them over and over. What a modern-day Thomas Jefferson!"

--- Lee Offield, Pacific Scales (Clackamas, Oregon), December 2010

Book Review

"*Frank Li presents a different and interesting view of American politics. Having grown up in China exposed to communist politics, his writings are uniquely different from the political pundits spawned here in the USA. It is my opinion that Frank Li's writings are well worth reading – and taken to heart!*"

--- Walter Young, a 90-year-old senior citizen, having experienced the battlefields of WWII, a corporate CEO, a religious leader, and currently active as Chairman/CEO and Owner of Emery Winslow Scale (Seymour, CT)

"*Frank Li is the kind of immigrant this country needs more of. He is educated and he is an entrepreneur. He is making with his writing contributions to a sane society and that is sorely needed. No handouts for him; he EARNED it!*"

--- Fred Herrmann, Owner, Indiana Scale (Terra Haute, IN)

"*I am an avid reader of Frank Li's writings, posts, and publications. I agree with Frank's position on almost every issue and even if I don't, I can see his viewpoint. I have all the emails that Frank has sent me, so I can refer back to them to forward them to someone at the appropriate time. This book will just make everything easier. What a great book!*"

--- Jim Bradbury, President, Kanawha Scales & Systems (Charleston, WV)

"I have read all of Frank Li's writings and find him to be right on target. His suggestion of limiting the American Presidency to one six-year term may be the right place to start. Obama could have been doing a better job the last four years if not for his primary concern of getting re-elected. Frank Li has a unique perspective of the need for government reforms, which makes this book for great reading."

--- Jack L. Clark, President and CEO, Technical Weighing Services (Griffith, IN)

"Frank Li is a deep thinker and a true American patriot. He is always engaged and always finding ways to apply his life lessons to the America he loves. Agree or not, his idea will inspire you to deep thought about the critical issues facing our culture, nation and especially our evolving worldview."

--- Rob Woodward, VP and GM, Pennsylvania Scale (Lancaster, PA)

"I was Frank's Ph.D. supervisor at Vanderbilt University many years ago. It has been exciting to see him move through life, now providing commentary on political aspects of the world scene. I hope you will take a look at the book - a lot of good stuff!"

--- John Bourne, Ph.D. (Nashville, TN)

Acknowledgements

A book like this requires a lot of work, not only by the author, but also by many people around the author. I am deeply indebted to several individuals for this book.

First and foremost, I would like to thank Jon Stimpson, Owner and President of National Scale Technology. Jon was merely a customer initially. But he and I clicked shortly after I started writing about politics in 2008. He is now my best pen pal on earth! Jon proofread all my publications over the past two years, including this book, and often significantly enhanced them with his insights. Jon also wrote the prologue for this book! Jon, I really feel lucky to have you both as a customer and as a friend! You are a great scale man and you are truly a patriotic American! Yes, you built that - your own business!

Secondly, I would like to thank Lee Offield, a scale man at Pacific Scales (Clackamas, Oregon). What he wrote in the December 2010 issue of the Weighing and Measurement magazine was so flattering that I included it in the copyright page at the beginning of this book!

Special thanks go to the following individuals who reviewed the book in advance and provided comments in the Book Review right before this page:
1) Walter Young.
2) Fred Herrmann.
3) Jim Bradbury.
4) Jack L. Clark.
5) Rob Woodward.
6) Dr. John Bourne.

I would also like to thank all the scale men and women on my email list. You have not only helped me succeed in the scale industry with your purchase orders, but also helped me sharpen my vision and pen for my writings with your passionate comments from time to time.

I would like to thank John Lounsbury, the editor at GEI (Global Economic Intersection), and Steve Hansen, the publisher at GEI, for giving me a platform of publication in May 2011 and for making me a better writer over time.

I would like to thank my wife Rebecca for keeping me sane all the time. Thanks to my two sons, Dan and Ben, for helping me understand what life is all about, ultimately. This book is more for them, the next generation and beyond, than for my own generation.

Finally, a big 'thank you' to my late father Li Dexin (Chapter 75) for giving me the good genes and upbringing that define my interest in politics and in writing, although I am an electrical engineer by training (Chapter 74).

Prologue

By Jon Stimpson
Owner and President, National Scale Technology
(Huntsville, Alabama)

Troubled times require clear vision and tough choices. This book provides the clear vision and even the tough choices.

The U.S. has a big problem: years of spending more than we could afford have left us monumental debt, increasing daily. Worse yet, many welfare (also known as "means tested") programs instituted by our political leaders to obtain votes have given the populace a dependency on no effort, no cost (to them) lifestyles and they are clamoring for more. The so called "poor" in the U.S. live better than most kings throughout history and better than the middle class in most other countries today, with cars, air conditioning, cell phones, and even cable for their big screen TV's.

The demand for more government largesse is limitless and the years from 2008 to 2012 have added 35 million new beneficiaries to the ranks of welfare recipients, even as the number of workers who provide the money for the benefits declines.

No country can survive the onslaught of an additional 11% of its population receiving government benefits every four years, paid with borrowed money; yet the rate is increasing with presidential and congressional candidates clearly competing with promises of ever more gifts to the voters!

Where to begin to fix the problem and protect our future? "Saving America, Chinese Style" provides concise answers and even recommends solutions to save our fundamentally flawed system. The U.S. electorate has become like Pavlov's dog, salivating at the election bell and the continued promise of more treats from the treasury.

It is ironic that a naturalized U.S. citizen born in Communist China has the clarity of vision and common sense to address the issues and offer ideas for remedial change. Perhaps there is truth in the belief that people too close to a problem can't envision its cause or cure.

Many of the recipients of government welfare programs will not appreciate this book, nor will the candidates and politicians who pander to them for their votes. That is not to say that those of us who are able should not provide for those who can't provide for themselves. This book is addressed to those who won't provide for themselves. With over half of the U.S. population receiving welfare benefits, many are in the "won't" category.

It is apparent from the magnitude of our debt, the threat is existential. "When the tick gets bigger than the dog, they both die."

Introduction

America is deeply in trouble, with high unemployment and huge national debt often cited as the top two problems. But what is the root cause for these problems?

To me, here are the two root causes:
1) The rise of BRICS (Brazil, Russia, India, China, and South Africa), led by China, as economic competitors to America.
2) The incompetence of America's political system, especially when compared with China's.

Cause 1) was inevitable, but cause 2) was not. How, then, can we make America's political system more competitive? Introducing strict term-limits for the top political offices, with the American Presidency being one-term (e.g. six years), plus more!

Overall, I believe I have the most accurate diagnosis for America, as well as the best solution. To sell them, I have been writing and publishing my ideas for more than four years. Very significantly, I have met with several top politicians for discussion. The photo below shows one example.

Photo: former House Speaker Dennis Hastert, author & wife, and Chicago Mayor Richard Daley.

Most importantly, I have been a weekly columnist at GEI (Global Economic Intersection) since May 2011, elaborating my ideas from various angles to a wide variety of readers.

It's time to further expound on it by writing a book for one simple reason: the 2012 U.S. election is over, thus concluding my first phase of "saving America".

This book is composed of 80 of my published articles, logically organized into a coherent whole in 12 parts as follows:
1) America: diagnosis and solution
2) What is an ideal government?
3) America: an overview
4) China: an overview
5) Democracy
6) China: in some depth
7) America: in great depth and breadth
8) America and China
9) America's foreign policy
10) Six democracy-communism similarities
11) Famous quotes and interpretations
12) My personal life

Each part contains several chapters. Each chapter is an article previously published, with some [significant] re-writing to fit it in context. Some articles have their original publication dates attached, with the events at the time as the background.

Part 1 defines the goal of this book. It contains two chapters as the diagnosis and solution for America, respectively.

Part 2 goes beyond America. It contains two chapters, addressing two vast subjects: "towards an ideal form of government" and "built to last: structure and conscience," respectively.

The remaining 10 parts are supporting materials for Parts 1 and 2.

This paperback is different from its sister ebook in several ways as follows:
1) Most of the color images in the ebook have been removed.
2) Like the ebook, there is not a bibliography at the end of this book. Since all the references are available on-line, I kept them in the form of hyperlinks. A reader can easily find them with a simple Google search by the title.
3) As in the ebook, the table of contents appears right after this page, with the hyperlinks being removed, obviously.

Here is a quote: *"you cannot open a book without learning something."* Who said it? **Confucius**!

Here is an interpretation of the comments by the book reviewers: *"you cannot open a good book without learning a lot of good stuff!"*

Now, just sit back and enjoy the book …

Table of Contents

Book Review 3
Acknowledgements 5
Prologue 7
Introduction 9
Table of Contents 12
Part 1: America: Diagnosis & Solution   17
    Chapter 1: Diagnosis for America: Cancer! 18
    Chapter 2: Solution for America: Term-Limits and More 26
Part 2: What Is an Ideal Government?   34
    Chapter 3: Towards an Ideal Form of Government 35
    Chapter 4: Built to Last: Structure and Conscience 46
Part 3: America: An Overview   54
    Chapter 5: What is America, Anyway? 55
    Chapter 6: Top 10 American Misconceptions about America 60
Part 4: China: An Overview   65
    Chapter 7: What is China, Anyway? 66
    Chapter 8: Top 10 American Misconceptions about China 73
Part 5: Democracy   80
    Chapter 9: 10-Point Democracy Manifesto 81
    Chapter 10: The Answer Is Democracy; the Question Is Why 84
    Chapter 11: A Country Must Be Run Like a Business 90
    Chapter 12: People vs. Business 95
Part 6: China: in Some Depth   100
    Chapter 13: Tiananmen Square 101
    Chapter 14: It Is The Political System, Stupid! ...103
    Chapter 15: Chairman Mao Is Smiling 106

Chapter 16: America: What is China's Political System, Anyway?...........107
Chapter 17: It Is June 4, Again...........112
Part 7: America: in Great Depth and Breadth 115
Part 7.1: American Democracy 116
Chapter 18: Pyramid Theory I...........117
Chapter 19: Loop Theory - Capitalism vs. Socialism...........123
Chapter 20: American Democracy: What Went Wrong and When?...........127
Chapter 21: American Democracy: Massive Falsehoods at the Top...........136
Part 7.2: American Presidency 140
Chapter 22: American Presidency: Why Is One-Term a Must?...........141
Chapter 23: American Presidency: Raising the Minimum Age to 55!...........144
Chapter 24: From NBA, to American Idol, to American Presidency...........147
Chapter 25: American Presidency: Let's Redefine It, Now!...........152
Chapter 26: An Open Letter to Mitt Romney......156
Chapter 27: An Open Letter to President Obama 159
Chapter 28: George Washington vs. Mao Zedong 163
Chapter 29: Mitt Romney vs. Deng Xiaoping.....167
Chapter 30: American Presidents: Three Best and Three Worst...........171
Chapter 31: The Myth of the Bill Clinton Presidency 177
Chapter 32: Top 10 American Misconceptions about 10 Recent Presidents...........180
Chapter 33: Top 10 American Misconceptions about Mitt Romney...........186
Chapter 34: American Presidency: Is It A Joke? 190

Chapter 35: Another Open Letter to Mitt Romney 195

Part 7.3: American Politics 197
Chapter 36: Blagojevich and Pearl Harbor: They Are Related! 198
Chapter 37: Caught on Tape: President Obama and Rod Blagojevich 207

Part 7.4: America: The Good, the Bad, and the Ugly 210
Chapter 38: American Dreams vs. America 211
Chapter 39: from Public Schools to Government, What Is Wrong? 214
Chapter 40: It Is The Out-Of-Control Spending on Military, Stupid! 220
Chapter 41: The Congressional Super-Committee: What A Joke! 223
Chapter 42: American Airlines & America: What Do They Have in Common? 225
Chapter 43: Unemployment Rate: What Is It and Does It Really Matter? 228
Chapter 44: Public-Sector Unions: From Wisconsin to America 231
Chapter 45: Obese: to Be or Not to Be 234
Chapter 46: Four Points to Ponder on America's 236th Birthday 237
Chapter 47: American Dreams: Oversold and Overbought! 242
Chapter 48: America: 10 Big Questions and 10 Honest Answers 247

Part 8: America and China   253
Chapter 49: Political & Economic Lessons from China 254
Chapter 50: Hello from China to America 259
Chapter 51: Warren Buffett and Chairman Mao: Something in Common? 264

Chapter 52: Freedom of the Press in America and in China 268
Chapter 53: Karl Marx and John Keynes 274
Chapter 54: America: Let The Rich Run The Country Like China Does! 281

Part 9: America's Foreign Policy — 287
Chapter 55: What's The Real Cost of The Iraq War? 288
Chapter 56: Emerging Economies: An Overview from 30,000 Feet 291
Chapter 57: Pyramid Theory II 295
Chapter 58: American Autumn vs. Arab Spring .300
Chapter 59: America: What to Do with North Korea? 303
Chapter 60: U.S. Middle East Policy: What Is Wrong? 308
Chapter 61: Top 10 American Misconceptions about the World 311

Part 10: Six Democracy-Communism Similarities — 318
Chapter 62: Democracy-Communism Similarity #1: Destruction of Capitalism..................................319
Chapter 63: Democracy-Communism Similarity #2: Brainwashing..326
Chapter 64: Democracy-Communism Similarity #3: Ideology..336
Chapter 65: Democracy-Communism Similarity #4: Kleptocracy 342
Chapter 66: Democracy-Communism Similarity #5: 'You didn't build that'...347
Chapter 67: Democracy-Communism Similarity #6: Stupidity 352

Part 11: Famous Quotes and Interpretations — 359
Chapter 68: America: What Did Winston Churchill Mean? 360
Chapter 69: What Did Ronald Reagan Mean? 363
Chapter 70: What Abraham Lincoln Mean? 366

Chapter 71: What Did Thomas Jefferson Mean? 369
Chapter 72: What Did George Washington Mean? 372

Part 12: My Personal Life ... 374
Chapter 73: The Battle Hymn of the Tiger Dad .. 375
Chapter 74: My American Dream Has Come True 378
Chapter 75: My Father Li Dexin 384
Chapter 76: Parenting in America: 25 Years Back and 25 Years Ahead 389
Chapter 77: My 30-Year College Graduation Reunion 393
Chapter 78: Swimming, Olympics, and More 396
Chapter 79: Olympics and Economies 399
Chapter 80: October 6, 1982 406

Epilogue 409
About the Author 411

Part 1: America: Diagnosis & Solution

Chapter 1: Diagnosis for America: cancer!
Chapter 2: Solution for America: Term-limits and More

Chapter 1: Diagnosis for America: Cancer!

America is deeply in trouble, with high unemployment and huge national debt often cited as the top two problems. But what is the root cause for these problems?

To me, here are the two root causes:
1) The rise of BRICS (Brazil, Russia, India, China, and South Africa), led by China, as economic competitors to America.
2) The incompetence of America's political system, especially when compared with China's.

Specifically, here is what happened to America after WWII:
1) America thrived from 1946 to 2000 for one key reason: America was the economic monopoly in the world! America's competitors either destroyed themselves through WWII (e.g. Germany and Japan) or screwed themselves up badly after WWII by adopting a fundamentally flawed system called "communism" (e.g. China and the former Soviet Union). As a result, America was left as the only game in town, making and inventing virtually everything and naming its own prices. This not only got America out of the Great Depression finally, but also created unprecedented prosperity in America throughout the second half of the 20th century. "Made in the USA" was the default; "Fair trade" was not even a phrase in American English, just "free trade"!
2) While America's superb capitalism has been driving the economy, democracy, as we know it today, has been progressively driving America

deeper and deeper into socialism. We became victims of our own success! However, no big problems showed up before 2000, because America, as the economic monopoly, could afford anything and everything, including democracy!

3) The bottom fell out at the turn of the 21st century, when BRICS began to show their strength. The rise of BRICS not only signaled the end of America's economic monopoly (e.g. America started crying for "fair trade" and emphasizing "Made in the USA"), it also revealed the naked truth about American democracy: It does not work! As a matter of fact, democracy is failing in America today for the same reason as it failed in "democratic" Rome (and Greece) more than 2,000 years ago: debts!

The rise of BRICS was inevitable, but the incompetence of America's political system was not. Unfortunately, American politicians have been trying to fix everything but the political system, which has made a bad situation much worse. In other words, we have a cancer, but we have been treating it like anything but a cancer!

1. What is the cancer?

Today, most American politicians are career politicians, working for one purpose only: getting re-elected *ad nauseam,* even if it means destroying America by emptying her public treasury! In other words, they serve themselves first, their constituents a remote second, and their country dead last! It is an insidious cancer, killing America from within, slowly but surely …

2. How was the cancer developed?

Let's look at Congress ...

1) Before WWI, America's members of Congress were unpaid for their services. In other words, first they had to make it (i.e. becoming financially independent), then they served with honor for a few years, and finally they returned home after doing their duty to the country. Serving was never meant to be a way of life – not even to make a living, let alone a career!

2) After WWI, America's members of Congress voted themselves stipends to cover the cost of living in Washington. Still no pay for any assistants – they could bring in as many as they wanted, as they were on their own.

3) After WWII, America's members of Congress voted themselves full pay, plus great benefits (e.g. pensions), and added salaries for many assistants, thus paving the way for "career politicians." All hell broke loose after that! Since then, most of them have been serving for one purpose only: getting re-elected *ad nauseam*. In other words, it stopped being about us, or about the U.S. – it became all about them! It is an insidious cancer, killing America from within, slowly but surely ...

3. How has the cancer been killing America from within?

For most, if not all, politicians, the re-election campaign starts as soon as they are elected. How do they keep getting themselves re-elected? By any and all means! Two examples:

1) Recklessly robbing business by supporting special interest groups (e.g. unions)! Still wondering about high unemployment? Wonder not! Our cost structure is too high!

2) Blindly robbing the public treasury by introducing socialistic programs such as affordable housing and affordable healthcare, to such an extreme now that in many cases, you are better off on welfare than by working! Still wondering about the huge national debt? Wonder not! The money has been used to buy votes!

Neither was a huge problem though, thanks to our superb free enterprise system, until 2000, when BRICS, led by China, showed up as economic competitors …

4. A few words on China

I was born in China in 1959 and grew up in the horrible days of the Cultural Revolution. So I know what socialism is: it destroys any incentive of work in people, resulting in a country being dirt poor! For example, in China before 1980,
1) Economy: It was totally ruined because the working class took over the economy from the rich in 1949, without knowing what to do with it!
2) Housing: Yes, it was basically free, but most urban families ended up living in dorms.
3) Health-care: Yes, it was basically free, but it was low-tech and long waits.

Then what happened? Chairman Mao died in 1976. China changed, fundamentally and big, thanks to a wise man named Deng Xiaoping! China started embracing capitalism in 1978, and is now more capitalistic than America in many ways. Overall, the Chinese system (i.e. capitalism + autocracy), albeit with many endemic problems of its own, appears to be slightly better than the American system (i.e. capitalism + democracy), especially in terms of running a country like a business. In fact, today's Chinese government is more pro-business than today's American government, even per Steve Wynn!

5. Our responses to the competition from China?

Complaints only! Worse yet, some American politicians have simply resorted to China bashing (e.g. currency), as they did to Japan in the 1980s. Here is a big problem though: It will not work this time! Four main reasons:
1) Unlike Japan and Germany, China has both the size and weight to fully compete with the U.S.
2) Unlike Japan and Germany, China is not a post-WWII U.S. "colony".
3) Like Japan, Germany, and even the U.S., China has been building its initial wealth through exports.
4) Like the U.S. in its early days, China has the potential for huge domestic consumption. China has been striving, and succeeding, in creating a domestic market fueled by its newfound wealth. For example, in 2011, more cars were sold in China than in the U.S.!

6. America's self-destruction

America has been self-destructing in two major ways:
1) By the extreme left: The politicians on this side keep driving America deeper and deeper into democratic socialism, with public-sector unions being the worst example. Spending and debts!

2) By the extreme right: The politicians on this side keep driving America deeper and deeper into democratic imperialism, with the Iraq War being the worst example. War and debts!

In short, it's the political system, stupid!

7. Is our political system really so bad?

Yes, it is! Because of this getting re-elected *ad nauseam* thing, the ugliness of our presidential re-election seemed to have seeped into the two wars in Iraq and Afghanistan.

1) President George W. Bush recklessly turned off the beacon to launch the Iraq War in 2003, at least partially, for the sake of his re-election. For more, read Chapter 55 ("What's the real cost of the Iraq War?").
2) President Obama chose to escalate the war in Afghanistan in 2011 (acceptable), but with a troop withdrawal plan so ridiculously hasty that there could have been only one possible explanation: it was perfectly timed for his re-election (totally unacceptable)! For more, read: For Obama the Road to Reelection Runs through Kabul.

So here are two serious questions:
1) Is our President, throughout his first-term, for nothing but his own re-election, with everything else being secondary?
2) If the answer is yes, which seems patently obvious, we cannot ever expect the President to always do the right thing for the country (vs. for himself) throughout his first-term, can we?

Fortunately for America, the Presidency is limited to two terms. For Congress, it's infinitely worse, because of the lack of term-limits! In other words, we cannot ever expect our members of Congress to always do the right thing for the country (vs. for themselves), as long as they are running for re-election!

Need a more concrete example to show what's profoundly wrong with American democracy? Here you go: voting vs. drinking.
1) Age 18-20: Too young to drink, but old enough to vote!
2) Age 18-20: Show ID to drink, but no ID is needed to vote!

For those who get it, no explanation is necessary. For those who don't, no explanation is possible!

8. What will happen if we stay the course?
We will become a second-class citizen in the world! To win (i.e. to be #1), what you think or do does not matter - you must actually be better than your competitor(s)!

Specifically, here are two projections if we stay the course:
1) By 2013, China will surpass us as the largest manufacturer on earth.
2) By 2030 (or sooner), China will overtake us as the largest economy on earth, thus ending America's leadership, not only economically, but also politically.

Frightened? Then change!

9. Is democracy doomed?
Yes, most likely! Any doubt? Read this classic piece: The Truth about Tytler. Here is an excerpt:

> *"A democracy cannot exist as a permanent form of government. It can only exist until the voters discover that they can vote themselves largesse from the public treasury. From that moment on,*

the majority always votes for the candidates promising the most benefits from the public treasury with the result that a democracy always collapses over loose fiscal policy, always followed by a dictatorship. The average age of the world's greatest civilizations has been 200 years."

"Great nations rise and fall. The people go from bondage to spiritual truth, to great courage, from courage to liberty, from liberty to abundance, from abundance to selfishness, from selfishness to complacency, from complacency to apathy, from apathy to dependence, from dependence back again to bondage."

Frightened? Then change!

10. What did the founding fathers think, really?

"Remember, democracy never lasts long. It soon wastes, exhausts, and murders itself. There never was a democracy yet that did not commit suicide."

--- John Adams

"A democracy is nothing more than mob rule, where fifty-one-percent of the people may take away the rights of the other forty-nine."

--- Thomas Jefferson

Frightened? Then change!

11. Closing

The diagnosis is cancer: getting re-elected *ad nauseam*! What's the cure? Stop the career politicians! For a complete solution, go to the next chapter ...

Chapter 2: Solution for America: Term-Limits and More

I believe I have the most accurate diagnosis for America, as well as the best solution. In Chapter 1, I presented my diagnosis. In this chapter, I will present the solution. But first, let me briefly defend my diagnosis.

1. In defense of my diagnosis
Here are two main arguments against my diagnosis:
1) Our political system is fine. We just need to elect the right people.
2) Our biggest problem is excessive spending. If we can just stop that, we will be fine.

Let's dispel these two arguments.

1.1 Why can't we just elect the right people?
Most people we elect are "right." It's the system that turns them "wrong"! Here is an extreme example: Senator Obama voted against raising the debt ceiling to $9T in 2006, which he labeled "unpatriotic". But under President Obama, our national debt has ballooned to over $16T!

1.2 Can't we just stop excessive spending?
No, we can't - it's inherent to our system, regardless of the party in charge! Simply put, the Democrats are for "tax & spend", while the Republicans are "strong on defense", which means "wars, borrow & spend". As a result, we are $16T in debt, and rising rapidly!

2. My solution
Constitutional changes! Specifically, here are three major changes absolutely necessary:

1) Limiting the American Presidency to one-term (e.g. six years). America can simply no longer afford to have a President who, throughout his first term, works solely towards his own re-election!
2) Raising the statutory requirements for the American Presidency, such as the minimum age to 55 and only after having served as a state governor for one full-term, at least. America can simply no longer afford to have a President who is inadequately prepared for the top job in America!
3) Introducing strict term-limits for Congress, preferably one-term (e.g. six years) as well. America can simply no longer afford to have Americans keep sending career politicians back to Congress as their representatives, who, as a whole, have garnered an approval rate of only 13%.

2.1 The first principle

"The business of America is business."

--- Calvin Coolidge

2.2 Two assumptions
1) A country must be run like a business, just like a family, or it will go bankrupt.
2) It's simply nonsense to argue that America is not like a business or family, because the U.S. government can always print money. Printing money can be very damaging, not the least of which is rampant inflation! More on this later.

Because there is little pure democracy in a well-run business or family, there should be little pure democracy in a well-run country! Now, you might argue why democracy worked for us before? Democracy seemed to have worked for us until recently because we, as the richest nation on earth, could afford it. While we enjoyed all kinds of "luxury" (e.g. entitlements and various missions to save the world), the rest of the world figured out their own ways of success, with Japan shaking us first in the 1980s and now China.

Still unconvinced? Just recall what happened to America's auto industry: It had its own monopoly for many years until better competition from Japan showed up. Soon America's auto industry was driven to bankruptcy! The same applies to the political systems: China's political system appears to be slightly better than America's. China, unlike Japan, has both the size and weight to truly compete with America.

In a competitive world today, all that a hiker needs to do, when chased by a hungry grizzly, is to run a bit faster than the other hiker!

2.3 Three propositions

1) Do not hate our competitors because they are better - just be better ourselves! Oh, do other people on earth have the same rights to "life, liberty and the pursuit of happiness" as Americans do? I assume your answer is "yes".
2) Do not hate China. It took China a long time (yes, centuries) to discover its own route to success, and it finally did - good for the Chinese!
3) Recognize that our political system, largely unchanged over the past 200 years, is obsolete. It's time to have it updated, if not over-hauled. No doubt, our founding fathers were smart men. But no human being could have been so foresighted as to see more than 200 years ahead!

2.4 More details on the solution

We need to introduce some elements of autocracy into our democracy, which means to run our country like a gigantic company, with a structure as follows:
1) The President runs the daily show.
2) The board of directors (or Senate) oversees the directions.
3) The shareholders (or House of Representatives) revolt only after some grave mistakes are made.

It should be better than China's system, with fairer representations, because of our long history of democracy.

Specifically, here are 10-point details:
1) Setting term-limits for the top elected offices:
   - President: One term (e.g. six years), firm!
   - Senator: Six years per term. One term, preferably.
   - House of Representatives: Six years per term. One term, preferably.
2) Raising the statutory requirements for the Presidency, such as the minimum age of 55 and having served as a state governor for one full-term, at least.
3) Abolishing the Electoral College! Just count votes, instead!
4) Spending must be controlled!
   - Limiting spending to a certain percentage of the GDP (e.g. 15%).
   - The budget must be balanced. If there is potential of growth, some deficit is allowed. However, always figure out how to pay for it first before introducing any new big spending program.

- Cutting the defense spending drastically. If not, we will soon have no country left to defend!
5) Minimizing the government, with the understanding that government does not create real jobs in quantity. The private sector does!
6) Dissolving all public-sector unions immediately and banning them forever, with an executive order to undo President Kennedy's Executive Order 10988.
7) Reforming Social Security and Medicare. Abolishing all entitlement programs (e.g. Medicaid) and replacing them with a minimal welfare system. Bottom line: No one should be better off on welfare than they are by working! To be more specific, the welfare benefit must not exceed half of the minimum wage!
8) Simplifying everything, from laws to the tax code, so as to reduce the number of lawyers and accountants. Most importantly, you don't have to be a lawyer to run for office.
9) Yes, a voter ID is a must, just like driving or drinking!
10) Raising the minimum voting age to 21, so that voting is at least as important as drinking!

3. In defense of my solution

Here are two main arguments against my solution:
1) Term-limits for Congress? It's already there – just stop electing the incumbents if you don't like them!
2) Debts? What debts? The U.S. government can print money, any time it wants and for as much as it wants.

Let's dispel these two arguments.

3.1 Term-limits for Congress

We must have explicit term-limits for Congress! Here is the cruel reality: aside from serving for themselves because of this "getting re-elected *ad nauseam*" thing, the incumbents have so many advantages over challengers that most of them keep getting re-elected. More worrisome, most Americans like their own members of Congress, because they bring "pork" back. What's pork? It's often a "steal" from the public treasury!

Here is a valid argument: it takes a newly elected member of Congress quite some time to learn the job. Here is the solution:
1) Abolishing all the committees in Congress! Let the executive branch run the country!
2) Simplifying our system, from laws to the tax code, so that you do not have to be a lawyer to serve.
3) Prolonging the term for House from two years currently to six years, for example.

3.2 Printing money

It's true that the U.S. government can print money and has been printing money in large quantity, because the U.S. dollar is "fiat money."

However, anybody who thinks printing money is a real solution must be insane. Domestically, printing money means money devaluation, which has a lot of implications, not the least of which is rampant inflation. Internationally, it could be even more terrible. For example, the Chinese know what fiat money is, as they invented it more than 1,000 years ago. They will therefore do everything possible to protect their "foreign investments". Specifically, here are three projections:

1) By 2014, China will surpass the U.S. as the largest importer on earth, on top of the fact that China is already the largest exporter. China will soon be able to dictate that trading with them be done in China's RMB, instead of the US dollar.
2) By 2016, RMB will practically, if not officially, become an alternative reserve currency to the US dollar. It may even replace the US dollar as the world's reserve currency!
3) By 2020, we will have printed so much money that few major economies will buy U.S. treasury bills any more. We may have to accept RMB from China in order to sell them some Boeing 787s and use RMB to buy goods from China. As a result, everything in Wal-Mart will be 10 times more expensive!

For a recent development, read: Is the Yuan About to Replace the Dollar as the World's Reserve Currency?

4. One big note about democracy

Democracy is not new. It was practiced by Rome and Greece more than 2,000 years ago. Both failed for the same reason: debts! Both were replaced by dictatorship. Will that be the fate for the western democracy today? Yes, very likely!

5. Closing

Human legacy includes a history of leadership changing hands. Rome, Egypt, China, and Britain all had their day in the sun. We, the USA, are having our own now. But our days are clearly numbered, if we keep sleeping on our 200-year-old political system and keep resisting changes. Or we can change, fundamentally and big. China did it. Why can't we?

Winston Churchill once said: *"democracy is the worst form of government except all the others that have been tried."*

Now, China appears to have a newer and better system. Let's get better, too.

Adapt and change!

Part 2: What Is an Ideal Government?

Chapter 3: Towards an Ideal Form of Government
Chapter 4: Built to Last: Structure and Conscience

Chapter 3: Towards an Ideal Form of Government

The world is in crisis! Europe has been turning out financial crises, country by country, over the past few years, non-stop. America is in no better shape, either financially or politically. In the Middle East and North Africa, the Arab Spring has resulted in several regime changes. In China, there are more and more protests against anything and everything ...

Is this the end of the world? Yes, this is the end of the old world, which is beginning anew. Therefore, there is no better time than now to discuss this profound subject: What is an ideal form of government and how to get there from here, as shown below in Figure 1?

This is a major break-away from traditional thinking, such as "*democracy as the universal form of human government*". For more, read the march of democracy and China: big changes coming soon.

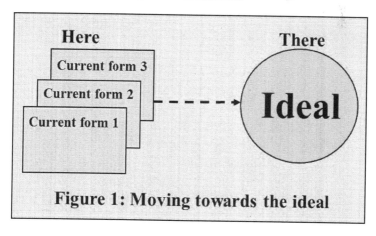

Figure 1: Moving towards the ideal

1. Definition: what is an ideal form of government?

To me, an ideal form of government can be defined by two key criteria as follows:
1) Individual freedom: the government must ensure maximum freedom for its citizens, including the right to choose their own leaders via free elections.
2) Government responsibility & accountability: the government must be responsible for what it does and be held accountable. What, then, should the government do? Do those things that are beyond the private sector! Three examples:
   - Embracing and maintaining capitalism. Capitalism has proven to be the only means to prosperity - no capitalism, no prosperity!
   - Defending the country while avoiding unnecessary wars.
   - Undertaking mega projects (e.g. highways and bridges).

2. Where are we today?

Today, there are chiefly three forms of government as follows:
1) Monarchy: It is *"a form of government in which the office of head of state is usually held until death or abdication and is often hereditary and includes a royal house"* (per Wikipedia). What about a dictatorship? A dictator with a family member in succession is essentially a king. Two examples: Saudi Arabia and North Korea.
2) Democracy: It is *"generally defined as a form of government in which all adult citizens have an equal say in the decisions that affect their lives"* (per Wikipedia). Two examples: Greece (nearly in bankruptcy) and the U.S. (advancing toward bankruptcy).

3) Autocracy: In this form of government, there is neither a king (as in a monarchy) nor any free election for people to choose their leaders (as in a democracy). Instead, a team of people chooses the next leaders for the country and they *"often take the form of collective presidencies"* (per Wikipedia). This form of government is also called "a dictatorship without a dictator" or "state capitalism." The one and only example: China.

Next, let's examine these three forms one by one.

2.1 Monarchy

This form of government represents the past. It has two characteristics as follows:
1) Individual freedom: People are not very free, and hence are not very empowered. As a result, this system just can't seem to advance from feudalism to capitalism, which means no prosperity. A free election? Forget about it!
2) Government responsibility & accountability: There is no doubt who is in charge: The king! Better yet, the king promotes permanency, with one supreme goal: passing the kingdom to his designated son (or daughter). A big problem is that the successor is often not as good as the king. As a result, a dynasty typically lasts for several generations only. Any doubt? Look at China's history over the past 2,000 years!

2.2 Democracy

This form of government represents the present. It has two characteristics as follows:
1) Individual freedom: People are free, and they elect their own leaders.

2) Government responsibility & accountability: It is becoming increasingly clear that democracy, as we know it today, will not last for two main reasons:
   - Everything is in short-terms, for the next election only. Nothing is in long-terms, let alone of permanency.
   - The government is neither responsible (e.g. it spends only, out of control) nor accountable (e.g. the Iraq War, for which no one in America has been held accountable). As a result, the entire West is now on the verge of bankruptcy. Several European countries are already there, with more to follow, including America!

2.3 Autocracy

This form of government is newer than democracy and appears to be the best available for now. China has it, with two characteristics as follows:
1) Individual freedom: People are relatively free, without the right, yet, to choose their own leaders though.
2) Government responsibility & accountability: The government is relatively responsible and accountable. Two examples.
   - After 1976, the government started embracing capitalism big time, which has brought prosperity to China on such a massive scale in such a short time span that it was simply unprecedented in human history!
   - The recent Chinese leaders have proven to be far more competent than many other world leaders, particularly Presidents George W. Bush and Barack Obama. Leadership matters!

Let me emphasize: In a competitive world today, all that a hiker needs to do, when chased by a hungry grizzly, is to run a bit faster than the other hiker!

In my humble opinion, China's political system is, overall, slightly better than America's. This is the key reason behind the rise of China and the decline of America (and the entire West) over the past two decades, with no end in sight!

2.4 Summary

Figure 2 illustrates, qualitatively, where the three forms of government stand with regard to "individual freedom" and "government responsibility & accountability": monarchy and democracy are at the two extreme ends, while autocracy is in the middle, with "balance." A big question is this: how to reach the ideal from here?

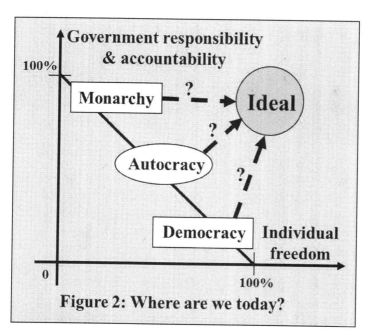

Figure 2: Where are we today?

3. How to get there from here?

Now, let's discuss how to reach the ideal in all three forms, one by one.

3.1 Monarchy

It has no future, either in theory as it does not represent the people, or in practice as most countries under monarchy are abjectly poor. However, revolutions (e.g. the Arab Spring) are unlikely to be the best solution. Two examples:

1) France: Here is what the French did via the French Revolution (1789–1799): *"A republic was proclaimed in September 1792 and King Louis XVI was executed the next year"* (per Wikipedia). Wasn't Libya's dictator Muammar Gaddafi executed recently? Do the Libyans want to go back 200 years to follow the footsteps of the French? Even if yes, it's unlikely to have an equally good result, because France already had some significant capitalism by then, but Libya has little today. The same analogy applies to Iraq – just replacing Muammar Gaddafi with Saddam Hussein!

2) China: China had several revolutions over the past 200 years. None of them changed anything in essence: China remained poor and weak until recently after it embraced capitalism.

Let me emphasize: there is not a single precedent of a third world country achieving prosperity via democracy. The key to prosperity is capitalism, not democracy!

What a monarchy country needs is a king like China's Deng Xiaoping. Deng was a dictator; not all dictators are bad for their countries! Deng used his power wisely for the good of the country: He laid the monumental groundwork for China, not only economically (i.e. capitalism), but also politically (i.e. a dictatorship without a dictator), which led to China's huge success today!

Personally, while I never had any hope for the old guards like Hosni Mubarak or Muammar Gaddafi, I think Syria's Bashar al-Assad had the potential of being a good reformer. But the protesters might have disrupted his plan. For your information, the Chinese protesters in 1989 briefly disrupted Deng's plan, too. Fortunately for China, Deng eventually prevailed. For more, read Chapter 13 ("Tiananmen Square").

3.2 Autocracy

China arrived at its current form of government for two main reasons:
1) The struggles over the past 200 years, at least. Give Mao Zedong credit for unifying China in 1949, although he ruined China's economy and caused the deaths of millions from 1949 to 1976.
2) By accident! Mao's only able son, Mao Anying, was killed in the Korean War, thanks to the West ('Amen'). Otherwise, today's China, under Mao Jr. or Mao III, could be just as bad as today's North Korea, which is the worst on earth!

Although China's political system appears to be the best available for now, it's fundamentally flawed in at least one critical aspect: who are these seven individuals in the Standing Committee of the CPC (Communist Party of China) Politburo?

As a matter of fact, these seven individuals are not even legitimate by the western standards, because they are not elected by the people! However, let's get out of the trap of western ideology and think basically and rationally: changing from a dictator (Mao) to "a dictatorship without a dictator" (after Mao) was monumental progress not only in Chinese history, but also in human history: a new form of government was born! Better (or worse, depending on your viewpoint) yet, this Chinese system has been succeeding over the western system of democracy for the past two decades, at least, with no end in sight!

As China changed its leadership in November 2012, its new leaders now face a huge challenge: how to further transform China's political system into a form that is progressively more and more truly of/by/for the people? Two notes:
1) This issue must be resolved for China's success to be long term. The only way to do it is via democracy: let people choose their own leaders! However ...
2) The new democracy in China must not be like the democracy in the U.S. today!

Leadership matters! The smooth ride set out by Deng will be over soon. A new greatness must appear for the next China!

3.3 Democracy

Democracy, as we know it today, does not work! Why did it "suddenly" stop working? Because of the rise of BRICS, led by China, and the incompetence of America's political system, or more generally, of the entire western system of democracy! Any doubt? Just look at this simple fact: China is now the largest foreign debt holder of both America and Europe. Did anyone envision this merely one decade ago?

More profoundly, democracy looks more and more like communism as a short-term fad. What a huge statement! How does democracy look like communism? Jump to Part 10 ("Six democracy-communism similarities") if you can't wait! Here, let's just focus on the fad part, with two points of explanation:
1) Evolution: Democracy has proven to be totally unable to adapt (e.g. it spends only; no big cut is ever possible). It is thus doomed, according to Darwin's proven theory of evolution.
2) History: Here is an excerpt from a classic piece (The Truth about Tytler):

> *A democracy cannot exist as a permanent form of government. It can only exist until the voters discover that they can vote themselves largesse from the public treasury. From that moment on, the majority always votes for the candidates promising the most benefits from the public treasury with the result that a democracy always collapses over loose fiscal policy, always followed by a dictatorship. The average age of the world's greatest civilizations has been 200 years.*

Is America's time up now, since we are already more than 200 years old? No, not yet! Before we give up on America, let's use reason and try three major changes as follows:
1) Limiting the American Presidency to one-term (e.g. six years). That way, it's more likely that we will end up with a President we can trust. The President would be there, as from the first day, truly for the country, instead of for himself (i.e. for re-election specifically). In other words, there will be no more pandering or raiding the public

treasury just for votes. Most importantly, there would be no more pretending to be governing but actually running for re-election all the time. Just serve with your heart and brain, and hopefully leave with a good and lasting legacy.

2) Raising the statutory requirements for the American Presidency, such as the minimum age to 55 and only after having served as a state governor for one full-term, at least. That way, it's more likely that we will end up with a capable President who knows what he is doing. Very importantly, a President must be able to match up, in substance, with any world leader, particularly the Chinese right now.

3) Introducing strict term-limits for Congress, preferably one-term of six years as well. That way, it's more likely that we will end up with many good and accomplished people serving in Congress, instead of career politicians who are good at nothing but running for office, to such an extreme now that they are bankrupting America by emptying her public treasury in their relentless quest for votes!

Like China today, a new greatness must appear for the next America! In other words, America is desperately in need of a great President to turn things around! How great? A combination of George Washington, Thomas Jefferson, Abraham Lincoln, and Ronald Reagan! For more, go to Part 7.2 ("American Presidency").

3.4 Summary

Figure 3 illustrates, qualitatively, how to get there from here: it's a two-way race between autocracy and democracy, with monarchy out.

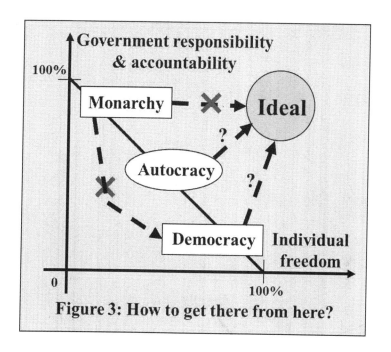

Figure 3: How to get there from here?

4. Bottom line

The political system does not matter, as long as it embraces capitalism!

5. Closing

The 20th century was clearly America's. The 21st century belongs to either China or America for sure. But which one is going to come out on top? It depends on who can adapt and change faster and better!

Over time, China needs democracy, but not the kind in the U.S. today. America urgently needs a new democracy by incorporating some elements of autocracy, but not necessarily the kind in China today. Why urgently? Because America is quickly heading toward bankruptcy, if we stay the course!

Chapter 4: Built to Last: Structure and Conscience

"If you think in terms of a year, plant a seed; if in terms of ten years, plant trees; if in terms of 100 years, teach the people"
--- Confucius, 500BC

A big challenge in life is durability, or "built to last", be it for your personal life (e.g. marriage), for your business (e.g. Built to Last: Successful Habits of Visionary Companies), or for your country (Chapter 11: "A country must be run like a business").

In this chapter, I will present a theory that simplifies "built to last" to only two keys: (1) getting the structure right and (2) having conscience. I will use three examples to support my theory: swim teams, the American scale industry, and America.

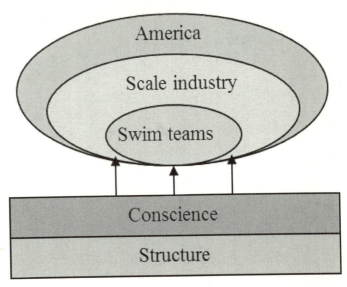

1. Built to last: a theory

Life is complicated. But some people are just more successful than others, be it in their personal life or in business. Why is that? Well, aside from the DNA (the older I become, the more I believe in genes), I think it all comes down to these two keys:

1) Getting the structure right. By "structure", I mean all the basics. For example, you can't expect a lasting marriage if you marry someone radically different from you, or if you do not understand the fundamental differences between men and women (e.g. a man rarely changes, but a woman continually changes).

2) Having conscience. It means you always try to do the right thing, which sometimes can be very difficult. For example, a successful marriage often means a lot of compromise and hard work on both sides for the sake of remaining together.

The same two keys apply to a business. Here the DNA means such things as a company's culture. The best example of a company built to last is GE, because it has got both the structure and conscience right, for the most part, at least.

The same two keys apply to a country. Here the DNA means a country's culture and, very importantly, the availability of natural resources. The best example of a country built to last, in recent human history, is America. But America's days seem to be numbered now. Why? America has been sleeping on the same political system for too long, resulting in an out-of-date structure and a total lack of conscience in its politicians!

2. Example 1: swim teams

I have two children, born in 1987 and 1989, respectively. I had them try several sports until 1997, when I, as a tiger dad (Chapter 73: "The Battle Hymn of The Tiger Dad"), "helped" them choose competitive swimming as their sport and enrolled them in a local YMCA swim team (called "NAPY" - Naperville YMCA). Both of them excelled and I was a happy father. Then a bad thing happened in May 1998: YMCA threw NAPY out! It turned out that NAPY was not a YMCA team *per se*. Rather, it was a team run by a parent board in conjunction with YMCA. YMCA had enough with the parent board and threw NAPY out!

The parent board struggled to form a new team, with pool times from various local facilities. It was the first time for me, a naturalized U.S. citizen from China, to experience American democracy up close. Man, it was ugly! In fact, it was so ugly that it was the first time I started having doubts about democracy. Specifically,
1) Most of the board members were in it for themselves (acceptable), but some acted without conscience (unacceptable): It was all about the best for "my kids", and for as long as they benefited, with everything else (e.g. team's longevity) being secondary.
2) Most board members played politics for control, using democracy selectively to their advantages, to such an extreme that the team's financials weren't even published to avoid "unnecessary controversies."

The good news is that a team called NAPV (Naperville Swim Team) was formed and it excelled, including winning a few age-group Illinois state championships (with this Li family earning more points than any other family)! The bad news is that NAPV existed only for about six years, because it was not built to last beyond one generation of swimmers, namely, the generation whose parents controlled the board at the beginning! If the ultimate criterion to judge the success of an organization is built to last, NAPV failed. What was wrong? Lack of conscience on the parent board!

In Chicagoland, there are only two swim teams that have proven to be built to last with sustainable glories (i.e. winning state championships for multiple generations of swimmers). What is so special about them?

1) Team 1 (in the west) is owned by an individual. It's a dictatorship. Team management is simple and straightforward - my way or no way: "If you don't like my way, leave," with parents having absolutely nothing to say about the running of the team! The team succeeded. The best swimmers in the area joined it, and the team succeeded more.

2) Team 2 (in the north) is owned by a parent board. Like NAPV, it's a democracy. Unlike NAPV, Team 2's parent board has conscience: They built the team with a good structure and they act conscientiously, which means to do the right thing not only for the small (i.e. the current members of the team), but also for the large (i.e. team, community, and future), in both short and long terms.

3. Example 2: the American scale industry

The American scale industry is estimated to be a $1B/year business. Like many other industries, it has been negatively impacted by globalization. However, we, the American scale industry, bear some serious responsibilities for losing the sales and manufacturing to

China. Let's focus on one issue here: a national organization that brings the American scale industry together.

No, there is no such an organization! Currently, there are at least four "national" organizations in America for the scale industry. They are:
1) ISWM: International Society of Weighing & Measurement.
2) SMA: Scale Manufacturers Association.
3) NISA: National Industrial Scale Association.
4) NCWM: National Conference on Weights and Measures.

They each act on their own, but together they undermine the American scale industry, including working against each other, especially on the fundamental issue of regulation vs. free-market. As a result, here are two simple facts:
1) All three private organizations are dying, due to declining membership.
2) The most active one is NCWM, a pseudo-government organization, for regulations.

I believe this is a snapshot of America: There are more and more takers than makers! Read: Government Employees and Manufacturing Jobs: Takers and Makers. Here is an excerpt: *"More Americans work for the government than work in construction, farming, fishing, manufacturing, mining, and utilities combined."*

In contrast, the Chinese scale industry is thriving. At the national level, it's simple and straightforward, with one organization (CWIA) representing everybody (i.e. manufacturers, dealers, and end-users), and with the government playing a minimum role in regulation.

How to change the American scale industry at the national level? We must have a right structure, which means to have one organization representing all (just like the Chinese do), and we must act with conscience, which means to do the right thing for America, not just for your own organization (yes, it's nice to be king). Specifically, the three private organizations must merge for one simple reason: there is room for only one! NCWM must realize that, at this time at least, the more it tries to regulate, the more it will hurt the American scale industry, because it has been over-regulated already, especially when compared with China!

Here is a quote: *"That government is best which governs least."*

Who said it? **Thomas Jefferson**!

4. Example 3: America's political system

America has good DNA (Chapter 5: "What is America, Anyway?"): our founding fathers left us with a good foundation. Very importantly, our land is replete with natural resources, which allowed us to screw up a lot more than many other nations (e.g. India). But still there is a limit to it and we are reaching that limit now!

I have already published a lot on this subject. Here is the bottom line:
1) Structure: we must get it right first. One key is to have term-limits, starting with one-term (e.g. six years) for the American Presidency!
2) Conscience: We may have all the laws on earth, but some people will find a way to beat the system. Therefore, it's critical that we elect the right people in the first place, namely, people with demonstrated accomplishments and people with

conscience. There is no bulletproof way to do it, but minimally we must raise the statutory requirements for the American Presidency, such as the minimum age to 55 (from 35) and only after having served as a state governor for one full-term, at least.

Still wondering why America is so deeply in trouble? Wonder not! Most of our politicians serve themselves first, their constituents a remote second, and their country dead last, thanks to this "getting re-elected *ad nauseam*" thing! How long do you think America, or any country, can last when it's structured like that, with its politicians totally out of conscience?

5. Discussion
What is the relationship among the three examples? Example 1 shows how democracy works in the small, with conscience being the key. Examples 2 and 3 are much bigger in size. Neither the American scale industry nor America had a big problem until China showed up as a competitor. Now, both are deeply in trouble, because of an inferior structure and because of the lack of leadership and conscience in their leaders!

Conscience, according to Wikipedia is "an aptitude, faculty, intuition or judgment of the intellect that distinguishes right from wrong." It's inherent to most of us as human beings. Any doubt? Read these three stories:
1) <u>Elderly Man Returns Cash Stolen from Sears in '40s</u>. Here is an excerpt:

> *"The man's conscience has been bothering him for the past 60 years."*

2) <u>Fatal hit-and-run suspect in custody</u>. Here is an excerpt:

> *"Nearly four years after a 20-year-old Joliet woman was killed in a hit-and-run accident, a Naperville man knocked on the woman's sister's door and admitted he was the driver."*

3) <u>Justice Roberts Inside Beltway: Did He Forget What's Outsides?</u> Here is an excerpt:

> *"Chief Justice John Roberts need fear no such fate because he has lifetime tenure on the Supreme Court. But conscience can be a more implacable and inescapable punisher — and should be."*

Bottom line: Always try to do the right thing, not just for yourself, but also for others!

6. Closing

Nothing is built to last, if we can't get the structure right first and if we don't always act conscientiously for the whole!

Here is a quote: *"Labor to keep alive in your breast that little spark of celestial fire, called conscience."*

Who said it? **George Washington**!

Part 3: America: An Overview

Chapter 5: What is America, Anyway?
Chapter 6: Top 10 American Misconceptions about America

Chapter 5: What is America, Anyway?

1. How was the country formed?

The bottom line version: many "disgruntled" Europeans sailed to this land, occupied it by any means, including killing many natives whom they wrongly labeled "Indians", and finally formed their own country, which is now known as "the United States of America."

If you are an idealist (e.g. a true human rights activist or a real democracy proponent) and if you are an American, you must denounce your American citizenship first before passionately pursuing your cause. Why? Because America, as a country, is totally illegitimate - America was built on occupied land appropriated from its rightful owners, the American Indians.

I am not an idealist. So I accept America as it is, with one critical condition: America will be forthright with other nations (e.g. China, Syria, and Iran) on such issues as human rights and free elections - Let them work these complex issues out by themselves, over time! For more, read Chapter 63 ("Brainwashing").

2. What was America built on?

America, as a country, has two corner stones: *capitalism* and *democracy*:

1) *Capitalism*: American capitalism was solidly built on rugged individualism, with two key characteristics as follows:
   - Freedom: "I can make it, as this is the land of opportunity." Three examples of successful individuals: Thomas Edison, Henry Ford, and Steve Jobs.

- Future: "Even if I must struggle, my children will be better off." Speaking from my own experience, I know this is the reason many immigrants came to America. I believe my two sons (read Part 12), grown up in America, are able to take advantage of the best opportunities in the world!
2) *Democracy*: American democracy was solidly built on two key documents: the Declaration of Independence and the US Constitution, provided for us by the founding fathers!

Additionally, and very significantly, America was built on a huge geographic area that was not only rich (i.e. basically un-farmed), but also replete with natural resources (e.g. coal and oil). The same thing can be said about America's two sister countries: Canada and Australia. But neither of them is close to being a beacon like America, largely because America became independent from the British much earlier!

It's freedom, stupid!

3. How did America do over its first 225 years (1776-2000)?

Very well! America succeeded over all other countries to rise to the top!

What happened to Europe? Europe was rising throughout the 19th century, but America was rising faster and better. Continuing through the 20th century, Europe became very self-consumed with WWI and WWII, while America kept moving strongly ahead. Europe, especially Germany, did come back strongly after WWII, but it was too little, too late to compete against the rising and relatively unharmed America.

What about Asia? China was self-destructive throughout the first 200 years of American history (1776-1976), in addition to being badly beaten by the Europeans and Japanese, both militarily and economically. Japan thrived for about 100 years from 1840 to 1940, before it made the huge mistake of attacking the U.S. at Pearl Harbor. Like Germany, Japan also came back strongly after WWII. But again, it was too little, too late to effectively compete against America.

After WWII, America dominated the world for three main reasons:
1) America's two major competitors, Germany and Japan, destroyed themselves during the war and became America's "colonies" after the war. In fact, today, almost seven decades after WWII ended in 1945, there is still substantial American military presence in both Germany and Japan.
2) The entire East, led primarily by the former Soviet Union and seconded by China, self-destructed by adopting a fundamentally flawed system called "communism", which proved to be a total disaster.
3) The inevitable result of democracy, namely, plundering the public treasury to win elections, had not manifested itself, yet.

Bottom line: the 20th century was America's!

4. What happened to America after year 2000?

A steep decline! Why is that? The rise of BRICS, led by China, and America's self-destruction because of the inferiority of America's political system! The former was inevitable, but the latter was not.

4.1 China's rise

America must be very concerned about the rise of China for two main reasons:
1) Economically: Unlike America's former competitors (e.g. Japan and Germany), China has both the size and weight to provide real competition for America.
2) Politically: Unlike the East vs. the West before the Cold War ended in 1989, China's political system is, overall, slightly better than America's, in my opinion and as supported by their continuing success during our decline.

To learn more about China, go to Part 4 ("China: an overview").

America still has two huge advantages over China: abundance of natural resources and vastly more advanced capitalism. However, these two advantages may be inadequate to compensate the inferiority of America's political system. For more, go to Part 10 ("Six democracy-communism similarities").

4.2 America's self-destruction

Simply put, America has already sacrificed too much capitalism for democracy – democratic socialism! It's time to re-balance with more capitalism and less (and better) democracy!

For more, go back to Chapter 1 or jump to Part 7.1 ("American Democracy").

Here is a quote: *"America will never be destroyed from the outside. If we falter and lose our freedoms, it will be because we destroyed ourselves."*

Who said it? **Abraham Lincoln**!

5. Closing

Rome was not built in one day, nor did it go down in one day. Where is America today as compared with Rome more than 2,000 years ago? Similar! Rome was destroyed by debts! So will America, unless America changes the course soon!

Chapter 6: Top 10 American Misconceptions about America

Misconception 1: America is not in decline

Here is an excerpt from President Obama's 2012 State of the Union Address:

> *"Anyone who is telling you that America is in decline does not know what he is talking about."*

False, misleading, and even an attempt at brainwashing (Chapter 63)! Here is the plain truth: America has been in a steep decline over the past decade, at least, although you rarely hear the American political-media complex say or admit it. Any doubt? Face the truth: our national debt has already exceeded $16T – It is rising rapidly, even accelerating. 23 million Americans are unemployed or underemployed. In short, we are pursuing Greece into our own bankruptcy! We may be able to print ever larger quantities of dollars to inflate our way out of bankruptcy but the result is the same: abject poverty and human misery down the road.

Misconception 2: We are in trouble, but everything will be alright

Why? Because America has always come out alright when facing crises before, right? Wrong! Prayer might have worked before, but not this time for two reasons:
1) Foreign competition. The China factor is totally different from before as follows:
    - Economically: Unlike America's former competitors (e.g. Japan and Germany), China has both the size and weight to provide real competition for America. Additionally, China now has the momentum.

- Politically: Unlike the East vs. the West before the Cold War ended in 1989, China's political system is slightly better than America's, in my opinion.
2) Self-destruction: Two extreme groups have been, purposely or not, severely undermining America over the past two decades, at least:
    - The extreme left: they promote destructive socialism.
    - The extreme right: they promote imperialism with out-of-control military spending and naked aggression against other nations (e.g. Iraq).

Misconception 3: Religion is important to America

No, religion is not (supposed to be) important to America, although it may be important to us individually. As a matter of fact, many Europeans sailed to America a few hundred years ago to escape religious persecution in Europe.

Church and State do not mix! Neither should impose on the other!

Misconception 4: If I get a college education, I can make it

History shows that a society needs and can only accommodate about 35% of its population college educated. Additionally, it's important that you major "correctly" in college (e.g. engineering and business vs. philosophy and history), in order to maximize your employability in this increasingly competitive global economy. For more, read Chapter 38 ("America: from public schools to government, what is wrong?").

Misconception 5: If I work hard, my American dream will come true

Everybody can work hard and anybody can have wonderful American dreams, but only a small percentage will actually make it to the top - You must be good <u>and</u> lucky! Any doubt? Just look at NBA: You have little chance (1) if you are less than six foot in height and (2) if you are not a black (e.g. not quick enough, not strong enough, or simply just not good enough). For more, read Chapter 18 ("Pyramid Theory I").

Very importantly, some American dreams are not good for America. For more, read Chapter 38 ("American Dreams vs. America").

Misconception 6: We are the richest country on earth

This claim is arguably still correct. But it's dangerous when used by the left-wing extremists to spend and spend like there is no tomorrow.

Our national debt has already exceeded $16T. What does that mean? Our days are numbered, if we stay the course. Rome was destroyed by debts more than 2,000 years ago!

Misconception 7: America's government is of/by/for the people

Think again! Two perspectives:
1) Are our children and their children people too? If yes, do you still think it right that we spend their financial futures like there is no tomorrow?
2) If Congress is of/by/for the people, why is its disapproval rating at 87%?

Misconception 8: Our government is the best form of government

Democracy, as we know it today, does not work! The entire West is now on the verge of bankruptcy. Several European countries are already there, with more to follow, including America. For more, go back to Chapter 3 ("Towards an ideal form of government").

Misconception 9: A big government is necessary for America today

Look at China: Its government is much bigger than ours. Because China seems to be doing better than we (e.g. booming economy and high-speed rail), we need a bigger government to match with China, right?

Wrong! The big government in China is both a blessing and a curse. It is a blessing, because of China's unique culture (e.g. vetting for the government "elites") and history. It is a curse because of its communist past, when everything belonged to the public.

America is very different from China. America thrived largely because of rugged individualism and unfettered capitalism. America has been in a steep decline, largely because of destructive socialism and an out-sized government.

Misconception 10: America is finished

Here are two recent assessments by two friends of mine:
1) "I'm afraid we have already passed the threshold of no return"
2) After reading my writing "American democracy: what went wrong and when?" (Chapter 20), a gentleman friend simply replied: "Since 1964, one person, one vote"! In other words, if we define

democracy strictly as one person, one vote, American democracy, according to this gentleman friend, was wrong from the start!

I disagree with these pessimistic assessments! I do not think it's too late for America yet, and that's why I have been relentlessly trying to save America with my pen over the past few years!

Part 4: China: An Overview

Chapter 7: What is China, Anyway?
Chapter 8: Top 10 American Misconceptions about China

Chapter 7: What is China, Anyway?

The 20th century was clearly America's. The 21st century will likely be either China's or America's, but which one? The Chinese seem unconcerned, but we Americans should be, because we are the "defending champion". Most importantly, if we relinquish our #1 position without knowing exactly why and how, there may be no end to our downhill slide, as China clearly proved in the past!

In order for America to have any chance in her head-on competition with China, America must understand China better. So it's time for me to "thoroughly" explain to my fellow Americans what China is.

1. China is a country with tremendous history (3000 BC - 1820)

America did very well for more than 200 years in her entire history. But that is "nothing" when compared with China, who mostly led the world for the first 1,800 years of its 2,012-year calendar!

1.1 Many great inventions

One prominent symbol of China is the Great Wall. Most Americans can easily imagine the incredible feat of building it more than 2,000 years ago – need a wall between the U.S. and Mexico?

But did you also know that China invented many things that fundamentally changed the lives of us all? Four examples: papermaking, printing, gunpowder, and the compass. Can you imagine your life today without these great inventions?

1.2 A great culture

One prominent figure who mostly defined the Chinese culture over the past 2,000 years was Confucius. Here is a description of Confucius per Wikipedia:

Confucius (551–479 BCE) was a Chinese teacher, editor, politician, and philosopher of the Spring and Autumn Period of Chinese history. The philosophy of Confucius emphasized personal and governmental morality, correctness of social relationships, justice and sincerity. His followers competed successfully with many other schools during the Hundred Schools of Thought era only to be suppressed in favor of the Legalists during the Qin Dynasty. Following the victory of Han over Chu after the collapse of Qin, Confucius's thoughts received official sanction and were further developed into a system known as *Confucianism*.

1.3 A great decline

Among all human civilizations of the past 5,000 years, China led more time than any other nation. However, as the calendar turned to the 14th century, Europe started ascending (again) via the Renaissance and the Industrial Revolution, while China basically stood still. In spite of that, by 1820, China's world share of GDP was still, according to Dambisa Moyo (How the west was lost), at an impressive 32.2%, while America's was a paltry 1.8% and Europe's was 26.6%.

2. China descended from heaven to hell (1821-1976)

According to Moyo,
1) By 1890, just 70 years later, China's world share of GDP was down to 13.8%, while America's was up to 13.8% and Europe's was up to 40%.
2) By 1952, China fell to 5.2%, while America and Europe were both 30%.

If that wasn't hell for China, tell me what is! Now, why did China's world share of GDP degrade so precipitously? Foreign competition and failure of domestic policies!

2.1 Foreign competition

The West developed both economically and militarily, while China languished. As a result, China ran huge trade deficits with the West. Worse yet, the West waged wars against China and China lost them all, from the two Opium Wars with the British, to the various territorial wars with Russia, and to the First Sino-Japanese War.

A poor country is a weak country!

2.2 Domestic failure

From 1821 to 1976, China had several revolutions, but none of them changed anything in essence: China remained poor, and became more impoverished after each and every revolution or war.

The worst damage was done in the communist era (1949-1976), during which Chairman Mao was in charge.

Mao made three huge mistakes:
1) He totally destroyed capitalism in China. As a result, China became dirt poor, so poor that a young man like me (born in 1959) thought of nothing but "getting the hell out of here". I did, in 1982. Many, who could, did, too!
2) He blindly embraced the "Mother Heroine" campaign by the Soviets and encouraged the Chinese women to have as many children as possible. As a result, the population ballooned,

growing from 540M in 1949 to 953M in 1976, on the way to explode to 2B by year 2000, which would be similar to being a poor family in Africa today with 20 kids – you will never see the light of the day!

3) He destroyed China with several campaigns such as the Great Leap Forward, which led to the Great Chinese Famine, and the Cultural Revolution, which led to the greatest destruction of a nation's culture and morality in human history!

3. China's comeback (1977-2012)

Mao died in 1976. China changed by embracing capitalism, thanks to one wise leader: Deng Xiaoping.

Deng was a dictator; not all dictators are bad for their countries! Deng used his power wisely for the good of the country: He laid the monumental groundwork for China, not only economically (i.e. capitalism), but also politically (i.e. "a dictatorship without a dictator"), which led to China's overwhelming success today. Furthermore, China is poised to become the largest economy on earth by 2030.

What is the secret behind China's success? Aside from embracing capitalism, China did two extraordinary things:

1) Focused on the economy, without blindly embracing democracy like Russia did, after the disintegration of the USSR. Yes, including the put-down of the pro-democracy demonstration in Tiananmen Square in 1989 (more in Chapter 13)! Any doubt about the benefits of not rushing to democracy blindly? Compare Russia with China today - they are decades apart in the standards of living!

2) Adopted a one-child policy. Otherwise, China's population today would likely be double her present 1.3B. Any doubt about the benefits of population control? Compare India with China today - they are decades apart in the standards of living!

Both were highly controversial, not only at home, but also in the West. However, they proved to be the right things for China at the time for one simple reason: survival! Any doubt? Recall this: <u>All 33 Chilean miners rescued after 69 days</u>. The miners were ready to eat the dead for their own survival right before the rescue team reached them! It's human nature to survive by any means, idealistic human rights notwithstanding!

Two photos below tell you a lot about China: 1975 vs. 2010.

Modernization has its drawbacks. But it's a lot more comfortable to cry in a Buick (the most popular American car in China) than on a bicycle!

4. China faces huge challenges ahead

Every success comes with a price! Here are two prices the Chinese are paying for their success:
1) Environmental pollution: China has become the world's factory, with bad air and bad waters.
2) Aging population: Although the one-child policy has been eased in recent years, the "damage" has already been done: China's population will decline soon, with a severely aging population.

Another huge problem in China is government corruption: It comes from two sources, largely because of its communist past and newfound wealth:
1) It's inherent to a one-party political system. The challenge is to keep it under control, while moving "towards an ideal form of government" (Chapter 3).
2) Despite the enormous growth of the private sector over the past three decades, the public sector still holds the bulk of the economy, from natural resources (e.g. oil and coal), to heavy industries (e.g. steel and telecommunication), to most of the land. If, when, and how to privatize them? One thing is known for sure: do not follow the path Russia took, which was to privatize everything overnight.

Given what China went through over the past 200 years, especially from 1949 to 1976, these problems are relatively minor. I am optimistic that the Chinese will solve them over time. The key is to keep capitalism going strong.

Capitalism is not everything; Capitalism is the only thing!

5. America and China

The Chinese are fascinated about America. They love American capitalism. They love American movies. They love America's values of freedom and justice, although the Iraq War has severely damaged America's image in the minds of many Chinese (and elsewhere in the world). They like English as a foreign language. They love NBA, and they are crazy about Jeremy Lin!

Today, an educated Chinese (e.g. college graduate) knows a lot more about America than the other way around. Why? Because the Chinese media is very open to international news! Very importantly, the Chinese political-media complex does not lie about America! Note: Chinese politicians lie about many things, but America is not one of them.

Unfortunately, the American political-media complex in general has not been forthright about China, thanks to "brainwashing" (Chapter 63)! Moreover, many China "experts" in the West focus too much on the technical details, without adequately understanding China (e.g. the essence of its political system and the culture). As a result, it's not surprising that a recent poll shows that most Americans see China unfavorably. For the top 10 American misconceptions about China, go to the next chapter.

6. Closing

China had her day in the sun for the first 1,800 years of our 2,012-year calendar. Then she sunk all the way to hell, with an incredible amount of human suffering and humiliation along the way. Now, China seems to have finally found her own path to success. Let's welcome her to the modern world, wholeheartedly with neither prejudice nor ideology!

Chapter 8: Top 10 American Misconceptions about China

Misconception 1: China is a communist country

China is no longer a communist country *per se*! China was a communist country from 1949 to 1976. China embraced capitalism after Mao died in 1976. Today's China is more capitalistic than today's America in many ways, even per Steve Wynn. Forging her own way of success, China is now poised to become the largest economy on earth by 2030.

The political system in China is a one-party system. The ruling party is called the CPC (Communist Party of China). This inconvenient name has given the American political-media complex a good excuse to keep calling China a communist country whenever it sees necessary. That is, however, a disservice to America, because it's misleading and it's brainwashing (Chapter 63)! For a good understanding of today's CPC, read China's political anniversary: a long cycle nears its end. Here is an excerpt:

1) *The party was established in 1921 in the name of people like him [a peddler]. But today it is widely seen as representing the entrenched interests of the wealthy elite – the kind of people who spend more on a single meal in Xintiandi than a peddler would make in an entire year.*

2) *With more than 80 million members, it is the world's largest political organization. In spite of its insistence that it remains true to its Marxist-Leninist, Maoist heritage, though, it is perhaps*

better described as the world's largest chamber of commerce.

3) *The first sentence of the manifesto of the CPC states that the party "is the vanguard of the Chinese working class". Yet today, fewer than 9% of its members are classified as "workers" while more than 70% are recruited from the ranks of government officials, businessmen, professionals, college graduates and military.*

To make it easiest to understand for my fellow Americans, let me give you two simple analogies:
1) Yesterday's CPC (1949-1976): Consider it to be the Democratic Party in America today, with the extreme left only. Hell?
2) Today's CPC: Equate it to the Republican Party in America today, without the extreme right (i.e. neo-cons). Heaven?

Bottom line: Do not be fooled by the word "communist" in CPC! It's largely historical, some cultural, and some still real, unfortunately.

Misconception 2: China is a threat to America

Economically, China is a competitor, not an enemy, to America. The use of the word "threat" is malicious and un-American.

Militarily, China has never been a threat to America! China's military budget in 2011 was $91B, while America's military budget in 2010 was $664B! China did increase its military spending in 2012 by 11%, which was characterized by the U.S. media as a ballooning military budget. Where else on earth could this kind of talk have been possible other than in America? All thanks to brainwashing (Chapter 63)!

Today, America's military spending is bigger than the next 16 biggest spending countries combined! Why is it so big? Because of that, America has been, since the Cold War ended in 1989, a major source of instability around the world, especially in the Middle East. For more, read: <u>Ron Paul on 9/11: Ask the right questions and face the truth</u>. Yes, Ron Paul has got this one right!

Misconception 3: China steals America's jobs

Capitalism is global by definition, from the resources (e.g. oil) to the markets (e.g. Buick is the most popular American car in China)! Two facts:
1) Over the past two decades, America lost more jobs to automation than to outsourcing.
2) The primary reason behind America's outsourcing is that America's cost structure is too high. The jobs that America "lost to China" would have gone to other places, such as the other BRICS countries, had China not developed over the past three decades!

Bottom line: America, do we still know what capitalism is. If yes, do we still want it?

Misconception 4: China trades unfairly with America
Free trades are fair trades!

The simple fact is that America has <u>trade deficits with more than 90 countries</u>. Are we going to argue with each and every one of them about "fairness"? Or, simply face the truth: Our cost structure is way too high!

Misconception 5: China is a currency manipulator

Every country has the right to defend its own currency for its best interests! Here is the latest example: Brazil "declared new currency war" against the U.S. and Europe.

Now, will further appreciation of RMB reduce the U.S. trade deficit with China in a meaningful way? Impossibly unlikely! Here are two sets of hard data, showing that "America's manipulation" of the exchange rate has worked with neither Japan nor China:

U.S. trading partner	Japan		China	
Year	1985	2011	2005	2011
U.S. trade deficit	$46B	$62B	$202B	$295B
Exchange rate ($1 =)	250 Yen	78 Yen	8.3 RMB	6.3 RMB

Bottom line: The only way to increase global competitiveness is through innovation (e.g. Apple) and hard work (e.g. lowering the cost structure), not the repeated use of steroids (i.e. stimulus packages like QE1 and QE2). Oh, by the way, QE1 and QE2 are also known as "printing money", which is the worst form of currency manipulation, by any definition!

Misconception 6: China steals America's IP (Intellectual Property)

Many countries have succeeded by copying first and then using their success for innovation! This applies to America 200 years ago, as well as to China today!

No doubt, the laws must be obeyed. Having said that, I would like to seek an "understanding" (not to defend IP theft) as follows: China invented, among many things, papermaking and gunpowder. What if the Chinese, 2,000 years ago, had set up a patent system that required that each and every one of us pay, for 5,000 years, the Chinese 1% of the price for each and every piece of paper we use and each and every bullet we shoot?

Another perspective: Japan "copied" a lot from China for thousands of years, from the language to the culture. I knew that before landing in Japan in 1982. However, it was not until I started writing my first academic paper in English that I realized the depth of the "copy culture" in Japan: as I was struggling with English (and Japanese), my Japanese professor advised me to "借文", which literally means "to copy text in the name of borrowing". "借文" are two Chinese characters in Japanese, but they are not Chinese!

Case in point: Copy is how human civilization has advanced! People look up to the leaders by "copying" them. Mimicking is the most sincere form of flattery!

Misconception 7: The Chinese are not free
Today's China is much freer than yesterday's China! So China is moving in the right direction. Remember: China was communist from 1949 to 1976. So China has come a long way to part from its communist past, and will only get better from now on. With more prosperity comes more freedom, and *vice versa*.

On the other hand, America will lose more freedoms, as its economy falters more. Here is a quote from Abraham Lincoln:

> "*America will never be destroyed from the outside. If we falter and lose our freedoms, it will be because we destroyed ourselves.*"

Case in point: Prosperity is, generally speaking, proportional to freedom, and *vice versa*! The key is to strike a balance between the two, country by country, people by people.

Having said the above, I do think China must improve on free speech, now!

Misconception 8: China has problems with human rights

The West must not apply the same standards to the East and *vice versa*! Here are two excerpts from two previous chapters in this book:

1) Chapter 5 ("What is America, Anyway?"): *If you are an idealist (e.g. a true human rights activist or a real democracy proponent) and if you are an American, you must denounce your American citizenship first before passionately pursuing your cause. Why? Because America, as a country, is totally illegitimate - America was built on occupied land appropriated from its rightful owners, the American Indians.*

2) Chapter 7 ("America: What is China, Anyway?"): *Both (i.e. not blindly embracing democracy and the one-child policy) were highly controversial, not only at home, but also in the West. However, they proved to be the right things to do for China at the time for one simple reason: survival! Any doubt? Recall this: <u>All 33 Chilean miners rescued after 69 days</u>. The miners were ready to eat the dead for their own survival right before the rescue team reached them! It's human nature to survive by any means, idealistic human rights notwithstanding!*

Bottom line: Given America's declining status, we Americans no longer have any right to lecture the Chinese on anything! Culturally, they have a far longer history than we do. Economically, we owe them money, more than $1T!

Misconception 9: China has issues with Taiwan and Tibet

Neither Taiwan nor Tibet is as big an issue today (i.e. China is prosperous) as they were 30 years ago (i.e. China was dirt poor). They will become non-issues within 20 years (i.e. China will be more prosperous). Meanwhile, no American intervention, no problem!

Misconception 10: The Chinese can't play basketball

Jeremy Lin is real! Although Jeremy was born in America and his parents came to America from Taiwan, I am sure he enjoys his enormous popularity in China, whose market is 1,000 times bigger than Taiwan's! I can guarantee you that Jeremy will have a mega endorsement deal from China in the near future, if not already!

Making money and being rich may no longer be fashionable in America, but they are still great in China! Should America sue China for copying capitalism from America?

Part 5: Democracy

Chapter 9: 10-Point Democracy Manifesto
Chapter 10: The Answer Is Democracy; the Question Is Why
Chapter 11: A Country Must Be Run Like a Business
Chapter 12: People vs. Business

"Democracy is when the indigent, and not the men of property, are the rulers."

--- Aristotle, 350BC

Chapter 9: 10-Point Democracy Manifesto

"Democracy is not new. It was practiced by Rome and Greece more than 2,000 years ago. Both failed for the same reason: debts! Both were replaced by dictatorship! Will that be the fate for the western democracy today? Yes, very likely!"

--- Frank Li

1) People, regardless of their race or ethnicity, have an inherent desire for freedom, justice, and power, after having their basic needs (e.g. food, clothing, and shelter) met. The most obvious way to obtain them, so far, has been via democracy.

2) Democracy has been successful mostly in the West only, after the initial success of capitalism. It has not been successful in India or Russia, largely because neither country has had much success of capitalism first. For this reason, democracy will not be successful in Iraq or Afghanistan. In fact, there is not a single precedent of a third world country achieving prosperity via democracy.

3) Democracy, in its advanced stage as in America and Europe, simply means spending, which is so out-of-control now that most of the West is heading towards bankruptcy. Several European countries are already there, with more to follow, including America.

4) Democracy, as we know it today, does not work. Instead, the Chinese system (i.e. capitalism +

autocracy), albeit with many endemic problems of its own (e.g. lack of basic *democracy*), has been faring far better than the other systems over the past two decades. Unless America changes soon, China will become the largest economy by 2030, thus ending America's leadership not only economically, but also politically.

5) What's the key difference between China and America, politically? In China, there is no election, just governing. In America, there is no governing, just election.

6) Diagnosis for America: Cancer (Chapter 1)! The career politicians work for one purpose only: getting re-elected *ad nauseam*. In other words, they serve themselves first, their constituents a remote second, and their country dead last!

7) America's political system today does not attract the best people to serve. Worse yet, it has turned many good people into bad ones. Two examples:
   - Senator Obama voted against raising the debt ceiling to $9T in 2006, which he called "unpatriotic". But under President Obama, the debt has ballooned to over $16T!
   - President Obama chose to escalate the war in Afghanistan in 2011 (acceptable), but with a troop withdrawal plan so ridiculously hasty that there could have been only one possible explanation: it was perfectly timed for his re-election (totally unacceptable)!

8) Many American Presidents damaged America severely by introducing programs, mostly as part of

their re-election, which were predestined to fail. Five examples:
- FDR: Social security - It's the biggest Ponzi scheme ever!
- JFK: Public-sector unions – It will prove, in less than 20 years, to be the most damaging act against America, ever!
- LBJ: Medicare and Medicaid - We are still borrowing to pay for them!
- GWB: The Iraq War – The beacon went off with it, and I believe it will eventually be marked as the beginning of the end of democracy as we know it (Chapter 55).
- BHO: Obamacare - It was introduced when we could least afford it.

9) Solutions for America: Constitutional changes (Chapter 2)!

10) Democracy could still be an ideal form of government (Chapter 3). For America, there must be term-limits for Congress and a one-term limit (e.g. six years) for the American Presidency, so as to give democracy another chance to work. For China, it must introduce democracy slowly but steadily.

Chapter 10: The Answer Is Democracy; the Question Is Why

"Remember, democracy never lasts long. It soon wastes, exhausts, and murders itself. There never was a democracy yet that did not commit suicide."

--- John Adams

Democracy, as we know it today, does not work! For the U.S., we must introduce term-limits for the top political offices, so as to give democracy another chance to work. For China, it must introduce democracy, slowly but steadily!

1. Four highly simplified definitions
1) Capitalism: The system in the U.S. today. Unfortunately, the "land of opportunity" is now filled with entitlements, thanks to democracy, as we know it today. In other words, America is becoming more and more socialistic!
2) Socialism: The system in Europe, featuring high taxes and generous entitlements. This system taxes the rich so much that it leaves little incentive of work. As a result, it has been nothing but only in a steep decline over the past few decades.
3) Communism: The system in the entire "socialist block" led by the former Soviet Union from 1945 to 1989, including China from 1949 to 1976. In this system, the proletarians came to power via violent revolutions. They did not tax the rich – they shot them, after (or before) confiscating their property! What happened next? A totally ruined economy! Why? The accumulated wealth of the

rich was quickly consumed and no new wealth was created to replace it, so all suffered. Today, there exist only two communist countries on earth: Cuba and North Korea. Both enjoy abject poverty and human misery. All others have failed and changed.

4) State capitalism: The system in China from 1979 to present. This system (i.e. autocracy + capitalism), albeit with many endemic problems of its own (e.g. lack of basic *democracy*), has been faring far better than the other systems over the past two decades, to the extent that we all now must ask ourselves this question: what is *democracy* and who needs it?

2. The U.S. vs. China

Let's focus on the U.S. and China for two obvious reasons:

1) "#1 is the winner, and the rest are all losers." The U.S. has been the #1 for the past few decades, but China is rapidly catching up, well on her way to surpassing the U.S. in GDP by 2030.
2) I love both the U.S. and China. I was so disgusted of China that I left in 1982. But today, I am more concerned about the U.S., because China is basically on the right track but the U.S. is not.

Now, let me repeat (from Chapter 1): the U.S. is deeply in trouble for two main reasons: (1) the rise of China as a competitor, and (2) the incompetence of America's political system – democracy, as we know it today, is a luxury we can no longer afford!

There are three ways to win in a head-on competition:
1) Our competitor self-destructs.
2) We become better ourselves.
3) We somehow manage to destroy our competitor.

3. Way #1: Will China self-destruct (again)?

Many westerners, especially some Americans, expect China to implode (again) for several reasons, such as history, based on some technical analysis, or their (subconscious) wish. My answer is "no, very unlikely". Here are five reasons:

1) The century we are now in is the 21st century. While the U.S. has dominated over the past some seven decades, China "ruled" mostly through the first 18 centuries! Then the Europeans took over the leadership and Napoleon knew it well: He called China "a sleeping lion" and advised the West to let China sleep. Fortunately (or unfortunately), the sleeping lion is now awake.

2) The Chinese know how to succeed when given the opportunities: how to make things and how to sell. In other words, business (or more broadly capitalism) is in their blood, which erupted in the 1990s, after being suppressed for a few hundred years. They also know, better than any other people, that punishing those who succeed, via death as in communism or taxes as in socialism, you end up without any success.

3) The current leadership generation in China (aged ~60) considers itself the luckiest generation of the Chinese ever, as this generation went from being extremely poor to being relatively rich in a short span of three decades! Their work ethic and drive to success are unmatched and unmatchable!

4) While an autocratic system like China's can bring in success quickly, it can also go wrong quickly. What makes it go wrong quickly? A strongman on the top! Fortunately, all strongmen in China are dead and it's impossible to have new ones unless something extraordinary happens, such as WWIII.

5) China calls itself, officially, a "socialist country with its own characteristics," but it largely followed the U.S. as the example throughout its economic reforms. Politically, however, there is no example to follow, nor much incentive left in China for democracy, as we know it, for two reasons: the Iraq War and the two bad examples of democracy in India and Russia.

Now, is lack of democracy a big problem in China? No, not yet, at least! What are the big problems for the Chinese? Environment pollution and government corruption! But these problems are minor as compared with what they have gone through over the past 60 (or 200) years. As a Chinese, I knew well how low China's international standing was, especially right after I arrived in Japan in 1982. Today, as a Chinese-American, I am glad that China has earned respect back from the rest of the world!

In short, being rich is much better than being poor, regardless of the political system!

4. Way #2: Can we become better ourselves?
Yes, we can, through changes. But it will not be easy and here is why:
1) I believe I have the most accurate diagnosis for America (Chapter 1) and the best and easiest possible solution (Chapter 2). But no positive change in democracy is easy.
2) Because most of our career politicians work for one purpose only (i.e. getting re-elected *ad nauseam*), the more they work, the more they seem to damage our country, with the wars in Iraq and Afghanistan being the worst examples.

3) The ruling party in China is called "the Communist Party of China." But today there are actually more communists in the U.S. than in China, as a percentage of the population. To me, most Democrats are socialists and the left-wing extremists are communists. Why? Because they sound so similar to the communists I experienced in China back in the 1960s and 1970s. Two examples:
   - Down with the rich; long live the proletarians!
   - They play God! Want a big help (e.g. housing or healthcare)? Count on me – I will give it to you by robbing the business or the public treasury, or both!
4) What about the Republicans? They are better than the Democrats for business; just as bad in spending; and worse in foreign policy (e.g. the wars).
5) The only way to increase our competitiveness is through innovation and hard work, not the repeated use of steroids, such as printing money! The government does not have any "real" money of its own. It's our money, all from business, ultimately!

5. Way #3: Can we somehow destroy China?

No, we can't! But will we try? If you had asked me this question 10 years ago, my answer would have been a resounding "no". But today I am not sure, given the Iraq War, and the reality that the U.S. will soon be a 2nd-class economy, with a 1st-class military …

More broadly, we, the U.S., have actually been the source of instability around the world since 1989, when the Cold War ended. Here are three facts (or observations):

1) Our military is by far the most powerful in the world. Today our defense spending is bigger than the next 16 biggest spending countries combined! Why? There are many war hawks in the military, plus jobs & votes for career politicians!
2) We destroyed the world order by launching the Iraq War! Modestly, it was the biggest mistake in the history of American foreign policy. More seriously, *"I believe March 20, 2003 will eventually be marked as the beginning of the end of democracy as we know it"* (Chapter 55: "What's The Real Cost of The Iraq War?").
3) We are the biggest arms dealer on earth, selling arms to "everybody," including Taiwan.

Now, a few words about Taiwan: a war between Taiwan and China is highly unlikely! Following the current trend, Taiwan will be somehow integrated into China economically, if not politically, within 20 years. No American intervention, no problem!

6. Closing

China fell hard a few hundred years ago and has finally turned itself around. Let's accept China's success and meet China's competition by becoming better ourselves. Here are two lessons from China:
1) Punishing success, via death as in communism or tax as in socialism, you will end up without any success.
2) Adapt and change! Or it's a long trip to hell!

Chapter 11: A Country Must Be Run Like a Business

"The budget should be balanced, the Treasury should be refilled, public debt should be reduced, the arrogance of officialdom should be tempered and controlled, and the assistance to foreign lands should be curtailed lest Rome become bankrupt. People must again learn to work, instead of living on public assistance."
--- Cicero, 55BC

1. Background

I am a technologist by training, armed with a Ph.D. degree in Electrical Engineering. However, soon after I started working in the real world, the ambitious me realized that I was on the wrong track: Why are most of the top guys in business sales people, not technologists like me? I learned and adapted – I have been running my own business since 2005. For more, go to Part 12 ("My personal life").

2. What is business?

To me, there are four basic principles in business:
1) Making money.
2) Sales are the only thing.
3) No democracy.
4) No unions.

2.1 Making money

Business is about making money and built to last (Chapter 4)! A company, no matter how big it is, can be simply divided into two parts: a profit center and a cost center. The former brings in money, while the latter spends it. So the management focus is almost always on the former, sales especially. When times get tough, without adequate money coming in, you must cut deep into the latter.

2.2 Sales are the only thing

Sales are not everything; sales are the only thing! Business is driven by sales, with the arrival of a purchase order triggering everything. Still wondering why it's almost always the sales people that make it to the top in a company? Wonder not!

2.3 No democracy

I learned this early in my career from my boss: "you guys discuss, but I will make the decision because I always have n+1 votes," where n equals the number of his direct reports.

2.4 No unions

The world is becoming increasingly "smaller" and more competitive. The damage a union can do is more obvious in an internationally competitive business than a non-international one. I worked for both NEC USA and Fujitsu USA, and learned one open secret in these Japanese companies: no unions allowed in America. Look around: there is no union in any of the Japanese companies in America! In fact, there is no union in any of the Asian companies in America! So unions in American companies, among many harmful things, are making American companies less competitive than their Asian counterparts. Plain and simple!

3. Running a country like a business

Now, let's apply the four basic business principles to running our country like a business:

3.1 Making money

The revenue of a country comes [chiefly] from taxes, and there is only one [chief] profit center in any country: business, the source of all taxes, corporate as well as personal. So a country must do everything possible to promote and support business. Everything else belongs to the cost center, which should thus be subject to big cuts when times get tough. In a simple business sense, America's #1 problem today is not jobs *per se*. Instead, it's the debts and deficits that are leading the country toward bankruptcy. Therefore, America must be restructured, as in business, getting its fiscal house in order first before anything else, such as hiring (i.e. jobs).

Oh, by the way, if you think America's #1 problem today is jobs, you either have a problem of your own (e.g. un-employed or underemployed) or have been brainwashed by the political-media complex (Chapter 63: "Brainwashing")! The politicians worry about jobs for the sake of their own jobs, only to destroy America by emptying her treasury systematically, however individually unintentional maybe. Let's be absolutely clear: There is no quick and easy solution to the jobs problem in America, other than change and time. Meanwhile, the more the government tries to do along the same old line of out-of-control spending, the worse off we are as a country, because it drives us down the road of total bankruptcy, faster and more disastrously! We should leave the economy alone to recover on its own.

3.2 Sales are the only thing

Sales, in terms of a country in this global economy, simply mean exports, or selling to other countries. Unfortunately, we have trade deficits with more than 90 countries. No country or company can keep going like this for long! So rather than fighting with those more than 90 countries one by one for fairness or currency, or both, why can't we be honest with ourselves once by simply admitting that we have a big problem?

What, then, is our big problem? Our cost structure is too high! Unconvinced? Just read this Worden Report: *"in 2011, there are nearly twice as many people working for the government (22.5 million) than in all of the manufacturing (11.5 million). This is almost exact reversal of the situation in 1960, when there were 15 million workers in manufacturing and 8.8 million collecting a paycheck from the government ... More Americans work for the government than work in construction, farming, fishing, manufacturing, mining, and utilities combined. We have moved decisively from a nation of makers to a nation of takers."*

What, then, is the most obvious solution in business terms? Restructuring! Cost cutting, especially in the public sector! Oh, by the way, do you believe in the "infrastructure bank" President Obama proposed in his bill some months ago? I do not and here is why: Everything we do must directly contribute to the "sales", or it's just yet another cost, making a bad problem worse! In other words, our sales are down largely because of our high cost structure. Is it time to borrow more money to keep some employees busy by having them shine the windows in the factory? You will never do that in business! Note that some infrastructure projects are necessary. Do them for the sake of business (i.e. shareholders), not for jobs!

3.3 No democracy

Democracy, as we know it today, is a luxury we can no longer afford. However, running a country may not be a pure business *per se*. For this reason, let's give democracy another chance by reforming our political system (Chapter 2).

3.4 No unions

Union, in its extreme form, is a *de facto* communist thing (i.e. the Soviet Union or China under Mao), with everything belonging to "the people". This everything will quickly be reduced to nothing when "the people", or the working class, are in charge, as history has repeatedly shown, from the ancient Rome to the modern Greece. Yes, everything of nothing is still nothing!

What about public-sector unions in the U.S.? Who are they unionized against - The United States of America? They should not have been allowed in the first place (blame JFK)! They must be abolished immediately and banned forever (Chapter 2).

4. Closing

Still unconvinced if America will lose its #1 position to China by 2030? It will happen unless America changes the course soon!

What's the secret behind China's surge? Running the country like a business!

Chapter 12: People vs. Business

"The business of America is business."
--- Calvin Coolidge

What is business, anyway? Business is about making money, which is also known as "profits." Profits often lead to more jobs for more profits. What about putting people or jobs before profits? No, that's charity, not real business!

Who are the people, anyway?

1. America
"We, the People", so begins the U.S. Constitution. But who are "the People" referenced? To the founding fathers, "the People" included certain rich white men only; others were excluded as follows:
- Point 1: women were not allowed to vote, nor were the minorities.
- Point 2: Only the rich were able to serve, unpaid in the top political offices (e.g. Congress and the American Presidency)! Yes, first you had to make it (i.e. being financially independent), then you served with honor for a few years, and finally you returned home after doing your duty to your country. No, serving was never meant to be a way of life - not even to make a living, let alone a career!

I think Point 1 was wrong but Point 2 was right. Point 1 was wrong because I, as a minority, deserve my right to vote. Point 2 was right because I believe only after you have become financially independent, are you likely to serve well, especially at the top, with your priorities absolutely right: country first, constituents next, and yourself last!

Over the past 200 years, America "fixed" not only Point 1 but also Point 2. As a result, today, all Americans (18 or older) can vote - a good thing! But the elected officials now are often not previously successful people. In fact, after WWII when the "servants" started being paid more than the "masters", most American politicians have been serving for one overwhelming purpose only: getting re-elected *ad nauseam*! In other words, they serve themselves first! Worse yet, they try to get re-elected at all costs, even if it means destroying America by emptying her treasury! As a result, most American politicians, including the President, have their priorities completely reversed: themselves first, constituents a remote second, and country dead last. Still wondering how and why America is so deeply in trouble? Wonder not - it's the political system, stupid!

2. China

In China, everything important is [still] named "the People's". Three examples:
1) The name of the country: The People's Republic of China.
2) The name of the army: The People's Liberation Army.
3) The name of the money: The People's money or Renminbi (or RMB for short).

However, just as in communism, the concept of "the People's property" exists, today in China, largely in name only! China changed from a theoretical form of of/by/for the people (1949 - 1976), which turned out to be a total disaster, to a practical form of of/by/for the business (1977 - present), which brought unprecedented

prosperity to China on such a massive scale and in such a short time span of only three decades that it was totally unprecedented in human history! What was the secret behind China's miracle? Running the country like a business! Specifically, among many things, China did two most anti-People things as follows:
1) Embracing capitalism and focusing on the economy, including brutally suppressing the student-led pro-democracy demonstration on June 4, 1989. For more, read Chapter 13 ("Tiananmen Square").
2) Enforcing the one-child policy to control the explosive population growth.

Extremely controversial as they were at the time, both of them are now widely accepted, inside China at least, as the absolutely right things to do for the betterment of the country! Big pain, but big gain - bad for the people at the time, but good for the country in the long-run!

Better still for the Chinese, China is now on the way to becoming the largest economy on earth by 2030 (or by 2020 per IMF's formula), thus ending America's leadership not only economically for sure, but also politically most likely.

3. Business and people

On one hand, we argue about people vs. business. On the other hand, we argue that corporations (i.e. business) are people too! Not only are corporations composed of people, corporations are also the ultimate source of all tax revenues for the country, including both business taxes and "people" taxes (e.g. income tax, property tax, and sales tax)!

4. Towards an ideal form of government

An ideal government (Chapter 3) should balance between the two: people and business. Unfortunately, neither America nor China is even close to this balance – they are two extremes at the opposite ends! Ultimately, the one who can find her own way of achieving this balance optimally will be the lasting winner. Meanwhile, the Chinese extreme seems to be more successful than the American extreme. Why? Because the talk of "people vs. business" is really the talk of "democracy vs. capitalism"! For prosperity, capitalism is a must, while democracy is merely an option. In other words, if you can't strike a balance between the two, choose capitalism over democracy! China has proven it with its recent ascension and the US's continued decline!

Bottom line: The Chinese embrace capitalism today, because it was capitalism in Europe 200 years ago that started China's steep decline, and it is capitalism in China today that has finally got China out of abject poverty that was totally devastating at the end of 27 years of socialism under Mao (which is more correctly known as "communism" in the West). America, on the other hand, has sacrificed too much capitalism for democracy over the past five decades, and will end up with having neither! Unconvinced? Just look at the protesters of Occupy Wall Street! What do they really want - a proletarian revolution to take over America? "Welcome on board, comrade America," Mao is cheering and waving, from hell!

5. Closing

The root cause of many American ills is its antiquated political system, nothing else! America's economic system (i.e. the free enterprise system) remains the best in the world, despite all its problems.

Do not let America be destroyed by the 47%, especially those permanent entitlement recipients, together with the self-serving politicians in the name of "the people"! They will become 51% within a few years if we stay the course. When that happens, and if you have trouble envisioning what that America would look like, visit Greece today or look at yesterday's China. It's terrible!

Part 6: China: in Some Depth

Chapter 13: Tiananmen Square
Chapter 14: It Is The Political System, Stupid!
Chapter 15: Chairman Mao Is Smiling
Chapter 16: America: What is China's Political System, Anyway?
Chapter 17: It Is June 4, Again

Chapter 13: Tiananmen Square

(Initially published at GEI on 6/4/2011)

Twenty-two years ago today, a tragedy occurred at Beijing's Tiananmen Square: The student-led pro-democracy demonstration was brutally crushed by the soldiers. Like many expatriate Chinese, I thought China was finished.

Guess what? China was not finished. To the contrary, it changed dramatically for the better, lifting some 400 million people out of poverty and becoming the second largest economy in the world. It's a miracle, totally unprecedented in human history! How can this be explained from June 4, 1989 on?

Looking back with the advantage of 22 years hindsight, three things are foremost in my thoughts.

First, let's acknowledge that what happened at Tiananmen Square on June 4, 1989 was a tragedy. I especially feel sorry for those families whose loved ones died on that day.

Second, I must say that the fatal ending of the demonstration turned out to be a hugely positive thing for China overall. Two main reasons:
1) The "miracle" has been the best thing ever for China. I simply cannot imagine how it could have happened any other way.
2) After Mao's death in 1976, Deng Xiaoping led China's economic reforms. It was hugely challenging, with constant fights between the left (i.e. Maoists) and the right (i.e. the reformers led by Deng). By June 1989, China was already well

on its way in the economic reforms with good results. But the tragedy not only disrupted the reforms, but also set it back by a few years, because it gave the left a reason, better than anything else they could have hoped for, to go back to the old days. Fortunately, Deng got his control back within a few years, and the reforms got rolling again. There is no way back now!

Third, was the students' demand for democracy valid? Yes, to me at the time; but no, in my view today. Why? Because the Chinese system has fared far better than other systems over the past 22 years, with no end in sight!

Finally, although 22 years are not a lot of time in history, it has been long enough to prove that Deng was the greatest leader in China's recent history, because he set the country on the right course not only economically (i.e. capitalism), but also politically (i.e. a dictatorship without a dictator).

Chapter 14: It Is The Political System, Stupid!

In Chapter 1, I identified the root causes of America's decline as (1) the rise of China and (2) the incompetence of America's political system, especially when compared with China's. I stated: "(1) was inevitable, but (2) was not."

So let's study a little bit of China's political system, shall we?

1. What is the political system in China?
Here is an excellent article: <u>Who will be China's next leaders?</u> It tells you, an American, everything you need to know about China's political system as well as its next leaders. Here are four highlights from the article:
1) System: *"It is a dictatorship without a dictator"*
2) Leadership: The next leaders (in 2013) will be President Xi and Premier Li.
3) Politicking: *"In this system, everyone is acting, everyone is fake; so we cannot really tell."*
4) Class: *"In the 1950s, Mao was trying to forge a classless society, but in the Beijing compounds where the families of senior officials lived, there was a highly stratified sense of status – the schools you went to, the shops you could visit and the car your family drove all depended on your exact-position in the bureaucratic hierarchy."*

2. The Chinese system explained in an American way

2.1 System
Imagine we have a one-party system in America today, with the Republican Party in charge, without the

right-wing extremes and without the burden of any election outside the party. It's not ideal at all, but will we be better off that way? This, roughly put, is China's political system today! Now, what was China's system under Mao (1949-1976) with the country being dirt poor? Imagine the same one-party system in America today, but with the Democratic Party in charge, with the left-wing extremists only!

2.2 Leadership

The next leaders in China have been long prepared by the current leaders, in a way similar to the GE way. How can the fortuitous leaders in America (e.g. President Obama) possibly compete against these Chinese leaders? Showmanship aside, President Obama is far shorter in experience and track records!

2.3 Politicking

This point may look ugly and foreign to an American, until you hear Joe Biden talking …

On July 10, 2010, Joe appeared on the Jay Leno show and said something like this: "Over the years, I have learned not to question people about their motives - just look at the things on the table (e.g. a proposed legislation) and deal with them." I was stunned upon hearing that: Joe is unreal, because motivation is often where I start in analysis (as I learned from CBS's CSI). Then I realized Joe could have been telling the truth (as he often does, awkwardly): There is only one true motivation among Joe's friends and foes: getting re-elected *ad nauseam*. Everything they do is motivated by this motivation! So if they would all question each other about the motivation, life would have stopped right there and then! In other words, it is the "don't ask, don't tell" thing in American politics that Joe inadvertently revealed to the world! How long shall we allow our politicians to fool around like that? Still unconvinced? Listen to Mayor [Michael Bloomberg on career politicians](#).

2.4 Class

Mao's class structure in politics still exists in China today. But it matters a lot less to the ordinary Chinese because of the new opportunities created by capitalism. Oh, America today is a class society more than China in many ways. Three examples:

1) Lying to Congress: It's a serious crime. But some members of Congress routinely lie to us, with no repercussion whatsoever.
2) Cop killer: Cops are more precious than ordinary people. So a cop killer deserves a more severe punishment than a murderer killing ordinary people.
3) Permanent welfare recipients: They get a living, without working, from those who work for a living. Properly called "parasites" in China, they can vote in America!

3. Closing

Everything is relative, including the political systems. While the Chinese system (i.e. capitalism + autocracy) has many endemic problems of its own (e.g. lack of basic democracy), it has fared far better than ours over the past two decades. As a result, unless we adapt and change soon, China will surpass us as the largest economy by 2030, thus ending America's leadership not only economically, but also politically.

How can we avoid that? Accept my diagnosis (Chapter 1) and solution (Chapter 2)!

Chapter 15: Chairman Mao Is Smiling

(Initially published at GEI on 4/20/2012)

Hello from China!

The Mao Memorial Hall is located on the south side of the Tiananmen Square in Beijing. It is a popular tourist attraction. I just visited it. While there, I imagined I saw Mao smile and mumble: "see, I told you so!"

I think I know what he meant …

Mao led the communists to power in 1949. After destroying the remaining parts of capitalism in China in the early 1950s, Mao kicked off his own "socialist" construction phase with two explicit and ambitious economic goals as follows:
- Goal 1: Surpassing the U.K. in 30 years!
- Goal 2: Surpassing the U.S. in 50 years!

What followed was a total disaster (read Chapter 7). But was Mao really such a big fool who did not know what he was talking about? It turned out that Mao's two mighty goals were quite obtainable - he just did not know how!

Mao died in 1976. China changed fundamentally for the better by embracing capitalism. As a result, China easily realized Goal 1 (1977-2007), and is now well on her way to realizing Goal 2 (1977-2027)!

Mao must be very happy about China today. That was why, I think, he smiled and mumbled: "see, I told you so!"

Chapter 16: America: What is China's Political System, Anyway?

(Initially published at GEI on 5/11/2012)

There has been a lot of political news coming out of China recently, from the purge (China Leadership Purge: Maoists Out, Liberals In), to the calls for political reforms (Chinese Premier Acknowledges Need for Political Reforms), to the latest Time's cover story "The People's Republic of Scandal." How should we view these news stories as a whole?

To me, all these news stories reflect positive changes for China. Here is why:

1) Purge: The purge of Bo is good for China. In fact, most of the purges over the past decade (e.g. Chen Xitong and Chen Liangyu) have been good for China.
2) Political reforms: It's positive to acknowledge the problems first and try to fix them via reforms. This is very different from the U.S., whose leaders are in total denial of its big problems! Remember: China was a hugely screwed up country, thanks largely to Mao. It takes major changes and a long time to fix it.

1. Overview of China's political system

Simply put, China's political system can be characterized in two points as follows:
1) System: It is a one-party system, with the ruling party being the CPC (Communist Party of China). How to view today's CPC? Equate it to the Republican Party in America today, without the extreme right (i.e. neo-cons). For more, read

Chapter 8 ("Top 10 American Misconceptions about China")!

2) Leadership: It is a dictatorship without a dictator.

Overall, this system, while far from being ideal as discussed in Chapter 3 ("Towards an ideal form of government"), appears to be slightly better than America's political system, in my humble opinion.

2. View China as GE

To best understand China, compare it to GE! Three positives in this analogy:
1) Leadership: Most of the leaders are accomplished people.
2) Management: It's like a company with the CEO at the top.
   - Jack Welch was perhaps a more imperial CEO at GE than President Hu Jintao in China, relatively speaking.
   - A dictatorship without a dictator has worked out well so far.
3) Built to last: The current leaders prepare the next generation leaders.

Two negatives in this analogy:
1) Mandatory compliance: because GE is the only game in town, you must kiss your way up for your career, or there is no place to turn.
2) Purge: purge is a part of the game by "design" (not necessarily 10% yearly as in GE), complicated by the traditional Chinese "palace politics." As a matter of fact, GE probably purges more often and larger in scale than China does. Recall this: When Jeff Immelt was chosen as Welch's successor, the two other candidates (i.e. James McNerney and Robert Nardelli) were "purged" out of GE.

3. Politics: The U.S. vs. China

Politicians are basically the same everywhere: they serve themselves first before serving anybody else. Here are three key differences between the U.S. and China:
1) Quality of the servants.
2) Cost of making a big mistake.
3) Permanency.

3.1 Quality of the servants
1) In the U.S, because of the abundance of opportunities in the private sector, if you are really good, you should not even think about working for the public sector before succeeding in the private sector! Using Steve Jobs' words: "Why join the Navy when you can be a pirate?"
2) In China, the best people serve in the government, traditionally and culturally, although the adoption of capitalism over the past three decades has changed that, because of the new opportunities in the private sector.

3.2 Cost of making mistakes
1) In the U.S., the cost of making a big mistake in the public sector is limited. Any doubt? Read this: Mel Reynolds Rap. What a big second chance!
2) In China, the cost of making a big mistake in the government can be huge; you can be basically done for the rest of your life or even executed.

3.3 Permanency
1) In the U.S., the culture of politics is to enjoy as much as you can for as long as you can. Few, not even the American Presidents, care about the well being of the country in the long run, thanks to "getting re-elected *ad nauseam*". Big problems?

Kick them down the road, while you benefit yourself now.

2) In China, there is a concerted effort, at the top at least, to perpetuate the CPC, which means you have to do things more responsibly, both short and long terms, without kicking the can down the road forever.

4. Discussion

Overall, while the best people do not necessarily make it to the top in China, the top leaders are all accomplished people, with their lifetime effort vested in it, just like in GE! Needless to say, there are many flaws in China's political system, not the least of which is the lack of "democratic" elections. But isn't that true for GE as well?

Of course, a country is not a company *per se*. So this analogy is mostly for illustrative purposes.

Bottom line: China is moving in the right direction basically, but the U.S. is not!

Here is a must-read article for all Americans who care about the U.S.-China relationship: Chinese Insider Offers Rare Glimpse of U.S.-China Frictions.

5. Closing

For Americans, Chinese politics is like Chinese food: Enjoy it but do not go into the kitchen to see how it is made - the closer you look, the more unsavory it becomes! Overall, few Americans, the author included, can live happily in China, either politically or economically.

It's disheartening that America is losing its head-on competition with China. Worse yet, I know America can be better than China, but we just seem unable to adapt adequately …

Chapter 17: It Is June 4, Again

(Initially published at GEI on 6/4/2012)

Once again, it is June 4. Once again, I feel compelled to write about it, adding to my prior writings on previous anniversaries (e.g. Chapter 13: "Tiananmen Square").

My position has evolved over the past 23 years as follows:
1) View 1: 23 years ago, I was with the students, totally.
2) View 2: I started moving in the opposite direction in 2005 and published my view in 2009. In fact, I just re-read my article entitled "Tiananmen Square" (Chapter 13). Not a single word needs to be changed!
3) View 3: The rest of the article reflects my view today, which is a further advancement to View 2.

In Chapter 77 ("My 30-Year College Graduation Reunion"), I state that my generation is *"perhaps the luckiest generation in Chinese history."* The students at Tiananmen Square on June 4, 1989 were about 10 years younger than I, hence the same generation. Therefore, I hope today they feel as lucky as I do. How, then, "unlucky" should they have felt 23 years ago? Moreover, how much did they really know about democracy before demanding it in such a radical fashion? Now, imagine: had the students succeeded in changing China the way they wanted at that time, what would China look like today? It's hard to imagine they would be as successful as they are today! For more on China, read Chapter 7 ("America: What is China, Anyway?").

History is the best judge for social changes, particularly for a big event like this. While we may need more time to draw a firmer conclusion on this, Nancy Pelosi might have already done it for us, as shown by the two photos below:

What was she doing in China in 2009? Asking China to bail the U.S. out of the financial crisis by buying more U.S. treasury bills!

What a huge difference 18 years made for Ms. Pelosi, as well as for China!

Winston Churchill once said: *"If you are not a Liberal at 20, you have no heart. If you are not a Conservative at 40, you have no brain."*

What did he mean? Two interpretations:
1) For China, he meant: the students at Tiananmen Square on June 4, 1989 were too young to understand what they were doing!
2) For America (Chapter 68: "America: What Did Winston Churchill Mean?"), *he meant: "in addition to raising the minimum age of the American Presidency to 55, raise the voting age to a minimum of 21 so that voting is at least as important as drinking, or perhaps even to 40 when you are wise enough to do so."*

Now, what about Nancy Pelosi in 1991? Apparently, at age 51 at the time, she did not understand what she was doing at Tiananmen Square, either! She had not yet reached the "brain" part of her life and apparently never will!

More broadly, given the world today (i.e. How the west was lost), isn't it time for all of us to profoundly question democracy in the same way as we questioned communism? For more, go to Part 10.

While we seek to find an ideal form of government (Chapter 3), China will continue to thrive, thanks to state capitalism, but the West will continue to decline, thanks to democracy, as we know it today ...

Part 7: America: in Great Depth and Breadth

Part 7.1: American Democracy
Part 7.2: American Presidency
Part 7.3: American Politics
Part 7.4: America: The Good, the Bad, and the Ugly

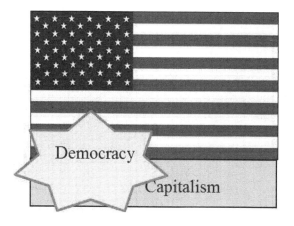

Part 7.1: American Democracy

Chapter 18: Pyramid Theory I
Chapter 19: Loop Theory – Capitalism vs. Socialism
Chapter 20: American Democracy: What Went Wrong and When?
Chapter 21: American Democracy: Massive Falsehoods at the Top!

"Remember, democracy never lasts long. It soon wastes, exhausts, and murders itself. There never was a democracy yet that did not commit suicide."

--- John Adams

Chapter 18: Pyramid Theory I

In this chapter, I will present Pyramid Theory I as a theoretical foundation for my work. But first, what is America, profoundly?

1. What is America?

America, as a country, has two corner stones: capitalism and democracy, as shown below. I explained them "basically" in Chapter 5. Now, let me explain them "profoundly".

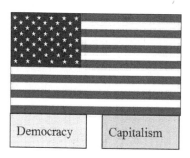

1.1 Capitalism

It's all about "making money" (or "profits"), nothing else such as "job creation" (which goes against efficiency) or "Made in the USA" (which goes against capitalism that is global by definition). The very essence of capitalism is "me first" and self-reliance: If each and every one of us can take care of himself/herself, we, as a nation, will take care of ourselves. I firmly believe this is the best system available on earth, and will remain so, as long as human nature prevails.

1.2 Democracy

It's all about "votes". In order to obtain more votes, our politicians pretend to be "you first" and made up such socialist schemes as "job creation" and "Made in the USA", totally going against capitalism, especially the self-reliance part. Worse yet, they are willing to win your votes at any cost, even if it means destroying America by emptying her public treasury! As a result, the "land of opportunity" is now filled with entitlements, to such an extreme now that America, as a country, is heading toward bankruptcy.

So *capitalism* and *democracy* are now on a collision course. What to do?

2. Richard Nixon and China's Mao

Here is a rumored dialog between China's Mao and Richard Nixon in 1972:
1) Mao: "Aren't you worried about a revolution, as guns are so widely available over there?"
2) Nixon: "No! Revolutions are not caused by guns, but by the smart people at the bottom. The American system allows the smart people to move up. So there will be no revolution in America."

Nixon was right! America, as the "land of opportunity", has been the beacon to attract the best to come here and to allow the best in America to make it.

3. Pyramid Theory I

Everything substantive in our society is pyramidal, with the "winners" sitting on the top and the majority filling in the middle and bottom. Three examples:
1) Wealth: Bill Gates and Warren Buffett are on the pinnacle. The rest of us fill in the middle and bottom.
2) Jobs: There are always more low-pay jobs than high-pay jobs (relatively). If you are good, get a high-pay one!
3) Business: There are always more workers than owners. If you are really good, be an owner!

The pyramidal shape not only follows physics (e.g. gravity), but also is the result of our capitalism at its best: You can make it if you work hard and if you are good (and lucky), even all the way to the 1% club! I am a modern-day example of an American dream come true (Chapter 74: "My American Dream Has Come True").

However, no matter how much our society advances (e.g. computers and the Internet), there are always the needs of having garbage collected and lawns mowed. In other words, while we are the best on earth to give anybody and everybody opportunities to move up (i.e. success), the majority of us will end up in the middle or bottom, as it should be. But politics changes that ...

4. Politics

American politics is all about obtaining votes. Because of the lack of term-limits, most, if not all, of the politicians work for one purpose only: getting re-elected *ad nauseam*. So they will do anything and everything to win your votes, including creating various socialist schemes in defiance of "Pyramid Theory I". Three examples:

1) Home ownership: If you want a bigger and better home than you can actually afford, no problem - we will have Fannie Mae or Freddie Mac help you out.

2) Job creation: We are willing to spend on such wasteful things as [a bridge to nowhere]() and [Marine One](), all in the name of job creation (or preservation), so that some of you can pretend to be working while the government can pretend to be paying you.

3) Made in the USA: Just compare GM with Toyota. One key difference between them is the UAW,

which is endemic at GM but nonexistent at Toyota.

Here is a big problem: the government has little money of its own (other than money printing). Instead, it subsidizes the "losers" by taxing the "winners". In other words, it punishes success! As a result, the pool of winners will become smaller and, at this pace, will be dried out or chased away soon. Still wondering about my statement "America is becoming yesterday's China"? Wonder not! Democracy, as we know it today, looks more and more like communism (i.e. China under Mao or the former Soviet Union), and it is destroying America faster than most Americans realize! Yes, punishing success, you will end up without any success!

5. What's the point?

Democracy is not a corner stone for America at all! Capitalism is, and the only one! In other words, capitalism is the foundation not only for America, but also for democracy, as illustrated below.

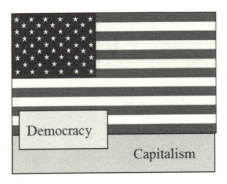

Furthermore, when democracy gets too big and too distorted, it will crash the foundation, resulting in a catastrophic collapse of America, as illustrated below:

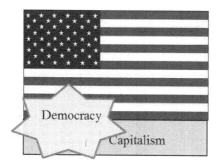

6. What should we do?

We must do three things in principle:
1) We must clearly recognize that capitalism is the foundation of our country, with democracy being merely an option. Sacrificing capitalism for democracy, we will end up having neither.
2) Clearly accept the human nature tenet: "me first". Yes, it applies to politicians too! However, unlike capitalists who have no problem admitting "me first", our politicians pretend to be "you first". In reality, they are all "me first", for which they care about your vote, not necessarily you. Worse yet, they are willing to win your vote at any cost, even if it means destroying America by emptying her public treasury! Worse still, they can be easily and openly bribed. Just look at this example: 81 House members just enjoyed an all-expense paid hiatus in Israel.
3) Design/change our political system to accommodate this human nature tenet, not denying or defying it, as it is now!

Specifically, we must stick to *capitalism* and dramatically improve our *democracy* with one fundamental change: Term-limits for the political offices, starting with the American Presidency: setting it to be one-term (e.g. six years) and raising the statutory requirements! For more, read Chapter 2.

7. Middle-Out Economics

During the 2012 campaign, President Obama fashioned something called "Middle-Out Economics". What is it? The diagram below visually compares it with Pyramid Theory I.

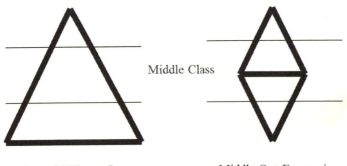

Middle Class

Pyramid Theory I   Middle-Out Economics

As is easy to see, middle-out does not even follow physics (e.g. gravity). Therefore, it is either trivial (e.g. just a physical shape) or unreal if it is deemed serious for anything in life.

Here is my take: Middle-Out Economics is unreal – it's just politics for votes!

8. Closing

Physics over politics! Pyramid Theory I over Middle-Out Economics!

Chapter 19: Loop Theory - Capitalism vs. Socialism

In this chapter, I will present a loop theory to further support my writings on politics. The loop theory is to simply and clearly define the relationship between capitalism and socialism. It was formulated by simply modifying Karl Marx's theory of societal development.

1. What's Marx's theory?

Figure 1 highlights Karl Marx's theory of societal development: evolution from some early societies (e.g. slavery) to feudalism, to capitalism, to socialism, and finally to communism.

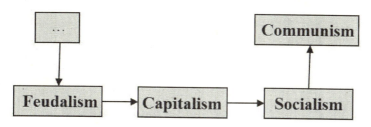

Figure 1: Marx's theory of societal development

At a very high level, this theory is right. Two individuals capitalized on this theory more than anybody else: Lenin and Mao. Both of them eventually failed for the same reason: They jumped from feudalism to socialism via a violent revolution that destroyed capitalism (in its primitive stage in their respective countries) first. Yes, the Soviet Union was a total disaster, as was China under Mao (1949-1976). China under Mao was actually feudalism, with Mao being China's last *de facto* emperor!

2. The loop theory

Figure 2 shows my loop theory by extending and truncating Marx's theory as follows:

1) Capitalism and socialism are in a loop, requiring balancing from time to time. Capitalism is a must for prosperity. Socialism, if poorly managed, may set us back to feudalism!
2) Communism is so far away that we all should ignore it.

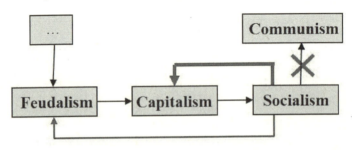

Figure 2: The loop theory

3. Where is everybody in societal development?

Let's examine four representative countries (or regions) one by one.

3.1 Middle East and North Africa

Most of them are in feudalism, both in form and in content. In form, a dictator with a family member in succession is essentially a king. In content, the #1 problem for all these countries is abject poverty, as none of them has had a boost from capitalism yet. In other words, capitalism is the only way to prosperity. Democracy *per se*, on the other hand, will inevitably lead to socialism, which, without capitalism, has proven to be a total disaster (e.g. the former Soviet Union and China under Mao). For this reason, I am not optimistic about the outcome of the Arab Spring. The region is likely to become the next India, with democracy being a liability for prosperity.

Once again, there is not a single precedent of a third world country achieving prosperity via democracy!

3.2 China

China moved from feudalism to capitalism after Mao's death in 1976, and is becoming more and more capitalistic, on track to becoming yesterday's America. What the West needs to understand is that the Chinese system (i.e. capitalism + autocracy) is like a military machine, [relatively] efficient and effective (far from being perfect though). What's even more perilous for the West is that this Chinese machine is moving in the right direction and this system of "a dictatorship without a dictator" cannot be easily derailed! Yes, there are many developmental bubbles in China (e.g. real estate). Yes, the economy will certainly slow down, especially when as compared with the current neck-breaking speed. But everything is under control – that's the beauty of the Chinese system! The Chinese government can pick and choose which bubble to deflate when it sees the necessity. Bottom line: there will be no financial crisis in China, as many westerners have been worrying about …

Needless to say, the Chinese system has a lot of problems, with government corruption and environmental pollution being the top two. But nothing is fundamentally and structurally wrong at this time, especially when compared with what the West is experiencing now.

3.3 Europe

Europe has had a good run over the past few hundred years. But it has so overspent its future for the present and gone so deeply into socialism now that Europe, as a whole, is on the verge of bankruptcy. Several countries are already there, with more to follow. What's the way out? No way!

3.4 America

America is marching toward more and more deeply into socialism, following Europe. To know how bad it can be, read this (After the London Riots) and this (The Social Degeneration Of The West). In case you do not know, there is absolutely no room for this kind of violence in China today!

More profoundly, why can't America compete against China? It's the political system, stupid! China's political system is, overall, slightly better than America's!

4 Closing

Human legacy includes a history of leadership changing hands. For the past 200 years, China went through hell, with nothing but human misery and humiliation. It appears that China has finally struck its own way of success – good for the Chinese! America, on the other hand, has had a wonderful run for the past 200 years, but is rapidly losing its way now.

America can still slow down the decline, if not stop it, by metamorphosing now as I suggested (Chapter 2). But it won't be easy and time is running against us.

Chapter 20: American Democracy: What Went Wrong and When?

Armchair generals can point out "what's wrong" about anything, especially for a vast subject like America.

I think I am uniquely qualified to do so, because I believe I have the most accurate diagnosis for America (Chapter 1), as well as the best solution (Chapter 2). In other words, nit picking is allowed only after you have offered a credible solution like I do!

1. The U.S. Constitution

Let me repeat my solution (from Chapter 2) that the U.S. Constitution should be amended as follows:
1) Limiting the American Presidency to one-term (e.g. six years).
2) Raising the statutory requirements for the American Presidency, such as the minimum age to 55 (from 35) and only after having served as a state governor for a full-term, at least.
3) Introducing strict term-limits for Congress, preferably one-term (e.g. six years) as well.

Why these major changes? In addition to my numerous writings on the subject, here is an excerpt from US Constitution Online:

> *"Thomas Jefferson himself was wary of the power of the dead over the living in the form of an unchanging Constitution. To ensure that each generation have a say in the framework of the government, he proposed that the Constitution, and each one following it, expire after 19 or 20 years."*

So these changes are long overdue! For example, 200 years ago, the average life expectancy in America was less than 55. Today, it's more than 75! Therefore, it's demographically correct to change the minimum age of the American Presidency from 35 to 55! More on this later in Section 8!

2. America: 1776 - 1918

America thrived economically throughout this period, largely because of rugged individualism and unfettered capitalism. The government played a relatively insignificant role in the economy, especially when compared with today. For example, Thomas Edison invented the light bulb and electricity without help from the government. Henry Ford invented the assembly lines in the same way.

Very importantly, throughout this period, all members of Congress served without pay, because they were successful (i.e. rich) people, and they truly served for the betterment of their country, with no monetary returns!

3. America: 1918 – 1945

The role of the government expanded substantially after WWI ended in 1918. Two things went very wrong during this period:
1) <u>The start of career politicians</u>: Read Chapter 1.
2) Great Depression: It was bad. The government initiated many social programs to fight against it, but none of them really helped America get out of the Great Depression. The advent of WWII, not the massive government spending on the various social programs, finally pulled America out of the Great Depression. Both Presidents Hoover and Roosevelt acknowledged it as a fact.

However, that has never dissuaded many left-wing extremists from stridently proclaiming the importance of excessive government spending, from the Great Depression to today's Great Recession.

Now, let's single out two issues that have profound implications to America today:
1) Government programs: Three major government programs that were all well intentioned to begin with, but turned out to be problematic, at least, down the road:
    - Smoot-Hawley Tariff: It actually helped worsen the Great Depression. It badly hurt Europe, America's chief trading partner at the time, which in turn hurt America, prolonging the Great Depression on both continents.
    - New Deal: This was the beginning of America as an entitlement society vs. unfettered capitalism based on rugged individualism.
    - Social Security: It is not an entitlement program *per se*, especially for those who have paid into it. Rather, it's a Ponzi scheme predestined to fail! In fact, it is such a big Ponzi scheme that it makes Bernie Madoff look trivial!
2) Keynesian economics: It is basically sound. It has two elements: <A> the government saves in good times and <B> the government spends extra in bad times. Unfortunately, many left-wing extremists (e.g. Paul Krugman and Robert Reich) conveniently forget about <A> while actively advocating an extreme version of <B>, as extreme as deficit spending is the only way to get

out of today's Great Recession. Total abuse of Keynes! For more, go to Chapter 53 ("Karl Marx and John Keynes").

For a comprehensive review of how the progressive movement flourished during this period of time, read: The Progressive Movement's Discredited Legacy.

4. America: 1945 – 1989

This was the Cold War period, in which the West, led by the U.S., competed against the East, led primarily by the former Soviet Union and seconded by China. By 1989, the West had won, unquestionably!

Throughout this period, the U.S. enjoyed prosperity unprecedented in human history. However, several time bombs were seeded which are now exploding! Three examples:

1) Public-sector unions: Here is a good article about them: The New Tammany Hall. Above all, I believe public-sector unions are totally communistic and must therefore go! In fact, this one has done so much on-going damage to America that I don't think history will be very kind to President Kennedy (more on this later).

2) Medicare and Medicaid: We have been borrowing to pay for them since their inception! Like Social Security, Medicare is a Ponzi scheme! What about Medicaid? It's purely an entitlement! They were perpetrated on us by President Johnson, as part of the Great Society.

3) Community Reinvestment Act (CRA): It was the key factor in the creation of the housing bubble that burst in 2008, with no easy way out, even today. The CRA was passed on President Carter's watch.

JFK, LBJ, and Jimmy Carter were all Democrats! Is that a coincidence? No! The Democratic Party has been the party of entitlements since FDR! Why? Because the beneficiaries of the entitlements form the bulk of that party! In short, it's money for votes, even if it means destroying America by emptying her public treasury!

The Republican Presidents during this period were better, with Ronald Reagan standing out as the best American President after WWII! For more, read Chapter 32 ("Top 10 American Misconceptions about 10 Recent American Presidents").

5. America: 1990 – 2000

Throughout this decade, America thrived again, largely because of the groundwork laid by President Reagan in the 1980s, including the end of the Cold War in 1989. There were two big problems during this period that have become increasingly clear now:

1) We failed to adjust adequately after the Cold War ended in 1989.
   - Our military was too big and we became a major source of instability around the world, especially in the Middle East. Yes, Ron Paul got this one right (Ron Paul on 9/11: Ask the right questions and face the truth)!
   - China embraced capitalism big time, and was on its way to becoming a formidable economic competitor to America.
2) CRA: President Clinton, another Democrat, amended it to its final, and lethal, form, thus ensuring a spectacular housing bubble that burst in 2008.

For more, read Chapter 31: "The Myth of The Bill Clinton Presidency".

6. America: 2001 – 2012
The bottom fell out! Here are two main reasons:
1) The rise of BRICS, led by China, has given America (and the West) the first real competition after WWII.
2) The incompetence of America's political system finally showed up and years of excessive government spending have eventually caught up with us.

As a result, we ended up with two worst Presidents in history:
1) George W. Bush: for "turning off the beacon" to launch the Iraq War.
2) Barack Obama: for being the biggest spender, by far, in U.S. history! Our national debt has skyrocketed from $9T in 2009 to $16T in 2012!

"Together the policies of these two Presidents have done more damage to America than all of America's enemies have done, combined! The biggest threat to America is its faltering economy, which is plainly visible now!" For more, go to Chapter 30 ("American Presidents: Three Best and Three Worst").

7. Discussion
Why is America so deeply in trouble today? It's the political system, stupid!

7.1 No competition, no problem
From 1945 to 2000, it did not really matter very much who the American President was, because America's economy was so much better than the East and so much larger than its competitors within the West (e.g. Germany and Japan). In other words, America, as the economic monopoly, simply could do no wrong,

including the push to sacrifice some capitalism for democracy, as a necessary expense to quell resentment of the prosperous. But not any longer! Democracy is now destroying capitalism, the engine of American success, in its inevitable march toward destructive socialism. For more, go to Part 10!

7.2 Competition

At the turn of the 21st century, China emerged as a true economic competitor for America for the first time after WWII. This competitor is different from the previous ones as follows:
1) Economically: Unlike America's former competitors (e.g. Germany and Japan), China has both the size and weight to provide real competition for America.
2) Politically: Unlike the East vs. the West before the Cold War ended in 1989, China's political system is, in my view, slightly better than America's.

Let me repeat (from Chapter 5): *"America still has two huge advantages over China: abundance of natural resources and vastly more advanced capitalism. However, these two advantages may be inadequate to compensate for the inferiority of America's political system."*

One huge difference between America and China is the leaders at the top! Just compare the resumes: President Obama vs. President Hu Jintao and Xi Jinping (China's VP and the next President). No comparison in substance! Barack Obama did not have any executive experience before becoming the American President, while the Chinese leaders all have great track records before taking the top jobs in China! It's the political system, stupid! In a nutshell, the American President is elected via a popularity contest, while *"the next leaders in China have been long prepared by the current leaders, in a way similar to the GE way"* (Chapter 16: "America: What is China's Political System, Anyway?").

Leadership matters!

8. The solution

Constitutional changes (Chapter 2)! It's the only way for America to have any chance in its head-on competition with China!

Now, why are term-limits for Congress not law yet, despite the fact that people have been crying for them for decades? Two main reasons:
1) They are not in the Constitution. They were not needed 200 years ago, because all Congressional positions were unpaid.
2) They are not in any amendments. They are unwanted by lawmakers, because most of them have been self-serving career politicians, since the end of WWII, at least.

Bottom line: How long can a country stay at the top when its top politicians, systematically and consistently, serve themselves first, their constituents a remote second, and their country dead last?

9. Closing

America is desperately in need of a strong leader, a commanding presence, to clean up the mess in Washington and move towards an ideal form of government (Chapter 3). My solution (Chapter 2) is the only workable proposal on the table!

Time is running out! Unless we can change our political system for the better soon, America will be finished.

Adapt and change!

Chapter 21: American Democracy: Massive Falsehoods at the Top

In the last chapter, I asked:

"How long can a country stay at the top when its top politicians, systematically and consistently, serve themselves first, their constituents a remote second, and their country dead last?"

In this chapter, I will highlight the massive falsehoods in American democracy at the very top around one theme: getting re-elected *ad nauseam*. I will use three examples: Vice President Biden; President Obama; and the American Presidency.

1. Vice President Joe Biden

On July 10, 2010, Mr. Biden appeared on the Jay Leno show and said something like this:

"Over the years, I have learned not to question people about their motives - just look at the things on the table (e.g. a proposed legislation) and deal with them."

I was stunned upon hearing that: Joe is unreal, because motivation is often where analysis should start (according to CBS's CSI, at least). Then I realized Joe could have been telling the truth (as he often does, awkwardly): There is only one true motivation among Joe's political friends and foes: getting re-elected *ad nauseam*. Everything they do serves that purpose! So if they would all question each other about the motivation, life would have stopped right there and then! In other words, it is the "don't ask, don't tell" thing in American politics that Joe inadvertently revealed to the world!

Still unconvinced about this "getting re-elected *ad nauseam*" thing? Listen to New York Mayor Michael Bloomberg: Mayor Bloomberg on politicians.

2. President Barack Obama

Like most American career politicians, President Obama serves, throughout his first term, for one supreme purpose only: getting re-elected *ad nauseam*. Three examples:

1) The Afghan War: Read: For Obama the Road to Reelection Runs through Kabul. Here is an excerpt: *"The real goals of the Afghanistan escalation are domestic and electoral ... The real purpose of these 300,000 soldiers is to make Obama look tough as he heads toward the next US presidential election."* While the reality is debatable, the perception alone is frightening! Michael Hastings's article ("The Runaway General") further confirms the perception. Worse yet, it is patently obvious that the troop withdrawal plan was timed perfectly for his re-election schedule. Apparently, no price is too high for us to pay for his re-election!

2) 2012 State of the Union Address: Here is what Senate Minority Leader Mitch McConnell said: "It was a campaign speech." While there should be no surprise to partisan talks nowadays, there is a lot of truth to his assessment. Any doubt? Watch the speech (again) by yourself!

3) 2012 Budget: Here is what Senate Majority Leader Harry Reid said: "No, I don't plan to bring a budget to the floor this year." It has been more than 1,000 days since the Senate last passed a

budget! Game on! Politics tops everything, and to hell with the country!

It's not entirely fair to blame President Obama alone for this. Rather, this has actually been a big part of the American Presidency! Any doubt? Let's review.

3. American Presidency

Like most American career politicians, an American President serves his first term, in modern time at least, for one supreme purpose only: getting re-elected *ad nauseam*. As a result, many recent American presidents damaged America severely by introducing, during their first term, mega social programs that were predestined to fail, or even launching a massive pre-emptive war as in Iraq. No, no price is too high for re-election. Five examples:

1) FDR: Social Security (introduced in 1935). It is the biggest Ponzi scheme ever!
2) JFK: Public-sector unions (permitted in 1961, via Executive Order 10988). They are totally communistic and must therefore go! This one has done so much on-going damage to America that I don't think history will be very kind to President Kennedy!
3) LBJ: Medicare and Medicaid (both introduced in 1965). We have been borrowing to pay for them since their inception!
4) GWB: The Iraq War (launched in 2003). I believe President George W. Bush launched the Iraq War, at least partially, for the sake of his re-election.
5) BHO: Obamacare. It was introduced in 2010 when we could least afford it.

Let me emphasize again: All five things mentioned above "happened" to occur during the first term of these

Presidents! Was that a coincidence? No! All of them were introduced to maximize the chance of their re-elections; each happened to be causing maximum damage to America after their term as President.

4. Closing

It's time to face the truth: American democracy does not work! My solution (Chapter 2) is the only workable proposal on the table! Many of our problems can be avoided and solved with one term for the American Presidency!

Part 7.2: American Presidency

Chapter 22: American Presidency: Why is One-Term a Must?
Chapter 23: American Presidency: Raising the Minimum Age to 55!
Chapter 24: From NBA to American Idol, to American Presidency
Chapter 25: The American Presidency: Let's Redefine It, Now!
Chapter 26: An Open Letter to Mitt Romney
Chapter 27: An Open Letter to President Obama
Chapter 28: George Washington vs. Mao Zedong
Chapter 29: Mitt Romney vs. Deng Xiaoping
Chapter 30: American Presidents: Three Best and Three Worst
Chapter 31: The Myth of the Bill Clinton Presidency
Chapter 32: Top 10 American Misconceptions about 10 Recent American Presidents
Chapter 33: Top 10 American Misconceptions about Mitt Romney
Chapter 34: American Presidency: Is It A Joke?
Chapter 35: Another Open Letter to Mitt Romney

Chapter 22: American Presidency: Why Is One-Term a Must?

I already identified the root cause of many American ills as the incompetence of America's political system -- (Chapter 1), and proposed a solution (Chapter 2), with one-term (e.g. six years) for the American Presidency being the core. This chapter focuses on the core.

America's political system is fundamentally flawed for two main reasons:
1) Representation: Democracy requires participation. Unfortunately, the majority oftentimes remains silent and the most vocal are heard most. Who, then, are the most vocal? Various special interest groups (e.g. unions)! Who are totally voiceless? The future generations! Still wondering why & how we have piled up huge debts on their back? Wonder not – The future generations have no representation in our system! Our politicians care more about the next election than about the next generation! President Obama cared more about his re-election than about anything else!
2) Constitution: We live in a world of changes, but our Constitution has hardly changed over the past 200 years. Is this a virtue or incompetence? To me, one big change is long overdue: setting one-term (e.g. six years) for the American Presidency.

American politics is said to have checks & balances. What are the ultimate checks & balances against the kind of extreme democracy in America today? Dictatorship! Before we surrender to this destiny, let's try a better solution: setting the American Presidency to be one-term (e.g. six years). Here are two main reasons:

1) A President limited by one-term is the closest to a dictator America needs today! This, together with some term-limits for Congress (preferably one-term of six years too), will give democracy another chance to work before the Chinese system prevails.
2) History shows that with the burden of re-election, a President could be reckless, trying to get re-elected at any cost, to such an extreme recently that presidential politics seemed to have played a huge role in the wars (e.g. Iraq and Afghanistan). In that sense alone, a democratically elected President is perhaps even worse than a worst dictator!

One legitimate concern, as expressed to me by former House Speaker Dennis Hastert during our meeting on April 4, 2011 (pictured below) is this: "six years may be too long to get rid of a bad President."

with former House Speaker Dennis Hastert, April 4, 2011

This problem is unique in America, as the American President is by far the most powerful person in the world, yet the statutory requirements for being the President are virtually nonexistent. For example, Senator Obama had no executive experience of running anything, not even a candy shop, and his resume was not good enough to run any big American company. But he won the popularity contest of the American Presidency! Now, has President Obama spent enough of your grandchildren's money to buy your vote for his re-election? Yes, apparently!

In addition to one-term, we must raise the statutory requirements for the Presidency, such as the minimum age of 55 (from 35) and having served as a state governor for one full-term, at least. That way, an American President can be as experienced as many other world leaders, such as China's. It's a competitive world out there and there is no substitute for experience!

Adapt or die! Human legacy is a history of evolution. Why should America's political system be so different? How long are we to continue to sleep on the 200-year-old system?

Chapter 23: American Presidency: Raising the Minimum Age to 55!

I already called America's political system inferior compared to China's and proposed that the American Presidency be limited to one term (e.g. six years) and the minimum age for the American presidency be raised to 55 (from 35). This chapter focuses on age.

The Chinese Constitution requires that the president be minimally aged at 45. Because the Chinese President is also the head of the ruling CPC (Communist Party of China) and a member of its Politburo Standing Committee whose age limit is 68 (for entry), a Chinese President typically takes office at about age 60, limited by two terms (five years/term). For example, President Hu is 69, while the next President Xi is currently 59.

With this kind of top-down age limit and a bottom-up laddered system for career advancement (i.e. mayor, governor, VP, and president), a Chinese President has an optimal combination of experience (i.e. neither too young, nor too inexperienced without going through the ladder) and judgment (i.e. not too old). Yes, both Hu and Xi served as both governors and VP, before taking the top job in China.

Applying China's criterion and system to America, there would have been neither President Obama (too young & too inexperienced – not being a governor) nor Presidential candidate McCain (too old & too inexperienced – not being a governor). Aren't we better off that way? Now, you might argue this: what about President Kennedy (too young) and President Reagan (too old)? Neither faced a formidable economic competitor like China! Times have changed! For more on Presidents Kennedy and Reagan, read Chapter 32 ("Top 10 American Misconceptions about 10 Recent American Presidents").

On top of the quality of its leaders, China's government today is far more pro-business than ours, even per Steve Wynn. Still wondering how and why China is now our biggest creditor? Wonder not! China's political system is, overall, slightly better than ours, and China's top leaders are far better than ours!

Here is a formula for disaster (especially in a competitive world today):

> young president + re-election = disaster

Yes, both Presidents George W. Bush and Barack Obama proved to be disasters for America! Are we just bad luck to have two bad Presidents in a row? No, it's the political system, stupid! The world has changed fundamentally and big, but we have not accordingly! In other words, unless our political system is fundamentally changed for the better as I suggested (Chapter 2), the streak of bad Presidents will continue.

One valid argument, as expressed to me by former House Speaker Dennis Hastert during our meeting on April 4, 2011, is this: "experience is important, not age."

Unfortunately, experience is not quantifiable, but age is. Besides, experience cannot be obtained without the time to do so. Therefore, I prefer a competitive minimum age without a loophole, especially when it is predicated by one term (e.g. six years).

Now, why is one-term a must for America, but China has two? Because America is a democracy, but China is not! An American politician with re-election in mind works for one purpose only: getting re-elected *ad nauseam*!

Chapter 24: From NBA, to American Idol, to American Presidency

(Initially published at GEI on 8/5/2011)

Democracy, in its "pure" form, simply means "one person, one vote" and the candidate with the most votes is declared the winner. It is a popularity contest by definition.

When a popularity contest becomes big, it inevitably becomes a showbiz. Now, does democracy really work in the showbiz? Let's see three showbiz examples: NBA, American Idol, and the American Presidency.

1. Showbiz #1: National Basketball Association

NBA honors some all-stars every year. Ten starters (i.e. five for the West and five for the East) are selected by the fans via votes, while the reserves are chosen by the coaches. Two issues:

1) The starting center for the West in the 2010-2011 season was Yao Ming, thanks to his millions of fans in China, despite the fact that Yao played only about five games before his season-ending injury and he missed the entire 2009-2010 season due to injury.
2) Why can't the fans vote for the reserves as well?

Pure democracy does not work - NBA knows!

2. Showbiz #2: American Idol

In this popular TV show (for more than a decade), 50% of the points of a contestant are decided by the fans via votes, while the other 50% by a panel of three judges. Two issues:

1) Why can't the fans decide the entire 100% points by votes?
2) Why is there such an outrageously anti-democracy rule called "save", by which the panel can "save" a contestant by totally ignoring the votes by the fans?

Pure democracy does not work - American Idol knows!

3. Showbiz #3: American Presidency

An American President is chosen much more democratically (despite the existence of the Electoral College) than NBA's all-stars as a whole or an American Idol. Why is that? If democracy does not even work for NBA or American Idol, how could we possibly expect it to work for a much more serious business like the American Presidency?

Maybe the American Presidency has not been a serious business at all, especially after WWII. It seemed to have worked out well for America [until recently] because America's free enterprise system was so much better than the other systems that America, as a country, could simply do no wrong. More modestly, America might have screwed up from time to time, but America's competitors screwed up a lot more (e.g. Germany and Japan in WWII, and the former Soviet Union and China throughout the Cold War). Now it does not seem to be working any longer because the rest of the world has finally caught up with America, especially China. China opened for business in the 1990s, with a copy of America's economic system (with a long way to go though) and a political system that is "slightly better" than ours. Worse yet, decades of the big screw-ups by American politicians in general and by the American

Presidents in specific have finally caught up with America too, bringing our economy down to its knees ...

Want some examples of the big Presidential screw-ups? Here is an excerpt from Chapter 21 ("American Democracy: Massive Falsehoods at The Top"):
1) FDR: Social Security (introduced in 1935). It is the biggest Ponzi scheme ever!
2) JFK: Public-sector unions (permitted in 1961, Executive Order 10988). They are totally communistic and must therefore go! This one has done so much on-going damage to America that I don't think history will be very kind to President Kennedy!
3) LBJ: Medicare and Medicaid (both introduced in 1965). We have been borrowing to pay for them since their inception!
4) GWB: The Iraq War (launched in 2003). I believe President George W. Bush launched the Iraq War, at least partially, for the sake of his re-election.
5) BHO: Obamacare. It was introduced in 2010 when we could least afford it.

Now, how about some examples showing that President Obama has become a laughing stock around the world? Three examples:
1) The world laughed when President Obama came out to speak against school bullying. Has President Obama trivialized himself to that level?
2) The Chinese laughed when President Obama issued a memorandum, establishing a task force on childhood obesity. Is this really a job for the government? Which government is more controlling: "communist" China or "free" America?

3) Americans laughed (or cried) after its government, led from behind by President Obama, finally solved the debt-limit crisis back in August 2011, which was created by the politicians in the first place. What is America's #1 problem? Jobs? No, that's the #1 problem for the politicians (yes, it's the votes, stupid!). America's #1 problem is debts! Do we really need another [super] committee to study the problem? What about the report by President's own committee chaired by Alan Simpson and Erskine Bowles (Chapter 41: "The Congressional Super-Committee: What a Joke!")? President Obama ignored it, completely! He again kicked the can down the road, just beyond his re-election bid this time, all the while America continues to suffer! Fool me once, shame on you. Fool me twice, shame on me!

Case made that the American Presidency has not been a serious business, after WWII at least? Can we afford to have more Presidents who are inexperienced and incompetent as compared with the other world leaders? Above all, can we afford to have another President who serves for no purpose but his own re-election at all costs?

On the other hand, the American Presidency may not be a "pure" business *per se*. For this reason, let's give it another chance to work by setting it to be one-term (e.g. six years) and raising the statutory requirements before it's determined by a popularity contest, shall we?

4. Conclusion

Given the fact that our country is so deeply in trouble, it's time for us to seriously examine the American Presidency in specific and American democracy in general, before it's really too late.

Rome was not built in one day, nor did it go down in one day! Should I also mention Greece?

Chapter 25: American Presidency: Let's Redefine It, Now!

(Initially published at GEI on 9/30/2011)

America is deeply in trouble. Nobody deserves more blame than President Obama as well as his predecessor, President George W. Bush. Out of disappointment and despair, many older (and wiser) Americans (i.e. age 50 and up) are reminiscent over Ronald Reagan (e.g. Looking for Ronald Reagan – and Not Finding Him). While I consider Reagan to be one of the best Presidents in American history, I doubt even President Reagan would be up to today's challenges. Why? Times have changed - it's the political system, stupid! It's the new China factor, stupid! Specifically, here are my two arguments:

1) From 1950 to 2000, the American Presidency mattered little - anybody reasonably intelligent could have been President without it having made a live-or-die difference for America. This is not true today, as evidenced by what America has been going through since 2000, with the far worse yet to come. Unconvinced? Read this: Behind the poverty number: real lives, real pain.

2) Since 2001, the American Presidency has mattered a lot more. Both Presidents George W. Bush and Barack Obama are proven disasters, far worse than the previous worst [in recent history]: President Jimmy Carter!

What was so special about the year 2000? The world had changed so much after the Cold War ended in 1989 that 2000 turned out to be a tipping point, with BRICS, led by China, becoming formidable competitors to the

West, like never before. China has not only the size and weight to compete with America, but also a totally different political system, which is, in my opinion, slightly better than America's political system. America, on the other hand, has not adapted adequately after 1989: America's foreign and economic policy has not changed enough. The political system has hardly changed at all over more than 200 years. By 2000, America had not only more economic competitors than ever, but also more political enemies (e.g. Islamic extremists) than ever. No American Presidents, from 1950 to 2000, faced such dual challenges, especially on the economic front. Two examples:

1) Job losses due to economic downturns had been temporary before, but more and more permanent after 2000.
2) Years of excessive spending and screw-ups by American politicians (e.g. Social Security, Medicare & Medicaid, and public-sector unions) have finally caught up with America.

As a result, the incompetence of America's political system in general, and specifically of the American Presidency, has become more and more evident: President George W. Bush recklessly turned off the beacon to launch the Iraq War, while President Obama has made a bad situation much worse by spending like there is no tomorrow.

What was the common thread between these two disastrous Presidents? Most damage was done during their first term! Why and how? Getting re-elected *ad nauseam*! Consequentially, today, America has not only even more economic competitors and political enemies than in 2000, but also much stronger duals than in 2000!

Worse still, further damage will be done to America's economy throughout President Obama's remaining time in office. Recently, he started a new class warfare against the rich for the sake of his re-election! Robbing the rich to help the poor? Everybody will be poor! Any doubt? Just ask the Chinese living under Mao or the citizens of the former Soviet Union! This is good politics for President Obama, but bad economics for America!

America is desperately in need of a great President to turn things around! How great? A combination of George Washington, Thomas Jefferson, Abraham Lincoln, and Ronald Reagan! Specifically, here is what must occur:
1) President Obama must not be re-elected!
2) Elect a Republican as the next American President! Neither Rick Perry nor Mitt Romney is perfect. But either will be far better than President Obama for two key reasons:
   - Both of them exceed my minimum requirements for the American Presidency: such as being older than 55 and having had a full-term governorship.
   - Both of them have a far better proven track record than President Obama, who had no track record as an executive of any kind before becoming the President and has had a terrible one as the President.

Now, how to choose between Rick Perry and Mitt Romney? Apply, if not demand, a litmus test as follows:
1) Commit to one-term (i.e. four years) only. No fooling around for re-election!
2) Commit to significant constitutional changes (Chapter 2).

Bottom line: The American Presidency matters now more than ever! Having a President serving for no purpose but his own re-election? Allowed no more!

America, change or die! Now it's time to redefine the American Presidency by electing a new President, who will get his priorities absolutely right without ambiguity: country first, constituents next, and personal agendas last!

Chapter 26: An Open Letter to Mitt Romney

(Initially published at GEI on 5/18/2012)

Dear Governor Romney,

Congratulations on your success in becoming the Republican nominee for President, soon!

As an independent, I wanted to let you know that I have already voted for you twice in the primaries (i.e. 2008 and 2012), and I intend to vote for you again in November.

As a writer, I strongly supported you (and Governor Perry) publicly on 9/30/2011 (Chapter 25). Here is an excerpt:
1) President Obama must not be re-elected!
2) Elect a Republican as the next American President! Neither Rick Perry nor Mitt Romney is perfect. But either will be far better than President Obama for two key reasons:
    - Both of them exceed my minimum requirements for the American Presidency, such as being older than 55 and having had a full-term governorship.
    - Both of them have a far better proven track record than President Obama, who had no track record as an executive of any kind before becoming the President and has had a terrible one as the President.

Now, will you win against President Obama in November? Most likely not! Here is why:
1) Our system favors the incumbents. This is especially true for President Obama, who has been

boldly running for re-election since his first day in the White House.
2) President Obama just launched a class warfare, which, I am afraid, will prove effective, ultimately.
3) Your neo-cons-flavored foreign policy could be even worse than President George W. Bush's! Most Americans do not like that (Weary Warriors Favor Obama).

Next, even if you win (Poll: Obama's gay marriage stance could hurt him), so what?
1) You are likely to be trapped into this "getting re-elected *ad nauseam*" thing, putting your personal interest of re-election way above our country's interest, like most of the recent American Presidents did!
2) Mathematically speaking, the difference between President Romney and President Obama is likely to be $5T: by 2016, our national debt will be $20T under President Romney vs. $25T under President Obama. Either way, we, as a country, will be screwed!

In short, even if you win by beating the unlikely odds, you are likely to merely increase the stats of "yet another bad President" by one! No, nothing personal - it's the political system, stupid!

But it does not have to be that way!

Here is a formula not only to guarantee you to win but also to save our country: Put the following two points on top of everything you already have!

1) You promise to be a one-term (i.e. four years) President, dedicating yourself to running the country without re-election.
2) You promise to fix the political system fundamentally by changing the Constitution as follows:
   - Limiting the American Presidency to one-term (e.g. six years).
   - Raising the statutory requirements for the American Presidency, such as the minimum age to 55 and only after having served as a state governor for one full-term, at least.
   - Introducing strict term-limits for Congress, preferably one-term of six years as well.

That way, not only will you become the next American President, you will also be remembered as one of the greatest American Presidents, ever!

Now, imagine this: On your 70th birthday (March 12, 2017), people will compare you with President George Washington as follows:
1) What did President Washington do? He created the Republic!
2) What did President Romney do? He saved the Republic!

What more do you want as a 70-year-old man by then?

How much greater than this do you think a human being can possibly be?

Thank you!

Chapter 27: An Open Letter to President Obama

(Initially published at GEI on 6/22/2012)

Dear President Obama,

Five weeks ago, I published an open letter to Mitt Romney, which has been so well received that it's only fair that I, an independent, write you an open letter now to balance it out.

To begin with, let me congratulate you, once again, for winning the election in 2008, fairly and squarely. Many of my Republican friends wouldn't give you a chance, but I did – I observed you for one year without judging, while constantly telling them: "Hey, give the guy a chance!"

Unfortunately, I am utterly disappointed at you today! Here are my two observations:
1) The job of the American Presidency has obviously been over your head: You did not have any executive experience before becoming the President. You have been learning on the job, which proved to be too little, too late.
2) While becoming an American President might have been an American Dream come true for you personally (Someday I want to be President), it has been a nightmare for America. Specifically,
    - You have proven to be the biggest spender in American history: Our national debt was enormous at $9T when you took office, but it will be more than $16T by the time you finish this term.

- You have been boldly running for re-election since your first day in the White House, instead of doing your job: running the country! Here is a basic question for you: Why do you want another term, if you are not even interested in being the President throughout your first term?

To be fair, I can't blame you for it all. Rather, "it's the political system, stupid!" Specifically,
1) Our system allowed an inexperienced person like you to become the President via a popularity contest, with few qualifications required.
2) Our system allowed you to serve in the White House for no purpose other than for your own re-election. What, then, is the best way to getting re-elected? Spending more and pandering more! No wonder you have been called "the food-stamp President" and "the first gay President"! Admittedly, some of your predecessors behaved similarly throughout their first terms as well. But you carried it to an extreme, such as waging a class warfare against the rich (read: Obama's Politics Are More Insidious Than Socialism), initiating a naked assault on capitalism (read: Obama: Bain attacks 'not a distraction'), and shamelessly playing politics with immigration (read: Obama takes a risk on immigration front).

Times have changed. The world has become much more competitive than ever. Consequently, America can simply no longer afford to elect an incompetent President who serves for no purpose other than his own re-election!

Today, America is not just deeply in trouble: fiscally, economically, and politically - it is heading in a totally wrong direction! For the near-term, look at Greece (i.e. running out of other people's money and running out of borrowing power). For the long-term, America could become yesterday's [Communist] China: robbing the rich to help the poor, thereby making everybody poor! Is this really where you want to take America? No, I bet not – you simply do not know what you are doing!

If you need a clue to what real governance is, ask Scott Walker, the Governor of Wisconsin! Here is what I state in Chapter 44 ("Public-Sector Unions: from Wisconsin to America"):

> *"What Governor Walker did was significant: It was a small step to undo the devastating damage caused by President Kennedy, but a gigantic step against the demise of America (Diagnosis for America: Cancer!)!"*

If you need to know how to tell the truth plainly (vs. pandering), watch this short video: You Are Not Special Commencement Speech from Wellesley High School.

Now, the re-election is just around the corner. I wish you would do two things as follows:
1) Stop blaming President George W. Bush for the economy! Did he do enormous damage to America? Yes, he did! Therefore, it's right for many Americans to blame him (Americans say Bush still more to blame than Obama for economy), but not for you. Why? Two reasons:
   - Without him, there would have been no President Obama!
   - You were elected to right his wrongs. You have had four years to do it, without success. It's time to let someone who is more capable do it!

2) Run a good re-election campaign against Governor Romney. As a result, you will bring the best out of him, especially the adoption of my proposal that he promises:
- To be a one-term President, dedicating himself to running the country without re-election.
- To fix the political system fundamentally by changing the Constitution as follows:
  - Limiting the American Presidency to one-term (e.g. six years).
  - Raising the statutory requirements for the American Presidency, such as the minimum age to 55 and only after having served as a state governor for one full-term, at least.
  - Introducing strict term-limits for Congress, preferably one-term of six years as well.

With that, not only will Governor Romney win in November, he will also have a chance to save America, thus becoming one of the greatest American Presidents, ever!

You, on the other hand, may still avoid being the worst American President in [recent] history, leaving that honor distinctively to President George W. Bush, whose legacy is surely defined in two points as follows:
1) The Iraq War. For more, read: "Blagojevich and Pearl Harbor: They Are Related!"
2) The creation of President Obama, the second worst American President in [recent] history!

In other words, with another term, you will surely take that honor away from President George W. Bush! Is that your desire?

Thank you!

Chapter 28: George Washington vs. Mao Zedong

(Initially published at GEI on 7/6/2012)

My niche in writing is the intersection between the U.S. and China. I often compare the two countries in various aspects, from the political systems to the college reunions (Chapter 77).

It's time to compare George Washington, "the Father of the U.S.", with Mao Zedong, "the Father of the People's Republic of China".

1. George Washington

Here is a description of George Washington per Wikipedia:

__George Washington__ (February 22, 1732 [O.S. February 11, 1731] – December 14, 1799) was the first President of the United States of America, serving from 1789 to 1797, and the dominant military and political leader of the United States from 1775 to 1799. He led the American victory over Great Britain in the American Revolutionary War as commander-in-chief of the Continental Army from 1775 to 1783, and presided over the writing of the Constitution in 1787. Washington became the first president, by unanimous choice, and oversaw the creation of a strong, well-financed national government that maintained neutrality in the wars raging in Europe, suppressed rebellion, and won acceptance among Americans of all types. His leadership style established many forms and rituals of government that have been used since, such as using a cabinet system and delivering an inaugural address.

Washington is universally regarded as the "Father of his country."

2. Mao Zedong

Here is a description of Mao Zedong per Wikipedia:

***Mao Zedong**, commonly referred to as **Chairman Mao** (December 26, 1893 – September 9, 1976), was a Chinese Communist revolutionary, guerrilla warfare strategist, Marxist political philosopher, and leader of the Chinese Revolution. He was the architect and founding father of the People's Republic of China (PRC) from its establishment in 1949, and held authoritarian control over the nation until his death in 1976. His theoretical contribution to Marxism–Leninism, along with his military strategies and brand of policies, are collectively known as Maoism.*

3. Washington vs. Mao

Here is my assessment:
1) Military strategy: Both Washington and Mao were brilliant military strategists. However, given the scale and speed of their respective victories, Mao achieved more. **Edge: Mao.**
2) Governance: Washington refused to be a king. He served for eight years and left the job, with his country well positioned for the future. Mao pretended to be a servant of the people, but turned out to be the *de facto* last emperor in China. China was ruined under his rule (1949-1976). With his country a shambles, Mao died heart-broken, as he spent his last decade, at least, scrambling for a succession plan, without success. **Edge: Washington.**
3) Influence upon the world: The country/system set up by Washington served as a beacon to the rest of

the world for more than 200 years (and counting), while Maoism has been clearly seen as a disaster all over the world. **Edge: Washington**.
4) <u>Legacy</u>: **Edge: Mao**. Here is why:
- If there is any truth to Patrick Fitzgerald's statement that Blagojevich's actions would make "*Lincoln roll over in his grave*" (<u>Fitzgerald regrets Lincoln Blagojevich comment</u>), then how would George Washington react upon reading this statement: "*The current form of the U.S government, as represented by the elected officials, is systematically corrupted by definition*" (Chapter 36: "Blagojevich and Pearl Harbor: They Are Related!")? Washington would be upset not because of any inadequacy in the original framework of our government, but because we have become so lazy and dumb that we failed to adapt to the changing times!
- Read Chapter 15 ("Chairman Mao is smiling").

Overall, Washington and Mao were even: 2 and 2.

4. Discussion

Obviously, it's impossible to "fairly" compare any two individuals who are (or were) almost 200 years apart, but 〃 ⸱et the point, hopefully.

A ∪untry/system built to last requires two types of exceptional leaders: (1) a creator to begin with and (2) many transformational reformers subsequently. The former builds the country/system on a solid foundation, while the latter keeps it going by adapting to the changing times.

China's extraordinary success today is largely due to the wisdom of one individual: Deng Xiaoping (Chapter 5: "America: What is China, Anyway?"). But Deng could not have done it without Mao's unifying China in 1949. Perhaps Mao was a necessary evil, given the enormous human suffering and misery under his rule. But for me, it's safe to say that no Mao, no Deng, no modern China!

The U.S. has had a good run for more than 200 years, but is desperately in need of a great transformational leader like China's Deng. Who will that great reformer be? Will that be Mitt Romney? For more, read Chapter 26 ("An Open Letter to Mitt Romney").

5. Closing
Comparing George Washington with Mao Zedong is part I. For part II, read the next chapter ...

Chapter 29: Mitt Romney vs. Deng Xiaoping

(Initially published at GEI on 8/10/2012)

After comparing George Washington and Mao Zedong, which was an exercise for fun, let's compare Mitt Romney with Deng Xiaoping, which may have historical significance.

Right now, Romney is of little significance as compared with Deng. However, Romney has the opportunity of besting any leader in human history, provided that he becomes the next American President, changes the U.S. Constitution, and retires after his first term, all as I suggested (Chapter 26: "An Open Letter to Mitt Romney").

1. Deng Xiaoping

Here is a description of Deng Xiaoping per Wikipedia:

***Deng Xiaoping** (22 August 1904 – 19 February 1997) was a Chinese politician, statesman, and diplomat. As leader of the Communist Party of China, Deng was a reformer who led China towards a market economy. While Deng never held office as the head of state, head of government or General Secretary of the Communist Party of China (historically the highest position in Communist China), he nonetheless served as the paramount leader of the People's Republic of China from 1978 to 1992.*

Inheriting a country fraught with social and institutional woes resulting from the Cultural Revolution and other mass political movements of the Mao era, Deng became the core of the "second generation" of

Chinese leadership. He is considered "the architect" of a new brand of socialist thinking, having developed Socialism with Chinese characteristics and led Chinese economic reform through a synthesis of theories that became known as the "socialist market economy". Deng opened China to foreign investment, the global market and limited private competition. He is generally credited with developing China into one of the fastest growing economies in the world for over 30 years and raising the standard of living of hundreds of millions of Chinese.

2. Mitt Romney
Here is a description of Mitt Romney per Wikipedia:

Willard Mitt Romney *(born March 12, 1947) is an American businessman and the presumptive nominee of the Republican Party for President of the United States in the 2012 election.* He was the 70th Governor of Massachusetts (2003–07).

America is desperately in need of a great transformational leader like China's Deng (read the last chapter: "Washington vs. Mao"). Will that be Romney?

3. Romney vs. Deng
Once again, the premise here is that Romney becomes the next American President, changes the U.S. Constitution, and retires after his first term, all as I suggested.

With that, fast forward to March 12, 2017. President Romney, now comfortably in retirement, invites me to his 70th birthday party. At that time, I will compare him with Deng as follows:
1) Economic reforms: Deng successfully transformed China's economy from communism to state

capitalism, while President Romney revived America's superior capitalism. Given the magnitude of the task, Deng achieved far more. **Edge: Deng**,

2) Political reforms: Deng transformed China's political system from communism (or more precisely, feudalism, with Mao being the *de facto* last emperor) to a new form that is best described as "a dictatorship without a dictator" (Chapter 3: "Towards an ideal form of government"). It appeared to be slightly better than America's political system until 2013, when Romney became the American President. President Romney fundamentally changed America's political system by changing the U.S. Constitution as follows:

- Limited the American Presidency to one-term of six years. Very significantly, President Romney set a good example and sacrificed himself by serving one four-year term only, opting not to run for re-election!
- Raised the statutory requirements for the American Presidency, such as the minimum age to 55 and only after having served as a state governor for one full-term, at least.
- Introduced strict term-limits for Congress. It is now one term of six years for both the House and Senate. No re-elections!

As a result, America's political system is, once again, superior to China's political system. Romney achieved far more than Deng. **Edge: Romney**.

3) Approach: Deng started with the economic reforms, saving China's political system as a by-product. Romney did it the other way: he started

with the political reforms, saving America's economy as a by-product. **Edge: Even.**

4) Legacy: Both Romney and Deng left their jobs with their respective countries well positioned for the future. **Edge: Even.**

Overall, Romney and Deng are even: 1 and 1.

4. Discussion

Deng's place in history is well set: Deng proved to be the greatest man in China's [recent] history. I believe he would prove to be one of the greatest "peaceful" transformational leaders in human history.

Romney's place in history is still tenuous and in the making ...

Governor Romney, you have a powerful choice: Heed sound advice ("An Open Letter to Mitt Romney") to become the next President and then be one of the greatest American Presidents ever, or remain a Nobody, including being just a spot filler President by luck!

5. Closing

Mr. Romney, be great! The path to greatness has already been shown to you! For all our sakes, please listen and just do it!

America simply cannot afford another term of Barack Obama, or a Romney Presidency that is less than the greatest!

Chapter 30: American Presidents: Three Best and Three Worst

(Initially published at GEI on 8/24/2012)

In the last chapter, I concluded: *"America simply cannot afford another term of Barack Obama, or a Romney Presidency that is less than the greatest!"*

What, then, is the greatest? Let's name the three best American Presidents, as well as the three worst in contrast, shall we?

1. American Presidents: the three best
The three best Presidents are easy to name: just go to Washington D.C. and look around, you will see three distinctive landmarks: Washington Monument, Jefferson Memorial, and Lincoln Memorial. End of discussion!

2. American Presidents: the three worst
The three worst are much harder to name for one main reason: there are too many bad Presidents! Here are my three selections: George W. Bush, Barack Obama, and John Kennedy, in that order!

I have mentioned, several times, that Presidents George W. Bush and Barack Obama are the two worst American Presidents in [recent] history. Why? Together the policies of these two Presidents have done more damage to America than all of America's enemies have done, combined! The biggest threat to America is its faltering economy, which is plainly visible now! Specifically,

    1) President George W. Bush turned off the beacon to launch the Iraq War, which I believe *"will*

eventually be marked as the beginning of the end of democracy as we know it" (read Chapter 55: "What's The Real Cost of The Iraq War?"). The launch of the Iraq War also showed government corruption in its worst form (read Chapter 36: "Blagojevich and Pearl Harbor: They Are Related!").

2) President Obama has proven to be the biggest spender in American history. Our national debt was enormous at $9T when he took office, but it has exceeded $16T before he finishes his first term. Worse yet, President Obama recently initiated a naked assault on capitalism (read Chapter 66: "Democracy-Communism Similarity #5: You Didn't Build That"), the very foundation of America!

Now, let me add President John Kennedy to the list as number three for this reason (Chapter 44: "Public-Sector Unions: from Wisconsin to America"):

"What Governor Walker did was significant: It was a small step to undo the devastating damage caused by President Kennedy, but a gigantic step against the demise of America!"

By allowing public-sector unions in 1961 (via Executive Order 10988), President Kennedy, knowingly against FDR's explicit warning, planted a time bomb in America that was doomed to explode in our faces, as it is now, with the far worse yet to come.

What, then, was FDR's explicit warning?

3. FDR's explicit warning against public-sector unions

Here is an excerpt from a Letter from FDR Regarding Public-Sector Unions dated August 16, 1937:

> *All Government employees should realize that the process of collective bargaining, as usually understood, cannot be transplanted into the public service. It has its distinct and insurmountable limitations when applied to public personnel management.*
>
> *The very nature and purposes of Government make it impossible for administrative officials to represent fully or to bind the employer in mutual discussions with Government employee organizations.*
>
> *Particularly, I want to emphasize my conviction that militant tactics have no place in the functions of any organization of Government employees.*
>
> *A strike of public employees manifests nothing less than an intent on their part to prevent or obstruct the operations of Government until their demands are satisfied. Such action, looking toward the paralysis of Government by those who have sworn to support it, is unthinkable and intolerable.*

4. Discussion

You may have your own list of the worst American Presidents. But history is always the best judge. Three notes:

1) President Obama could easily be the worst, guaranteed, if he gets re-elected.

2) President Kennedy might well be recognized as the worst American President ever twenty years from now, as America finally realizes the magnitude of the damage he caused by allowing public-sector unions in 1961.
3) With regard to President George W. Bush ...
   - If you argue that President Obama is worse than President George W. Bush, consider this: there would have been no President Obama without President George W. Bush! Nevertheless, your argument may be valid in four years, if President Obama gets re-elected.
   - If you want to replace George W. Bush with Jimmy Carter on the worst list, you are too Republican (vs. American) and you may have been too brainwashed (Chapter 63)! To be objective, [again] read: Chapter 55 ("What's The Real Cost of The Iraq War?") and Chapter 36 ("Blagojevich and Pearl Harbor: They Are Related!"). Now, if you are still unconvinced about President George W. Bush's place in history, here are some stats about the Iraq War: Tens of thousands of Iraqis died. What about the U.S. casualties? 4,486 deaths and over 100,000 wounded! It was a crime against humanity! For more, read: Tutu: Bush, Blair, should face trial at the Hague.

Still wondering why America is so deeply in trouble? Wonder not! America has been having only bad (or mediocre) Presidents since 1933, at least, with Ronald Reagan being the sole exception!

Why so many bad Presidents? It's the political system, stupid! More specifically, it's getting re-elected *ad nauseam*, stupid! Most, if not all, of the bad

American Presidents did most of the damage to America during their first terms, for the sake of re-election!

Let me repeat (from Chapter 18: "Pyramid Theory I"): *"unless our political system is fundamentally changed for the better (as I suggested), the streak of bad Presidents will continue"*.

Now, if you still want to argue about who is worse and who is the worst American President, feel sorry for (1) America, for having this subject become such a hot topic, and (2) yourself, for missing the case in point: It's the political system, stupid, not any individuals!

5. What's the solution?
It's time to re-define the American Presidency (Chapter 25)!

America is desperately in need of a great President to re-define the American Presidency and start turning things around in 2013! Who will that person be? President Obama is a not-good-enough President at best – He is all flash and no substance, on top of being the biggest spender in American history! Nor can it be Mitt Romney, who, as is, will not be good enough, either! Bad news for America!

Here is the good news for America: Romney can be a lot better, if we demand it, as I suggested (Chapter 26: "An Open Letter to Mitt Romney")!

6. Closing
Human legacy includes a history of leadership changing hands. Rome, Egypt, China, and Britain all had their day in the sun. We, the USA, are having our own now. But our days are clearly numbered, if we keep

sleeping on our 200-year-old political system and keep resisting changes. Or we can change, fundamentally and big. China did it. Why can't we?

How did China do it? With a great transformational leader named Deng Xiaoping!

How can America do it? Expect President Romney? Romney has the opportunity of besting any leader in human history (Chapter 29: "Mitt Romney vs. Deng Xiaoping"). But will he?

Chapter 31: The Myth of the Bill Clinton Presidency

(Initially published at GEI on 9/21/2012)

Today, there are four living past American Presidents: Jimmy Carter, George Bush, Bill Clinton, and George W. Bush. How do their respective parties view them?

In the 2012 Republican National Convention, neither Bush showed up.

In the 2012 Democratic National Convention, Jimmy Carter did not show up. However, Bill Clinton not only showed up, he also played a prominent role as the keynote speaker.

How, then, should President Clinton be viewed by America today and in history?

1. Overview

Overall, as compared with Presidents George W. Bush and Obama, President Clinton looked like a "genius" for his time in office. But the simple truth is that he was one of the luckiest American Presidents in history, thanks to the four big factors as follows:

1) The groundwork laid by President Reagan in the 1980s, particularly the end of the Cold War in 1989, created an environment for success.
2) The dot.com boom: President Clinton benefited hugely from a financial blockbuster he had nothing to do with; it was his presidency's lottery winnings! It made the difference between his term in office being viewed as a success or a failure.
3) The Republican Congress forced him to accept transformational acts that balanced the budget and

reformed the welfare programs, which he claimed for his own after passage despite his resistance to it.

4) BRICS had yet to show up - America enjoyed her last decade of the economic monopoly.

As for his place in history, aside from surviving the impeachment as a result of the Monica Lewinsky scandal, President Clinton made two costly mistakes ...

2. President Clinton's two costly mistakes

1) He amended the CRA (Community Reinvestment Act) to its final, and lethal, form, thus contributing to a spectacular housing bubble that burst in 2008. For more, read: How the CRA Fueled the Housing Bubble?

2) He failed to significantly adjust America's foreign policy after the Cold War. As a result, America actually became a major source of instability around the world, especially in the Middle East. A strong case in point: The seeds for the 9/11 tragedy were sowed on President Clinton's watch. For example, President Clinton actually refused Sudan's offer to turn Osama Bin Laden over to the U.S.! Ron Paul has got this one right (Ron Paul on 9/11: Ask the right questions and face the truth)!

3. Discussion

In Chapter 30 ("American Presidents: Three Best and Three Worst"), I stated: *"President Kennedy might well be recognized as the worst American President twenty years from now, as America finally realizes the magnitude of the damage he caused by allowing public-sector unions in 1961."*

History will judge President Clinton in the same way: The long-term impact of his two costly mistakes is yet to be known. As a matter of fact, America has yet to widely acknowledge they were even mistakes. A complicit media, more intent on helping elect Democrats, has kept them out of the public's sights. For more, read Chapter 63 ("Brainwashing").

Still wondering why America is so deeply in trouble today? It really started in earnest after 1989, when the Cold War ended. America failed to adequately adjust to the new world characterized by two points as follows:
1) For the U.S., the world should have been much more peaceful (e.g. without thousands of Soviet nuclear weapons aimed at us), but we made it worse than ever, with the worst being the wars in Iraq and Afghanistan. For more, read Chapter 55 ("What's The Real Cost of The Iraq War?").
2) The rise of BRICS, led by China, as economic competitors to the U.S.

President Clinton had the opportunity to set America on a new course to new historical greatness, but he did not. For that, he will never be counted as a great President. Rather, he will eventually be remembered as one of the luckiest American Presidents in history – no more than that!

Chapter 32: Top 10 American Misconceptions about 10 Recent Presidents

(Initially published at GEI on 10/12/2012)

In Chapter 30 ("American Presidents: Three Best and Three Worst"), I state: "Still wondering why America is so deeply in trouble? Wonder not! America has been having only bad (or mediocre) Presidents since 1933, at least, with Ronald Reagan being the sole exception!"

What a big and sweeping statement! In this chapter, I will elaborate it by talking about 10 recent American Presidents, from 1933 to present. This is very important, because no history is more relevant than recent history and the next presidential election is just a few weeks away.

Misconception 1: FDR was great

FDR would forever be remembered as "the War President" in America, because he led America to victory in WWII, brilliantly!

Unfortunately, FDR also severely damaged America. Starting with the New Deal, he fundamentally changed America for the worse. Here is an excerpt from Chapter 53 ("Karl Marx and John Keynes"):

FDR faced formidable challenges (e.g. The Great Depression) when he was elected to the American Presidency. He did everything possible to remain popular, including raiding the public treasury and introducing Social Security, thus ensuring his repeated re-elections (yes, three times)! Consequently, America was fundamentally changed from a society based on rugged individualism and unfettered capitalism to an entitlement society. It has only been progressively getting worse since then, with the government getting so big and fat now that its massive weight is crushing America.

Misconception 2: JFK was great

Many Americans remember JFK as a great President for two main reasons:

1) <u>His Moon Speech</u>, in which he boldly predicted that America would land on Moon "before this decade is out". It came true.
2) Some great sound bites, such as "ask not what your country can do for you, but what you can do for your country."

In reality, JFK asked, more than anybody else ever in America, what America could do for him and his supporters than what they could do for America! Specifically, here is an excerpt from Chapter 30 ("American Presidents: Three Best and Three Worst"):

President Kennedy might well be recognized as the worst American President ever twenty years from now, as America finally realizes the magnitude of the damage he caused by allowing public-sector unions in 1961.

Misconception 3: LBJ was good

LBJ was just as bad as FDR in expanding socialism at any costs, with his Great Society being "inspired" by FDR's New Deal and the introduction of Medicare and Medicaid just like FDR's Social Security, a worst Ponzi scheme ever! Specifically, when LBJ passed Medicare in 1963, the estimated cost for 1990, including inflation, was $12 billion/year. The actual cost in 1990 turned out to be $190 billion/year! Worse yet, it has nearly quadrupled since then! If this is not a reason for America's bankruptcy, tell me what is!

Misconception 4: Richard Nixon was a crook

Richard Nixon should be considered one of the greatest American Presidents in [recent] history, perhaps even ahead of President Reagan, except for the Watergate scandal and Nixon's subsequent resignation.

President Nixon did two extraordinary things that fundamentally changed America (and the world) for the better:
1) He established diplomatic relations with China, which was really the beginning of the end of the Cold War.
2) He created the petrodollar by convincing the Saudis (and the OPEC) to price and sell their oil in the US$ (in exchange for the U.S. military protection of the kingdom). As a result, the U.S. can "buy" oil by printing the US$, while all other countries must earn the US$ to buy oil. Three questions for you:
   a. Can you possibly imagine a better deal for America than this?
   b. Do you know this is a key reason behind America's prosperity over the past four decades?
   c. Do you also know this is about to end if we stay the course?

Misconception 5: Was Jimmy Carter really so bad?

Although Jimmy Carter did not make my three-worst (Chapter 30), he was a bad President, by any standard! In fact, we are still suffering severely under his misguided policies and actions such as the CRA

(Community Reinvestment Act) which was a root cause for the housing bubble that burst in 2008, the Mariel boatlift, and the creation of both the Departments of Education and Energy that are a combined unaffordable $150 billion/year boondoggle!

Misconception 6: Ronald Reagan was good

Ronald Reagan was not good - He was great! As a matter of fact, President Reagan was in the top four (Chapter 30) for three reasons:
1) President Reagan fixed the huge mess left by President Carter.
2) President Reagan was the only American President, after WWII, who reversed the advancement of socialism in America.
3) President Reagan won the Cold War for America!

Misconception 7: George Bush was not good, because he was not re-elected

George H.W. Bush was better than most Americans think for two reasons:
1) He knew how/whether to start a war, and when/where to stop! The Gulf War was brilliantly executed, especially in hindsight today!
2) He was honest enough to raise taxes, with the realization that a just war must be properly funded, even if it meant to break his promise of "no new taxes". He paid a steep price for his honesty and responsible governance: he was not re-elected!

Misconception 8: Bill Clinton was a genius

He was not! Bill Clinton was one of the luckiest American Presidents in history. For more, read Chapter 31 ("The Myth of The Bill Clinton Presidency").

Misconception 9: George W. Bush was not very smart

Many Americans think George W. Bush is a good man, who is just not very smart. As a result, he made several big mistakes, such as the Iraq War.

In reality, President George W. Bush is a lot smarter than you think. He went to Yale and had better grades (i.e. C) than Barack Obama at Columbia (i.e. too bad to be published)!

President George W. Bush "recklessly turned off the beacon" to launch the Iraq War, at least partially for the sake of his re-election. When he realized there was no way out, he effectively played dumb for the rest of his presidency. After all, it was better to be dumb than evil.

Oh, how evil is President George W. Bush? Not only did he severely damage America, he also might have permanently damaged the GOP.

Misconception 10: Barrack Obama is very smart

Many Americans acknowledge that Barack Obama was not very experienced when he became the President, but believe he is a very smart man.

Here is an excerpt from Chapter 66 ('You Didn't Build That'):

> *If that's true, why is it so hard for him to reveal his grades in college (<u>Obama campaign makes case for releasing his college transcripts</u>)? ... All signs indicate that Barack Obama received a lot of "help" from the government throughout his life ...*

As a matter of fact, Barack Obama may truly be an "Affirmative Action" President! For more, read: <u>Obama: The Affirmative Action President</u>.

Here is a warning to America: if President Obama is re-elected, America will be so deeply into socialism that there will be no return!
1) How do I know so much about socialism (and communism)? Been there, done that - I escaped it by coming to the U.S. (read Part 12)!
2) How bad is socialism (and communism)? It's hell! For more, read Chapter 67 ("Stupidity").

In conclusion, watch this short video: <u>Obama is going to pay for my gas and mortgage!</u>!

Chapter 33: Top 10 American Misconceptions about Mitt Romney

(Initially published at GEI on 10/26/2012)

The Presidential election is imminent. This is a historical make or break moment for America: continue with President Obama in his inexorable march toward socialism or seek a big change with Mitt Romney, who is a rare talent not only in the U.S., but also in the world! Unfortunately, Romney's reputation has been so distorted over the past one year that many Americans harbor many misconceptions about him.

Let's try to correct the top 10 misconceptions about Mitt Romney for the sake of our fellow Americans and for the future of our country ...

Misconception 1: Romney does not believe in anything

Romney believes in capitalism! That is good enough for America today, because President Obama obviously believes in socialism! How do I know so much about socialism (and communism)? Been there, done that (read Part 12)! Romney is a living proof that you can make it big in America, if you work hard and if you are good and lucky!

Misconception 2: Romney is an extremist

Absolutely not! In today's presidential politics, you need the extremists in the primary (i.e. the extreme right for Republicans or the extreme left for Democrats), before you have a chance to be in the middle for the general election. It's the middle 5% of the independent voters like you and me that decide a close election like this one!

Misconception 3: Romney has flip-flopped

Which top politician has not? As President Obama has amply proven, some degree of populism is required to win. Romney was first bracketed by the extreme right in the primary, and then by the extreme left after the primary. However, he remains the same good man!

Misconception 4: Romney had a questionable tenure in the private sector

Romney had "a stellar performance" in the private sector, as even admitted by President Clinton (Romney's Stellar Performance)!

Misconception 5: Romney had a questionable tenure as Governor in Massachusetts

Romney did a good job in Massachusetts, especially by working with Democrats and eliminating their perennial deficits! Romney became a governor in Massachusetts, which, in itself, was a remarkable achievement for a Republican!

Misconception 6: Romney is too rich

It's so un-American to even think that way! We, as Americans, cherish success, not condemn it! Romney earned his wealth!

As a matter of fact, Romney's wealth is far less than John Kerry's, who married his. Yet, there was no outcry about Kerry's wealth when he ran for President in 2003. Do we really want a "loser" who can't even make a good example living (e.g. as a community organizer) to be our President?

Being rich is a good thing! For more, read Chapter 54 ("America: let the rich run the country like China does!").

Misconception 7: Romney does not understand average Americans

It's not difficult to understand average Americans! An average American wants to figuratively have a beer with an average-Joe President like George W. Bush or Barack Obama. But should the average American be happy with the job performance of these two Presidents? They both are among the worst American Presidents in history (Chapter 30: "American Presidents: Three Best and Three Worst").

Misconception 8: Romney is too hawkish in foreign policy

You may be right! But do not worry! The President's highest priority should be the defense of the U.S.! Romney has been polarized by the extreme right, but will regain his senses once in office. Romney is no George W. Bush!

Misconception 9: Romney is too tough, or not tough enough, with China

China is a competitor, not an enemy! America is deeply in trouble because of its own internal struggles! As Abraham Lincoln stated:

> *"America will never be destroyed from the outside. If we falter and lose our freedoms, it will be because we destroyed ourselves."*

Romney is smart enough to understand it!

Misconception 10: I still do not trust Romney

President Romney will be far better than President Obama for America, in both short and long terms, guaranteed! Let's give Romney a chance for five reasons:

1) Romney is an exceptional leader with "a stellar performance" as a businessman and as a governor. He is a rare talent not only in America, but also in the world!
2) Romney is not a career politician. Romney knows who built America mostly: the private sector!
3) Romney is not just a businessman like Ross Perot. Romney served in the public sector.
4) Romney is not a neo-con! Romney is no George W. Bush!
5) President Obama is just not good enough, at best.

In conclusion, if you are an independent who likes Ron Paul, do what his son Rand Paul does: vote for Mitt Romney! For more, watch this video: Rand Paul and Why He Endorsed Mitt Romney for President.

Chapter 34: American Presidency: Is It A Joke?

(Initially published at GEI on 11/2/2012)

The answer is "No, not yet, but getting close". Three examples:
1) Barack Obama did not have any executive experience by 2008, but was elected the American President!
2) John McCain selected Sarah Palin as his running mate in 2008, A questionable choice by any standard, Palin actually had more executive experience than Obama at that time!
3) George W. Bush recklessly launched the Iraq War, at least partially, for the sake of his re-election.

There is no better time than now to talk about the subject, as the election is imminent.

1. Who is qualified to be an American President?
Just be a U.S.-born citizen and older than 35 - that's it! No experience required! For more, read: So you want to run for president? Just sign here. It asks "*far fewer questions than a McDonald's job application*"!

2. How will the next American President be determined?
Ideally, we should be demanding something as follows:
1) For the incumbent, a solid track record - President Obama's record is dismal!
2) For the challenger, a new and bold vision for America – Does Mitt Romney have one?

But practically, these three numbers will likely determine the next American President.
1) The unemployment rate!
2) The price of the gas.
3) The Dow Jones average.

For more, read: 3 Numbers That Will Determine the Next President.

3. The American Presidency

The American Presidency is a powerful job for two predominant reasons:
1) Unlike the British Prime Minister, who needs to be bestowed by the Queen, or the Chinese (or Russian) President, who shares power with the Prime Minister, the American Presidency is a one-man show.
2) It is armed with the power to launch a host of nuclear weapons that can destroy much of the world instantly.

Unfortunately, the American Presidency is limited in power for addressing domestic issues, largely because of the 535 "tribal leaders" in Congress. They are elected to defend their own turfs, including the duty to "steal" their "fair share" from the public treasury (Chapter 65: "Kleptocracy"). That makes the American Presidency less fun.

The President is no king, domestically!

Here is the good news for the American Presidency: it is almost unlimited in power for international affairs, including launching a war without Congressional approval. Although the Constitution clearly states that only Congress can declare a war, no Presidents since

WWII have followed this law. So why bother now? That makes the American Presidency a lot more fun.

The President is more than a king, internationally!

4. American Presidents

All great human beings, including the American Presidents, strive for greatness, which, over time, simply means a great legacy.

One prerequisite of a great legacy for an American President is to get re-elected. President George H.W. Bush understands it very well, as he was deeply humiliated after losing his re-election, leaving a lasting impression on his elder son, George W. Bush.

A great President is often a war President. George W. Bush knew it (George W. Bush, War President).

Now, how about getting re-elected and being a war President all with one action like launching the Iraq War? "Yes, take it" - one stone, two birds! That was exactly what President George W. Bush did in 2003, using 9/11 as an excuse (Ron Paul on 9/11: Ask the right questions and face the truth)! What about Congress at that time? It was just a bunch of tribal leaders who cared more about their own re-election than about anything else (Chapter 36: "Blagojevich and Pearl Harbor: They Are Related!"). "So just cajole them in now and buy them out later with such things as the MMA!" So thought and did President George W. Bush, at the time.

For the real cost of the Iraq War, read Chapter 5! For another perspective, read: Tutu: Bush, Blair, should face trial at the Hague.

Okay, that was President George W. Bush. What about President Obama? He used the war in Afghanistan for his political gains! Specifically, he chose to escalate the war in Afghanistan in 2011 (acceptable), but with a troop withdrawal plan so ridiculously hasty that there could have been only one possible explanation: it was perfectly timed for his re-election (totally unacceptable)! For more, read: <u>For Obama the Road to Reelection Runs through Kabul</u>".

Additionally, Barack Obama may truly be an "Affirmative Action" President! For more, read: <u>Obama: The Affirmative Action President</u>.

Now, what about President Clinton? Read Chapter 31 ("The Myth of the Bill Clinton Presidency").

For more about more American Presidents, read Chapter 31 ("Top 10 American Misconceptions about 10 Recent American Presidents").

5. Discussion

Still wondering why America is so deeply in trouble? Wonder not! It's the American Presidency, stupid!

Instead of demanding greatness, Americans want our President to be like one of us, so that we can figuratively have a beer together. Well, we got exactly what we asked for in George W. Bush and Barack Obama, at least!

Experience matters! Leadership matters! A good track record matters!

How can America (or any country) possibly survive so many bad Presidents (Chapter 32: "Top 10 American Misconceptions about 10 Recent American Presidents")?

Lucky no more! Joke no more!

6. The solution
Let's give Mitt Romney a chance for five reasons:
1) Romney is an exceptional leader with "a stellar performance" as a businessman and as a governor. He is a rare talent not only in America, but also in the world!
2) Romney is not a career politician. Romney knows who built America mostly: the private sector!
3) Romney is not just a businessman like Ross Perot. Romney served in the public sector with excellence.
4) Romney is not a neo-con! Romney is no George W. Bush!
5) President Obama is just not good enough, at best.

7. Closing
Will America recognize and adopt the Romney solution or continue the joke with President Obama? Let's find out in a few days. Meanwhile, watch this animated movie (again): Reagan vs. Obama: Social Economics 101.

Chapter 35: Another Open Letter to Mitt Romney

(Initially published at GEI on 11/30/2012)

Dear Governor Romney,

How was your lunch with President Obama yesterday?

As a staunch supporter of your campaign (Chapter 34), I was disappointed at the election result. But was I surprised by it? No, not at all! As a matter of fact, in my open letter to you dated 5/18/2011 (Chapter 26), not only did I predict the eventual outcome, I also spelled out a virtually guaranteed path to success for you. Unfortunately, you did not listen …

How could I have guaranteed you sure success? Two reasons:
1) I believe I have the most accurate diagnosis for America (Chapter 1) as well as the best solution (Chapter 2).
2) I believe Americans will buy my diagnosis and solution if enough people will listen, especially after an endorsement by a Presidential candidate, who is willing to put his support behind it for the sake of America.

Anyway, the 2012 election is over. President Obama won, which means America will continue her slide down to hell. How come?

Domestically, it's simple: Most of the "blue" states that President Obama won happen to be the most fiscally troubled states (e.g. California and Illinois).

They will be in bankruptcy soon, like many European countries (e.g. Greece and Spain), dragging down America with them!

Internationally, let's see a perspective from a former communist country: Hungary. Read this: Hungarian-born Billionaire makes anti-socialism case in TV ad. Now, click here to watch the TV ad.

Sad, isn't it? Yet, more than 47% of Americans do not know, or care!

Here is a quote: *"A democracy is nothing more than mob rule, where fifth-one-percent of the people may take away the rights of the other forty-nine."*

Who said it? **Thomas Jefferson**!

Is America finished? No, not yet, but very close! Let's do our best to save it! Specifically, how about endorsing my diagnosis (Chapter 1) and solution (Chapter 2) for America?

I thank you very much for your attempt to save our country and look forward to your reply!

Best Regards,
Frank Li, Ph.D.
P.S., You may find this short video interesting: Obamacare at work!

Part 7.3: American Politics

Chapter 36: Blagojevich and Pearl Harbor: They Are Related!
Chapter 37: Caught on Tape: President Obama and Blagojevich

"My choice early in life was either to be a piano player in a whorehouse or a politician. And to tell the truth, there's hardly any difference."

--- Harry Truman

Chapter 36: Blagojevich and Pearl Harbor: They Are Related!

(Initially published at GEI on 12/16/2011)

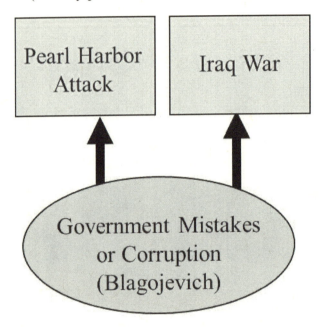

Here are the top two news stories on December 7, 2011:
1) Blagojevich Sentenced to 14 Years.
2) Pearl Harbor Attack Remembered at 70th Anniversary.

Upon seeing these two titles, I immediately linked them together, via the similarities to the basis for the Iraq War, as shown by this diagram above.

Next, let's look at these three blocks one by one.

1. The Pearl Harbor attack

Let's view it from both sides: Japan and the U.S., respectively.

1.1 From the Japan side

Two Japanese individuals were chiefly responsible for the Pearl Harbor attack:

1) Isoroku Yamamoto: He was a Japanese Naval Marshal General and the commander-in-chief of the Combined Fleet during WWII. He directed the Pearl Harbor attack.
2) Hideki Tojo. He was a general of the Imperial Japanese Army, and the 40th Prime Minister of Japan from October 17, 1941 to July 22, 1944. He ordered the Pearl Harbor attack.

By 1940, Japan pretty much occupied the entirety of East Asia, including Korea, China, and the Philippines. The only military threat to more Japanese expansions was America, the Pacific Fleet specifically. So there was a big debate between the Japanese Army and the Japanese Navy about what to do with that threat. The Army, led by Tojo, wanted to attack Pearl Harbor, where the Pacific Fleet was headquartered. The Navy, led by Yamamoto, was against the idea of an attack. Below is a rumored conversation between the two:

Tojo: Can you wipe out the Pacific Fleet in a few days?
Yamamoto: Yes, I can. But then what?
Tojo: Hmm ... Let's worry about that later.

Yamamoto was a Harvard graduate and a well-traveled man, knowing the potential of America. Tojo, on the other hand, was limited in his knowledge about America. The debate between them was over as soon as

Tojo became the Prime Minister on October 17, 1941. Tojo ordered Yamamoto to attack Pearl Harbor, which was carried out on December 7, 1941.

What a huge mistake by the Japanese! That got America into WWII, which ultimately led to a total defeat of Imperial Japan!

1.2 From the U.S. side
The Pearl Harbor attack was by far the largest attack by a foreign force to a U.S. territory. The U.S. responded decisively, correctly, and eventually victoriously.

2. The Iraq War
Let's also view it from both sides: the U.S. and Iraq, respectively.

2.1 From the U.S. side
I have been highly critical of the Iraq War. Additionally, I often use the analogy that invading Iraq after Al-Qaeda attacked us on 9/11 would be like retaliating against Canada for the Japanese attack of Pearl Harbor. Totally illogical and wrong! Two reasons:
1) Iraq was not part of the 9/11/2001 attack on America.
2) Saddam Hussein, the dictator in Iraq at the time, was not friendly with Osama bin Laden, the mastermind behind the 9/11 attack, and there was no Al-Qaeda in Iraq before the Iraq War!

Now, a question: before the Iraq War was launched, was there a debate inside the Bush administration similar to the one between Tojo and Yamamoto before the Pearl Harbor attack? I bet yes, especially the "then what?" part! Even citizen at the time Barack Obama was opposed to the war as far back as 2002 (Barack Obama's Stirring 2002 Speech Against the Iraq War)!

The Iraq War represents not only the worst mistake in American foreign policy, which has been somehow acknowledged within the U.S., but also, in my view, the worst form of government corruption in American history (more on this later). In fact, it was so bad that I predicted that the Iraq War *"will eventually be marked as the beginning of the end of democracy as we know it"* (Chapter 55).

2.2 From the Iraq side

Is Iraq better off today than in those days under Saddam? I don't think so! Furthermore, are you excited about the Arab Spring? Do not be! Here is an excerpt from Chapter 19 ("Loop Theory: Capitalism vs. Socialism"):

> *Most of them (referring to the countries in Middle East and North Africa) are in feudalism, both in form and in content. In form, a dictator with a family member in succession is essentially a king. In content, the #1 problem for all these countries is abject poverty of the mass population, as none of them has had a boost from capitalism yet. In other words, capitalism is the only way to achieve prosperity. Democracy per se, on the other hand, will inevitably lead to socialism, which, without capitalism, has proven to be a total disaster (e.g. the Soviet Union and China under Mao). For this reason, I am not optimistic about the outcome of the "Arab Spring" over there. The region is likely to become the next India, with democracy being a*

liability for prosperity. Again, there is not a single precedent of a third world country achieving prosperity via democracy.

My fellow Americans, we destroyed Iraq via the Iraq War, and it will take the Iraqis several decades at least to restore Iraq to its pre-war condition in terms of prosperity. So keep this in mind: just as we remembered the Pearl Harbor attack after 70 years, the Iraqis will be remembering the Iraq War in 70 years!

3. Government mistakes or corruption

The Pearl Harbor attack proved to be a huge mistake by the Japanese government. Who made that mistake specifically? Tojo, as he was a *de facto* dictator! Tojo was eventually held accountable - he was hanged on December 23, 1948!

The Iraq War was obviously a huge mistake by the U.S. government. Who made that mistake specifically? President George W. Bush? Perhaps, but he was not a dictator. Who has been held accountable for that mistake? No one! Where is the basic justice?

3.1 U.S. government corruption

To me, the Iraq War was a crime against humanity! It was the result of the worst possible form of government corruption, from President George W. Bush to Congress, for three main reasons as follows:

1) Here is an excerpt from Chapter 1: *"Is our President, throughout his first-term, for nothing but getting himself re-elected, with everything else being secondary? If the answer is yes, which seems patently obvious, we cannot ever expect the President to always do the right things for the*

country (vs. for himself) throughout his first-term, can we?"

2) Although many reasons were given for the Iraq War (e.g. "for WMDs" per some initially; "for oil," per Alan Greenspan; and "for spreading democracy," per President George W. Bush), the simple truth is that with the start of the Iraq War, President Bush's re-election was secured.

3) Now, let's recall how the Iraq War bill was passed in Congress: with a heavy push by the Bush administration, it was passed with an overwhelming majority! Why and how? Because there was tremendous political pressure to do something about Iraq at the time and few could afford to vote against the bill, which would have been a re-election killer for sure. Voting for it, on the other hand, had absolutely no negative consequences personally whatsoever. In other words, whether it was just or not was a non-issue. Nor was whether it was right or good for America. It was about "me" and it was the re-election, stupid!

Corruption, according to Wikipedia, is "in *philosophical, theological,* or moral discussions, *spiritual* or *moral impurity* or deviation from an *ideal.*" Is it an American ideal for a member of Congress to vote for no purpose but his (or her) own re-election? No! When most in the same institution (e.g. Congress) deviate from that ideal, it's institutional corruption. When that institution represents a government, it is government corruption!

3.2 Why the Iraq War, anyway?

Here is my account for the Iraq War, in a Sherlock Holmes style!

While *"the Pearl Harbor attack was by far the largest attack by a foreign force to a U.S. territory,"* the 9/11 attack was by far the largest attack by a foreign force to the U.S. mainland in modern times. Like our response to the Pearl Harbor attack, our response to the 9/11 attack was decisive and correct: We launched a war in Afghanistan on October 7, 2001, to go after Osama bin Laden. However, by the summer of 2002, it became clear that the war in Afghanistan was not easily winnable and therefore could have put President Bush's re-election in jeopardy. Something bigger must be done to turn the public's attention away from Afghanistan - Iraq was chosen! That, to me, was the real reason behind the Iraq War! In other words, Iraq was simply a casualty of American politics at the time! That was the key reason behind my argument that *"George W. Bush has proved to be the worst American President in history."*

The truth will prevail eventually!

3.3 Now, enter Blagojevich …

Rod Blagojevich was a career politician who "served" in Congress for six years before becoming the Governor of Illinois in 2002. He spent most of his career enriching himself and was finally caught on tape trying to sell the U.S. Senate seat vacated by President-elect Obama, which eventually led to his conviction in 2011. In case you were unaware, his predecessor, George Ryan, is still serving his 6½-year jail term for corruption. As a matter of fact, four out of the past nine Governors of Illinois went to jail! So while I am proud to be a long-time resident in Chicagoland, I am not proud of Illinois politics.

Are we Illinoisans just unlucky to have so many corrupted politicians at the top? Or are we Illinoisans lucky to have so many of them brought to justice? Neither! Corruption is wide spread among the elected officials throughout the U.S. at all levels! In other words, there are many Blago-likes still active and there will be many more Blago-likes brought to justice in the coming years,

While I applaud the efforts to bring Blagojevich and Blago-likes to justice, I must point out that it's not the real solution to stop, or even to slow down, corruption in the U.S. government, just like killing the insurgents in Iraq or in Afghanistan is not the real solution over there – they are being produced faster than being killed! We must identify the root cause first and then fix it! What is the root cause of insurgence in Iraq or in Afghanistan? Our mere presence over there! What is the root cause of corruption in the U.S. government? It's the political system, stupid!

Blagojevich is perhaps the most severely punished politician in America for corruption. However, the corruption involved in the launch of the Iraq War was at the highest level and thus infinitely worse than Blagojevich's crime! Who is going to be held accountable for the Iraq War? No one! Who is pursuing it? No one!

3.4 Back to U.S. government corruption

The current form of the U.S government, as represented by the elected officials, is systematically corrupted by definition! Here is an excerpt from Chapter 1:

American politicians serve themselves first, their constituents a remote second, and their

country dead last! It is a cancer, killing America from within, slowly but surely ...

More pointedly, over the past decade at least, the corrupted U.S. political system has caused most damage not only at home (e.g. pandering to the special interest groups to the point of bankrupting the country), but also abroad (e.g. the Iraq War).

Here is the common thread between the Pearl Harbor attack and the Iraq War: Both are blatant acts of naked aggression!

4. Closing

Admittedly, it's a long stretch to link Blagojevich with the Pearl Harbor attack. But hopefully, you get the point: it's time to fix our "broken" political system once for all!

Chapter 37: Caught on Tape: President Obama and Rod Blagojevich

(Initially published at GEI on 4/13/2012)

Two recent news stories:
1) <u>Ex-Illinois Governor Rod Blagojevich enters federal prison</u>.
2) <u>Obama caught on tape assuring Russian President more flexibility after U.S election</u>.

Are these two stories related? Yes!
1) Both stories again prove this point: American politicians work for themselves first, with everything else being secondary.
2) Both President Obama and Blagojevich made the same mistake: being caught on tape!

1. Blagojevich

Rod Blagojevich was a career politician who "served" in Congress for six years before becoming the Governor of Illinois in 2002. He spent most of his career enriching himself and was finally caught on tape trying to sell the U.S. Senate seat vacated by President-elect Obama, which eventually led to his conviction in 2011.

Like many career politicians, Blagojevich does not seem to even know the real world anymore, living in his own fantasyland instead. Two examples:

1) He kept saying that what he tried to do was "horse trading," as a standard practice in politics, without realizing that "horse trading" in this case was corruption.

2) He campaigned until the end (Blagojevich speaks on last free day), never acknowledging the harsh reality. Perhaps, his 14-year sentence is a bit too harsh, but I believe his non-stop public campaign after his arrest in December 2008 contributed to the harsh sentence.

Welcome to the real world the rest of us live in, Governor! You got what you deserve (Read: Illinois' lost decade)!

2. President Obama

In Chapter 21 ("American Democracy: Massive Falsehoods at the Top"), I stated: *"Like most American career politicians, President Obama serves, throughout his first term, for one supreme purpose only: getting re-elected ad nauseam"*. This news story is just yet another example to prove the point!

Is this "mistake" by President Obama as bad as Blagojevich's mistake in content? Yes, even worse! In China, it would have been considered treason. In America, it will be brushed off, just as the Iraq War was - nobody, either President George W. Bush or any of the members of Congress who voted for the war, has been held accountable for "the worst mistake of American foreign policy in history"!

Americans seem to punish personal mistakes (e.g. Blagojevich's), but not system mistakes (e.g. President Obama's), though the latter damages America a lot more than the former! As a result, American politicians will keep making system mistakes, without being punished.

3. The American Presidency

In Chapter 21 ("American Democracy: Massive Falsehoods at the Top"), I listed out five Presidential "mistakes". Here is a new example: General George Patton said, at the time, it was a huge mistake allowing Russia to take Berlin at the end of WWII. Eisenhower made the political choice of holding U.S. troops back. It furthered his presidential ambitions, but cost the U.S. and the world dearly! Ultimately, Patton was proven correct, but Ike became the President! To Eisenhower, that was all it mattered!

4. Closing

Blagojevich and President Obama proved to be the same in two aspects, at least:
1) Both of them work for themselves first.
2) Both of them got caught on tape.

However, the realities are very different for them now: one is in jail, while the other will keep running for re-election, from the White House ...

Should we blame them individually? Yes, but only to some extent! Far more importantly, it's the political system, stupid! Our political system simply does not attract the best people to serve in the first place. Worse yet, it turns many good people into self-serving politicos once elected, all due to this "getting re-elected *ad nauseam*" thing!

It's time to face the truth: American democracy does not work! My solution (Chapter 2) is the only workable proposal on the table!

Part 7.4: America: The Good, the Bad, and the Ugly

Chapter 38: American Dreams vs. America
Chapter 39: America: from Public Schools to Government, What Is Wrong?
Chapter 40: It Is Out-Of-Control Spending on Military, Stupid!
Chapter 41: The Congressional Super-Committee: What A Joke?
Chapter 42: American Airlines & America: What Do They Have in Common?
Chapter 43: Unemployment Rate: What Is It and Does It Really Matter?
Chapter 44: Public-Sector Unions: from Wisconsin to America
Chapter 45: Obese: to Be or Not to Be
Chapter 46: Four Points to Ponder on America's 236th Birthday
Chapter 47: American Dreams: Oversold and Overbought!
Chapter 48: America: 10 Big Questions and 10 Honest Answers

Chapter 38: American Dreams vs. America

(Initially published at GEI on 9/16/2012)

With the opening of the Martin Luther King, Jr. monument, it's a perfect time to reflect on the subject of American Dreams (e.g. what is your American Dream?) and, more importantly, to expand it to a new horizon: is your American Dream good for America?

Personally, coming to America in 1985 was a dream come true for me (i.e. a Chinese Dream then). Since then I have realized my own American dream: to achieve modest financial independence and then do whatever I want (e.g. Writing about politics). For more, read Chapter 74 ("My American Dream Has Come True").

Sweet!

Unfortunately, there are many bad American Dreams too. Two examples:
1) Owning a house bigger than you can actually afford.
2) Spending much more money than you actually have, both personally and as a country, and it has finally caught up.

Sour!

More profoundly, while "realizing my own American Dream" is almost always a good thing for the person himself (or herself), is it good for America? Here is an extreme example: Many people around the world cheered after Barack Obama was elected as the first black American President, as a real, modern-day, pinnacle example of an American Dream come true. But has President Obama been good for America? I think not.

Now, let's move from race to gender in the face of political correctness. Sarah Palin might have realized her own American Dream of becoming rich and famous, as a direct result of being the running mate of John McCain in 2008. But was she good enough to be just one heartbeat away from an American President? Next, enter Michele Bachmann - she knocked Tim Pawlenty out of the race after the straw poll in Iowa in 2011, which again proved this: American democracy is not a serious business, not even as serious as American Idol (Chapter 24). Michele, prove yourself as a governor first before dreaming of becoming the President! Study some economics first before making such unintelligent promises as $2/gallon gas! Stop mixing religion with politics by making such a "joke" as "Irene is God's message for Washington"!

Bluntly, neither the Obama dream nor the Palin/Bachmann dreams would have had any chance in China, because of its more stringent requirements for the top political offices. This is a key reason behind China's rise and America's decline over the past decade. Overall, the Chinese system has simply outperformed the American system, exposing some foundational flaws in America's antiquated political system for the first time ever in American history.

Fundamentally, the right order of priorities for our politicians should be country first, constituents next, and personal agendas last. But most, if not all, of our politicians have their priorities reversed. Why? It's the

political system, stupid! Our system not only allows it, but also enables it! Now, two basic questions:
1) How long must we continue to live with Congress with a disapproval rating of 87% before changing the system?
2) How much more can we put up with an inexperienced and incompetent President before raising the statutory requirements?

Unless we change soon, there will not be many sweet American Dreams, either left or to pursue, on the way to 2030, when China will surpass America as the largest economy on earth!

Chapter 39: from Public Schools to Government, What Is Wrong?

(Initially published at GEI on 10/21/2011)

"A government big enough to give you everything you want is strong enough to take everything you have."
--- Thomas Jefferson

I have been thinking about writing on this subject for a while. This article (Should the starting salary for a teacher be $60,000?) set me on fire. Here is how it begins:

> *How would the nation's school system be different if teachers were paid like engineers?*
>
> *Secretary of Education Arne Duncan proposed last month that a significant boost in teacher salaries could transform public schools for the better by luring the country's brightest college graduates into the profession.*

Here is my reaction in three points:
1) Both the private sector and the public sector have their roles in our society. However, public-sector employees must never compare with private-sector employees in pay. Want more money? Join the private sector! More altruistic, with a desire to serve? Work in the public sector!

2) In America, the brightest college graduates have never worked, upon graduation, and should never work, in the public sector.

3) The public school system is failing overall. The solution is not to pour more money into it! Reform it instead! First and foremost, abolish all teachers unions immediately and ban them forever (Chapter 2)!

Next, let me explain these three points one by one.

1. The private sector vs. the public sector

As the "land of opportunity", America has produced far more successful individuals than everywhere else in the world. Just to name three: Thomas Edison, Henry Ford, and Steve Jobs! These people, on top of being very bright, were successful for two main reasons: (1) they lived in America and (2) they succeeded in the private sector.

Success in the public sector, on the other hand, is much harder, if not impossible, to define. Does becoming an American President symbolize the pinnacle of success in the public sector? If yes, why have so many recent American Presidents so severely damaged America (Chapter 32: "Top 10 American Misconceptions about 10 Recent American Presidents")? If becoming a member of Congress is a symbol of success, why is Congress's disapproval rating at 87%?

Bottom line: America has been great largely because of the excellence of its private sector. The public sector supports it by creating the environment for success. America is deeply in trouble now, largely because of its antiquated political system, which is well reflected in the public sector. Here are two simple facts:

1) The public sector is too big! Read: <u>Government Employees and Manufacturing Jobs: Takers and makers</u>. Here is an excerpt: *"More Americans work for the government than work in construction, farming, fishing, manufacturing, mining, and utilities combined."*
2) Public-sector workers are overpaid! Read: <u>Comparing Privte Sector and Government Worker Salaries</u>. Here is an excerpt: *"state and local government employees earned total compensation of $39.60 an hour, compared to $27.42 an house for private industry workers, a difference of over 44%!"*

How and why has the public sector become so out-of-control that it is destroying America? It's the political system, stupid! President Kennedy sowed the seed in 1961 by allowing public-sector unions, which has finally caught up with us! For this reason, I stated (in Chapter 30): *"President Kennedy might well be recognized as the worst American President twenty years from now, as America finally realizes the magnitude of the damage he caused by allowing public-sector unions in 1961."*

It's time for us to fundamentally reform our political system, including significantly reducing the size of the government, before the Great Recession is turned to the Great Depression II, out of which America may never come!

2. Luring the brightest students into teaching

With a Ph.D. degree in Electrical Engineering and with two sons recently graduated from college (Yale/Economics, class 2009 and Michigan/Business, class 2011), I think I am well qualified to speak on this subject, with two points as follows:

1) The brightest college students major "correctly" (e.g. Economics, Business, or Engineering), not in such majors as Teaching, Political Science, or Sociology. Yes, they generally follow money. Surprised?
2) Over the past two years (i.e. tough times), only the top students with the right majors have had the limited opportunities to land top jobs, in the private sector, of course! Some less fortunate students are now a part of Occupy Wall Street, I suspect.

Bottom line: There is not a single reason for the brightest college students to even think about working in the public sector upon graduation. Why? Because, despite all its problems, America's private sector remains not only far better than the public sector, but also the best in the world, with the best possibility of achieving your full potential!

Now, why did Barack Obama (Columbia/Political Science, class 1983) and Arne Duncan (Harvard/Sociology, class 1987) major "incorrectly" in college and then start their careers in the public sector? Well, they were obviously not the brightest students! Don't get me wrong: both of them are bright - not only were they bright enough to have made it into the Ivies, they are also bright today. They are just not the brightest, which, unfortunately, appears to be required for their current jobs. Worse yet, their lack of experience in the private sector seems to have finally caught up with them: They do not understand the economy, and they do not know how to run America like a business! All what they seem to know is politicking and spending, as if money were unlimited!

Just to be fair to the Democrats: neither George W. Bush nor Dick Cheney was the brightest student, either. Bush was a C student at Yale, while Cheney was a Yale dropout.

3. The public school system

After having my two sons go through the public school system, I must say that I am happy with my school district (203, Naperville, IL). On top of that, I believe the top 20% students in America are, overall, better than their counterparts in China (Chapter 73: "The Battle Hymn of The Tiger Dad"). Two changes are absolutely necessary though:

1) Abolishing the teachers' unions immediately and banning them forever (Chapter 2)! Public-sector unions are anti-America by definition! Additionally, how could we possibly attract the brightest college graduates to a public school system that is poised with such silly union rules as LIFO (last in first out)?

2) Mind-set change: you work in the public sector to serve, not to profit more than the "masters", namely, the taxpayers who foot the bill!

I believe these two changes must occur before anything else is even attempted, such as those suggested by some experts recently (e.g. Fix this education).

Overall, however, the public school system has failed, especially in big cities like Chicago. How could we possibly educate our children to be the best when more than 50% of them are from broken families? How could we possibly expect much excellence from the teachers when their seniority trumps over individual performance? As a total solution, unless we can come up with a new form of government as I suggested (Chapters

2 and 3), I think America's public school system should be privatized. Remember, America's best universities are mostly private. They are the best in the world!

4. Closing

In an open and free society like ours, most of the brightest students understand the value of education, know what to major in college, and know what to do upon graduation, which is to join the private sector for a chance to achieve their full potential. This has been the case throughout America's history and should remain so forever.

The public sector, on the other hand, should be minimized and reformed to make sure its role is to serve, truly serve, starting with the American President.

Here is a quote: *"The best minds are not in government. If any were, business would steal them away."*

Who said it? **Ronald Reagan!**

Chapter 40: It Is The Out-Of-Control Spending on Military, Stupid!

(Initially published at GEI on 11/18/2011)

"America will never be destroyed from the outside. If we falter and lose our freedoms, it will be because we destroyed ourselves."

--- Abraham Lincoln

This recent article (Counter China, US sets training in Australia) set me on fire. Here are three simple messages to my fellow Americans:
1) China is a competitor, not an enemy!
2) We, the U.S., already have too many enemies! The last thing we need is to make yet another new enemy, be it China or any other country!
3) We have been spending too much on military, often disguised as defense spending. This excess, as epitomized by the two wars in Iraq and Afghanistan, has significantly contributed to the fact that we, as a country, are broke!

Below are five excerpts from my five chapters in this book:
1) In Chapter 9 ("The answer is democracy; the question is why"), I state: *"we, the U.S., have actually been the source of instability around the world after the Cold War ... Today our defense spending is bigger than the next 16 biggest spending countries combined!"*
2) In Chapter 55 ("What's the real cost of the Iraq War?"), I state: *"The U.S. defense industry is so well entrenched that it has to have enemies to survive. After the Cold War, the obvious pick was*

China, with all kinds of accusations from communism to human rights. However, most of these accusations went away with the Iraq War. China rapidly moved forward (without much distraction from the U.S.) and has doubled its GDP since then."

3) In Chapter 25 ("American Presidency: let's redefine it, now!"), I state: "*What was so special about the year 2000? The world had changed so much after the Cold War ended in 1989 that 2000 turned out to be a tipping point, with the emerging economies, led by China, becoming formidable competitors to the West - like never before ... America, on the other hand, has not adapted accordingly after 1989: America's foreign and economic policy has not adequately changed. The political system has hardly changed at all over more than 200 years. By 2000, America had not only more economic competitors than ever, but also more political enemies (e.g. Islamic extremists) than ever.*"

4) In Chapter 25 ("American Presidency: let's redefine it, now!"), I also state: "*After two disastrous Presidents in George W. Bush and Barack Obama, today, America has not only even more economic competitors and political enemies than in 2000, but also much stronger duals than in 2000!*"

5) In Chapter 2 ("Solution for America"), I state: "*cut the defense spending drastically. If not, we will soon have no country left to defend!*"

Why are we so out-of-control on military spending, way beyond the need of self-defense? It's the political system, stupid! First of all, there is the deep entrenchment of the defense industry. Then, as you would expect, there are many war hawks in the military, eager for career advancement with more stars to wear. Finally, there are votes and jobs for the career politicians!

How to fix the problem? Reform the political system (Chapter 2)!

Chapter 41: The Congressional Super-Committee: What A Joke!

(Initially published at GEI on 11/25/2011)

So the Congressional Super-Committee has just failed miserably. What a joke! Surprised? You should not! It was set up to fail three months ago! The politicians got the political cover by passing the buck to the committee: the Democrats got the debt limit increase they needed, while the Republicans allowed it without meeting their ultimatum of no new taxes. This whole thing was a mutually agreed conspiracy to kick the can down the road yet again, postponing the day of reckoning ...

America's political system is essentially a two-party system. To succeed as a member of Congress, which was paved as a career by the law-makers after WWII (Chapter 1), you must pledge allegiance to your party, which will help you not only get elected in the first place, but also get re-elected again and again, without term-limits! As a result, serving the country has become an abstraction with a lower priority, but serving the party is of primary importance with tangible personal benefits day in and day out. Furthermore, because a party is supported by various special interest groups (e.g. unions and the defense industry), serving the party simply means serving the special interest groups! Still wondering how and why our national debt is so out-of-control now? Wonder not! The system is designed to spend only, for various special interest groups. We can't cut, because any cut would offend one special interest group at least, which is much more costly for politicians than to simply hand out more – it is out of the public treasury, anyway!

Yes, the Super-Committee was a joke! Saddened? Don't! The American Presidency looks more and more like a joke too: Virtually no qualifications are required, just sign up to run: "It's easier to sign up as a candidate for president than it is to apply for a job at McDonald's"! Winning is, of course, a lot harder, but it's a popularity contest not even as serious as American Idol (Chapter 24)!

Saddened by such a miserable reality check of the American Presidency? Don't! While George W. Bush will prove to be the worst American President in recent history, President Barack Obama has proven to be a joke. Here is an excerpt from Chapter 22 ("American Presidency: Why is One-Term a Must?"):

"Senator Obama had no executive experience of running anything, not even a candy shop, and his resume was not good enough to run any American company. Yet he won the popularity contest of the American Presidency! Now, has President Obama spent enough of your grandchildren's money to buy your vote for his re-election?"

How to fix the problem? Change the political system, starting with one-term (e.g. six years) for the American Presidency, on top of raising the statutory requirements! For Congress, some kind of term-limits is a must, preferably one-term (e.g. six years) as well (Chapter 2)!

The oldest democracy Greece (and Rome) died more than 2000 years ago because of debts. America will die for the same reason, unless we change the course soon!

Chapter 42: American Airlines & America: What Do They Have in Common?

(Initially published at GEI on 12/2/2011)

The headline business news this past Tuesday (November 29, 2011) was this: American Airlines files for bankruptcy protection. Here is how it begins:

> *"American Airlines and its parent company filed for bankruptcy protection as they try to cut costs and unload massive debt built up by years of high fuel prices and labor struggles."*

Were you surprised to hear the news? No, if you are reasonably intelligent! A more profound question is this though: what do American Airlines and America have in common? Here is my 3-folder answer:
1) Both are deeply in trouble financially.
2) Both have seen their respective peers go down, without adequate effort to avoid the same destiny. Specifically, both are stuck with special interest groups (e.g. unions) with no [easy] way out.
3) What's the destiny? Bankruptcy! American Airlines is already there; America will be there soon, if we stay the course.

There is a huge difference between the two though: American Airlines is a company, but America is a country. As a company, American Airlines should consider bankruptcy, because it is, overall, the best option for the company at this time. As a country and the only superpower in the world, America must be very careful: A bankruptcy for America could be a total disaster to the world, both economically and politically, to the point of a possible WWIII.

Here is the good news: I believe I have the best diagnosis for America (Chapter 1), as well as the best solution (Chapter 2).

Here is the bad news: America has proven inadaptable. Here is an excerpt from Chapter 41 ("The Congressional Super-Committee: What a Joke!"):

> "We spend only and we can't cut, because any cut would offend one special interest group at least, which is much more costly for the politicians than to simply hand out more – it is out of the public treasury, anyway!"

Worse yet, according to the proven Darwin's theory of evolution, the "winner" is often neither the smartest nor the strongest, but the most adaptable. We are therefore destined to be a "loser" because of our inability to adapt.

Worst of all, here is an excerpt from a classic piece ("The Truth about Tytler"):

> "A democracy cannot exist as a permanent form of government. It can only exist until the voters discover that they can vote themselves largesse from the public treasury. From that moment on, the majority always votes for the candidates promising the most benefits from the public treasury with the result that a democracy always collapses over loose fiscal policy, always followed by a dictatorship. The average age of the world's greatest civilizations has been 200 years."

We, the U.S.A., are certainly more than 200 years old already! Is our time really up? I don't think so and that's why I have been trying to save America with my pen, or keyboard, to be precise.

Will America listen?

Chapter 43: Unemployment Rate: What Is It and Does It Really Matter?

(Initially published at GEI on 12/9/2011)

Last Friday (December 2, 2011), the top business news was this: Unemployment Slips to 8.6% as Private Sector Adds Jobs. I found it misleading for two main reasons:

1) It is my understanding that we must create 125,000 jobs per month just to keep up with the population growth in the workforce. In November, the private sector created 120,000 non-farm jobs, which means that the real unemployment rate should have gone up, especially given the rise of new weekly jobless claims above 400,000!

2) It is also my understanding that the current method of calculating the unemployment rate is severely flawed (Q&A: A look behind the drop in the jobless rate). But still it should not have been so imprecise as to be off by about 0.4%, or about 500,000 jobs! Have all those some 500,000 unemployed people stopped looking? If so, shouldn't that be the top news story?

While I agree that creating 120,000 non-farm jobs in November was good news, I was troubled by the following news on the same day:

1) The media headlines shouted: Unemployment rate drops to lowest since 2009!
2) President Obama hailed at the news.

I doubt the media and President Obama are deliberately misleading the public, knowing that (1) our method of calculating the unemployment rate is severely flawed and (2) the overall situation in America is no better now than in 2009, in almost all aspects, from unemployment, to job prospects, to poverty, to debts and deficits (national, state, and local)! Unconvinced? Read this (Meet the Jobless in Iowa), or this (College Graduates Face Record High Debt in the Age of Record High Unemployment), or this (Hidden America), or this (Santa finds kids giving shorter lists in recession). Need you read more?

Why so doubtful? Because neither President Obama nor the media can be trusted for two main reasons:
1) President Obama has been doing his job as President for one primary purpose only: getting re-elected, with everything else being secondary, including the long-term well-being of the country! Just to be fair, President George W. Bush acted the same way throughout his first term.
2) The American media, especially the established and for-profit ones, pander to the politicians. Two examples:
   - Together with the politicians, the media have created a perception that jobs are the #1 problem in America. I disagree! It's a symptom, not a diagnosis! I believe *"America's #1 problem today is not jobs per se. Instead, it's the debts and deficits that are leading the country toward bankruptcy. Therefore, America must be restructured, as in business, getting its fiscal house in order first before anything else, such as hiring)."* For more, read Chapter 11.
   - The media failed to question the insanity behind the launch of the Iraq War, which is so consequential that I believe it *"will eventually be marked as the beginning of the end of democracy as we know it"* (Chapter 55).

Now, let me answer the two original questions in the title:
1) Unemployment rate: what is it? The real unemployment rate is definitely above 15%. We need a new method to more truthfully reflect the reality!
2) Unemployment rate: does it really matter? Yes, it does, because people are suffering! Even so, it's not as important as the long-term survival of our country!

America is deeply in trouble! Everything will get much worse before it becomes better, including the real job prospects, which, according to Christine Romer, former Chair of the Council of Economic Advisers for President Obama, could take 40 years. Why are we so deeply in trouble? Because our problem is structural and years of excessive spending have finally caught up with us! Yes, it's payback time - either we pay now or our children will pay later at a much higher price! Any doubt? Look at Europe today!

America is deeply in trouble! If someone gives you an easy solution, don't trust it! Want a real solution? Introducing term-limits for the top political offices, starting with one-term (e.g. six years) for the American Presidency! For more details, read my diagnosis (Chapter 1) and solution (Chapter 2)!

Finally, here are three profound questions for you to answer:
1) Does it matter to you who the President is?
2) Who can you still trust in American politics today?
3) Will your children be better off than you, if we stay the course?

Chapter 44: Public-Sector Unions: From Wisconsin to America

(Initially published at GEI on 6/8/2012)

"A strike of public employees manifests nothing less than an intent on their part to prevent or obstruct the operations of Government until their demands are satisfied. Such action, looking toward the paralysis of Government by those who have sworn to support it, is unthinkable and intolerable."

--- Franklin D. Roosevelt

On June 5, 2012, in what was called "the second most important election this year", the people of Wisconsin spoke out loud and clear: keep Governor Scott Walker in office!

What did Governor Walker do to deserve such a recall attempt? He offended the unions by curbing the rights of public-sector unions! It was the right thing to do, not only for Wisconsin, but also for America! For more, read: The whine from Wisconsin.

Unfortunately, such a clear-cut issue is not clear at all in America today, thanks to decades of practice of democratic socialism and brainwashing (Chapter 63). Here is a good example: a publication (High stakes for Big Labor in Wisconsin recall vote) muddles the water from the title to the contents! Two notes:
1) Private-sector workers can be correctly called "the laborers". But public-sector workers cannot - they are the proud "public servants"!

2) Unions should exist to protect the laborers, not to create a protected class of public employees who earn more and have vastly better benefits than their employers, the laborers!
   - For the private sector, unions are valid. I believe everything will work out by itself. For example, when the UAW became too big, it nearly killed the U.S. auto industry. Some correction has occurred, although the UAW is still too big today.
   - For the public sector, unions are not valid. Who are they unionized against? The laborers! More bluntly, public-sector unions are more than socialistic - they are *"totally communistic and must therefore go!"* For more, read Chapter 20 ("American Democracy: What went wrong and when?).

Here is an excerpt from a Letter from FDR Regarding Public-Sector Unions dated August 16, 1937:

All Government employees should realize that the process of collective bargaining, as usually understood, cannot be transplanted into the public service. It has its distinct and insurmountable limitations when applied to public personnel management.

The very nature and purposes of Government make it impossible for administrative officials to represent fully or to bind the employer in mutual discussions with Government employee organizations.

Particularly, I want to emphasize my conviction that militant tactics have no place in the functions of any organization of Government employees.

> *A strike of public employees manifests nothing less than an intent on their part to prevent or obstruct the operations of Government until their demands are satisfied. Such action, looking toward the paralysis of Government by those who have sworn to support it, is unthinkable and intolerable.*

When and how did public-sector unions (i.e. the *"unthinkable and intolerable"*) start in the U.S.? In 1961, thanks to President Kennedy (Executive Order 10988)! Why did President Kennedy perpetrate such a communistic thing on America? For the sake of his re-election!

Tolerable no more!

What Governor Walker did was significant: It was a small step to undo the devastating damage caused by President Kennedy, but a gigantic step against the demise of America!

Two messages out of Wisconsin are loud and clear:
1) Wisconsin is not like France or Greece, which recently elected *"socialists to fix the problems caused by socialism"* (Chapter 64: "Democracy-Communism Similarity #3: Ideology").
2) Democracy worked in this case!

Governor Walker, keep up the good work to save Wisconsin! It was a good start! Yes, divide and conquer, until they are all gone!

Governor Romney, heed my advice to win the most important election this year, in order to save America (Chapter 26: "An Open Letter to Mitt Romney")!

Chapter 45: Obese: to Be or Not to Be

(Initially published at GEI on 6/15/2012)

Americans are fat (Statistics – Obesity in America). People are rightfully concerned about it (How Obesity Threatens America's Future). But what is the real solution (Why God Wants You to Be Thin)?

Here is the latest solution from New York City: New York City poised to Limit Size of Sugary Drinks. Do you like it? I don't. Here is why:
1) Obesity is a "traditional" sign of prosperity.
2) Obesity is a "modern" life style of choice.
3) There should be no law against that choice – freedom of being fat!

1. Obesity is a "traditional" sign of prosperity
In Buddhism, being fat is glorified, as it represents prosperity.

Can you easily spot fat people in Africa? No!

America is obviously the most obese country in the world. Coincidentally, it happens to be most prosperous too. It's known as a country of "plenty", including (junk) food and obesity!

I grew up in China, where everything was rationed, especially during the Cultural Revolution. We had ration stamps for everything (e.g. rice, meat, sugar, cooking oil, and even tofu). Malnutrition was the norm and obesity unheard of.

As China becomes more prosperous, so does obesity. Today, there are no more ration stamps in China, but a lot of McD's and KFC's instead! Oh, computer games are adding to obesity too, as people become less mobile and lazier!

I lived in Brussels from 1988 to 1991, and noticed that the Europeans were, and still are, much thinner than Americans. You may have your own explanation for this. But to me, it is simple: food in Europe is at least twice as expensive as that in America!

Personally, I lost 20 pounds three months after I moved to Brussels (from America) in 1988, but gained 20 pounds three months after I moved back to America in 1991!

2. Obesity is a "modern" life style of choice

I am six feet tall. For the past decade, my "stable" weight has been 220 pounds, which is about 30 pounds over my ideal weight. I knew all along that diet (i.e. eating right and eating less) was really the only way to go, but I just could not do it. Instead, I tried all kinds of "easier" ways, including working out every day for the past decade, without success. Yes, I am fit, but overweight!

My dad passed away about two months ago (Chapter 75: "My Father Li Dexin"), in the same way as several relatives on that side of the family (i.e. stroke as a result of high blood pressure). That finally got me serious about losing weight: I started eating right and eating less, in earnest. As a result, I lost 15 pounds already! 15 more to go and keep it down!

3. No law against the choice of obesity!

Americans value freedoms, including the freedom of being fat!

The government should stay out of our lives! When you start limiting the size of sugary drinks, what's next? Where is the end? So do not even start!

Now, what about the medical insurance for all kinds of problems caused by obesity? An insurance program, be it privately-run or government-run, should be allowed to charge more premiums for the obese people. The same applies to airline seating: If you overflow from your seat, pay for two (or even three)! It's simple economics, not discrimination!

4. Closing
What's going on with New York City Mayor Michael Bloomberg?

Chapter 46: Four Points to Ponder on America's 236th Birthday

(Initially published at GEI on 6/29/2012)

July 4th, 2012, marks America's 236th birthday. As usual, we shall celebrate it with fireworks. Extraordinarily, let's think, harder than ever, about four points as follows:
1) Who are we as a country?
2) What is our trouble, really?
3) Why are we so deeply in trouble?
4) What's the real solution?

It's now or never!

1. Who are we as a country?
Three readings:
1) Chapter 5: "What is American, Anyway?"
2) Chapter 6: "Top 10 American Misconceptions about America."
3) Chapter 20: "American Democracy: What Went Wrong and When?"

2. What is our trouble, really?
We are deeply in trouble fiscally, economically, and politically.

2.1 Fiscal trouble
Fiscally, our trouble is very obvious: our national debt has already exceeded $15T (and growing rapidly), which is more than our annual GDP. It was $9T in 2009 when President Obama took office.

2.2 Economic trouble

Economically, our trouble is also obvious:
1) Although the official unemployment rate is at 8.2% today, the real number is about 15% (Unemployment rate: How many Americans are really unemployed?). The jobs being created now are not enough to even keep up with the population growth. Still wondering why 53% of all young college graduates in America are either unemployed or underemployed? Wonder not!
2) The housing market has been down since 2008 and will remain down for the foreseeable future.
3) Read: The Student Loan Bubble: Only Stupid People Will Be Surprised When It Bursts.

2.3 Political trouble

Politically, our trouble is perhaps the least obvious for most Americans. So let's have a simple reality check of the three branches of our government, one by one, as follows:
1) Legislative: 87% in US disapprove of Congress.
2) Judicial: Only 44% of Americans approve of the Supreme Court.
3) Executive: Have you noticed that Americans no longer talk about how great their Presidents are/were, but which one is/was worse and who is/was the worst? Two examples:
   - George W. Bush's favorable rating lowest of any living president, poll shows.
   - President Obama's Place In U.S. History: Debt Monger.

Personally, I think George W. Bush and Barack Obama are the two worst American Presidents in [recent] history. Why? Here is an excerpt from Chapter

20 ("American Democracy: What went wrong and when?"):

> "*Together the policies of these two Presidents have done more damage to America than all of America's enemies have done, combined! The biggest threat to America is its faltering economy, which is plainly visible now!*"

For more, read Chapter 27 ("An Open Letter to President Obama").

3. Why are we so deeply in trouble?
Read Chapter 1!

Highlight: The root cause of our problems is neither fiscal nor economic, but political! Yes, it's the political system, stupid! Specifically,
1) Democracy, as we practice it in the U.S. today, no longer works.
2) China's political system (Chapter 16: "America: What is China's Political System, Anyway?"), albeit with many endemic problems of its own, appears to be slightly better than America's, which is all that is necessary for China to win its head-on competition with the U.S. Worse yet, it's shaping up to be winner take all, just like what the U.S. had throughout the second half of the last century!

Let me emphasize that our problems are big and structural! Three examples:
1) Gridlock has paralyzed our government for years.
2) When the two parties finally manage to get something done together, it's often a wrong thing

(read: <u>Bipartisanship Is Behind Government's Worst Programs</u>)!

3) The launch of the Iraq War showed that there were neither checks nor balances within our government. Instead, it was, and still is, corrupted to its core. For more on U.S. government corruption, read Chapter 36 ("Blagojevich and Pearl Harbor: They Are Related!").

4. What's the real solution?
Read Chapter 2!

Highlight: We must fix the political system fundamentally by changing the Constitution as follows:
1) Limiting the American Presidency to one-term (e.g. six years).
2) Raising the statutory requirements for the American Presidency, such as the minimum age to 55 and only after having served as a state governor for a full-term, at least.
3) Introducing strict term-limits for Congress, preferably one-term of six years as well.

Now, how can we have the solution implemented? Two possible ways:
1) NATO could support an Occupy Wall Street military takedown of the "massively unpopular" Obama regime in the protection of the 99%, in the same way as it did in Libya. Or, if you prefer, NATO could support a Tea Party military takedown of the "tyrannically oppressive" Obama regime in the defense of America's Constitution and founding principles. For more, read Chapter 63 ("Brainwashing").
2) Elect Governor Romney the next American President. This, obviously, is the preferred way.

Unfortunately, Governor Romney is not guaranteed to win in November, unless he heeds my advice (Chapter 26: "An Open Letter to Mitt Romney") that he promises
1) To be a one-term President, dedicating himself to running the country without re-election.
2) To fix the political system fundamentally by changing the Constitution as I suggested above.

With that, not only will there be President Romney, but also he will have a chance to save America, thus becoming one of the greatest American Presidents like George Washington!

But, will Governor Romney listen?

5. Closing
Read and think - Have a great July 4th!

Chapter 47: American Dreams: Oversold and Overbought!

(Initially published at GEI on 7/13/2012)

Have you seen the recent Time magazine cover (July 2, 2012)? What an important subject! Its inside is even better, with the cover article entitled "Keeping the Dream Alive," by Jon Meacham.

Unfortunately, like many good articles in America's established media today, Meacham's article falls short of being great, largely because it fails to recognize the root cause of many American ills. It therefore falls short of possibly offering any real solution to "keeping the dream alive".

To have a real solution, we must have a truthful diagnosis first (Chapter 1), which requires being honest with ourselves. One simple truth is that American dreams have been oversold and overbought!

1. Definitions

Today, the notion of the "American Dream" is often accompanied by the notion of the "middle class". So let's define these two terms first. According to Meacham's article,

1) American Dream: It is the *"perennial conviction that those who work hard and play by the rules will be rewarded with a more comfortable present and a stronger future for their children."*
2) Middle class: Middle class families are defined by *"their aspirations more than their income. Middle-class families aspire to homeownership, a car, college education for their children, health and*

retirement security and occasional family vacations."

2. American dreams: my view

Many people, Americans or not, have American dreams, such as coming to the U.S. to "make it", President Obama's early dream of <u>Someday I want to be President</u>, and hitting a mega-lottery tomorrow.

I have written about American dreams several times. Here are two representative publications:
  1) Chapter 38: "American Dreams vs. America".
  2) Chapter 74: "My American Dream Has Come True".

In short, I consider myself a modern-day example of an American dream come true. But I can't emphasize more that not all American dreams are good for America.

3. American dreams: what went wrong?

Some American dreams went wrong because America went wrong. America went wrong because America failed to adapt to the changing times. For more, read:
  1) Chapter 5: What is American, Anyway?
  2) Chapter 6: Top 10 American Misconceptions about America.
  3) Chapter 20: American Democracy: What Went Wrong and When?

Bottom line: America, as a country, must ask and answer two basic questions:
  1) Do other people on earth have the same rights to <u>life, liberty and the pursuit of happiness</u> as Americans do?

2) If yes, how can America possibly compete against the emerging economies (Chapter 56), which have joined the fray with hundreds of millions of cheap laborers?

Unless these two questions are answered correctly and corresponding actions taken, America will continue to decline; at this pace, that means there will soon be no more sweet American dreams left for anyone to pursue.

Unfortunately, rather than asking and answering these two basic questions, American political leaders have largely ignored them. Immune to the changing times, they focus on one thing only: "getting re-elected *ad nauseam*". How do they keep getting themselves re-elected? Spending more and pandering more, including choosing to whom the same old American dreams can be dispensed, in exchange for votes ...

4. American dreams: oversold and overbought

American politicians have oversold American dreams in their relentless pursuit of votes. The willing Americans have overbought them, because they forgot, or never knew, about who we are (e.g. "we are a nation of self-made men", as per Henry Clay). It's money for votes, all at the expenses of the long-term well-being of America! Four examples:
1) Home ownership: At its peak, close to 70% of Americans owned their homes (U.S. Census Bureau News), a ratio boosted by poorly thought out laws (e.g. Community Reinvestment Act) against the free market. Worse yet, many Americans owned homes bigger and better than they could actually afford, resulting in a huge housing bubble that burst in 2008, with little sign of relief in sight to date.

2) College education: It's true that college graduates, in general, earn more than non-college graduates. But everything must follow "Pyramid Theory I" (Chapter 18), with the understanding that only a small percentage can actually make it to the top (Too Many Waiters And Janitors Have Degrees). Today, the total amount of student loans is at more than $1T. This bubble, just as volatile as the housing bubble, will explode in our faces soon (read: The Student Loan Bubble: Only Stupid People Will Be Surprised When It Bursts)!
3) Unemployment: Although the official rate is at 8.2%, the real rate is above 15%. The situation is particularly bad for the young people (e.g. 53% of all young college graduates in America are either unemployed or under-employed).
4) State and local government bankruptcy: Read: Stockton, California: Belly Up. More will follow! Who is to blame? Public-sector unions, with President Kennedy being the ultimate culprit! For more, read Chapter 44 ("Public-Sector Unions: from Wisconsin to America").

Need you have more examples?

5. Discussion

Why so wrong? It's the political system, stupid! We have been sleeping on the same political system for more than 200 years, and it's getting worse and worse, thanks to "getting re-elected *ad nauseam*". It's time to fundamentally change it by amending the Constitution as I suggested (Chapter 2)!

An important note: American dreams should be mostly for the private-sector workers, epitomized by Steve Jobs and Bill Gates, two outstanding self-made men! Public-sector workers are "servants", whose [outsized] American dreams not only are wrong by definition, but also have been clearly and severely damaging America - there are simply too many "servants" enjoying their American dreams by living way better than their "masters"! This must be reversed, if America wants to have any future. For more, read Chapter 44 ("Public-Sector Unions: from Wisconsin to America")!

6. Closing

Meacham was right in his conclusion that *"This year the choice for President comes at a time when specific ideas about relieving and growing the middle class — education reform and access, for instance — seem less important than the present and the future of the overall economy."* It should be obvious that we will all be below the "middle class" if our political system fails us, finally and totally.

But where is Meacham's solution to "keeping the dream alive"? He does not have one!

Here is my solution: Not only is it essential that Governor Romney win in November, but he must follow my suggestion to fundamentally change America's political system, so as to really "keep the dream alive!" For more, read Chapter 26 ("An Open Letter to Mitt Romney").

Chapter 48: America: 10 Big Questions and 10 Honest Answers

(Initially published at GEI on 9/7/2012)

Did you watch the 2012 Republican National Convention as well as the 2012 Democratic National Convention? If yes, are you now confused - whom to believe?

Do not feel very bad about yourself, because many career politicians are professional liars. What about the mainstream media? It is part of the establishment intoxicated in brainwashing (Chapter 63)!

America is deeply in trouble and here are some simple facts:
1) The poverty level is at a record high (The State of Poverty in America).
2) Our national debt has just exceeded $16T, namely, more than $50K per person for everybody in the U.S.!
3) The official unemployment rate has been above 8% for several years, while the real rate is above 15%, with no relief in sight ...

I believe I have the most accurate diagnosis for America (Chapter 1), as well as the best solution (Chapter 2). To fully appreciate them, we Americans must be very honest with ourselves. I will try to do just that in this chapter. It asks 10 big questions about America today and answers them honestly.

Question 1: Is the Great Recession over?
Yes, the Great Recession was over more than two years ago, according to the official definition. But it's

still here, practically, especially for those 23 million unemployed.

Question 2: When can we get out of the Great Recession, really?

Not within 10 years, unless we dramatically change our course! Why not? Can the morbidly ill have any real hope, without first having a sound diagnosis and then following a strict regimen (Chapter 2), however painful, to recovery?

Once again (from Chapter 47: "American Dreams: Oversold and Overbought"), America, as a country, must ask and answer two basic questions:
1) Do other people on earth have the same rights to <u>life, liberty and the pursuit of happiness</u> as Americans do?
2) If yes, how can America possibly compete against the emerging economies, which are joining the fray with hundreds of millions of cheap laborers?

Unless these two questions are answered correctly and corresponding actions taken, the Great Recession is the new norm. Do not believe in any easy solutions - they are just more "feel good" lies!

Question 3: How bad can the Great Recession get?

It can be as bad as the Great Depression, or even worse, unless we change our course! Two examples:
1) The job market will not improve in the foreseeable future. Why not? Simple math: with the economy growing at less than 2%, we are unable to accommodate even the population growth!
2) Competition from the emerging economies will only become fiercer.

Question 4: How did we get out of the Great Depression?

WWII, not the massive government spending! Both Presidents Hoover and FDR acknowledged it as a fact!

Question 5: How can we get out of the Great Recession?

Two possible ways:
1) Fundamentally changing America's political system for the better, starting with the American Presidency, as it already has been suggested (Chapter 2).
2) WWIII! Here is an excerpt from Pyramid Theory II (Chapter 57):

> *After all, it was WWII that finally got America out of the Great Depression, although Keynesians like to credit the massive government spending, which was the biggest lie of the 20th century. In other words, America did win WWII. But more significantly, America's competitors either destroyed themselves through the war (e.g. Germany and Japan) or screwed themselves up badly after the war by adopting a fundamentally flawed system called "communism" (e.g. China and the Soviet Union). As a result, America was left as the only game in town, making and inventing virtually everything and naming its own prices. This not only got America out of the Great Depression finally, but also created prosperity in America for the ensuing five decades. Analogously, it may well take WWIII to get America out of the Great Recession. The only difference is this time America may be the culprit, as*

America has both the capability and incentive to provoke WWIII, especially if the neo-cons get their way! In fact, the seeds of WWIII might have already been sowed with the Iraq War.

Most Americans adamantly oppose wars, despite various attempts by both the left (e.g. Death by China) and the right (e.g. US: Missile defense for North Korea threat, not China). So let's focus on way (1): fundamentally changing America's political system.

Question 6: Why must the change start with the American Presidency?
Two reasons:
1) It's rotten up there! For more, read Chapter 21 ("American Democracy: Massive Falsehoods at the Top"). Falsehood and incompetence trickle down!
2) Barring a bloody revolution, a fundamental change like this can only start from the top.

Question 7: How can the change start with the American Presidency?
Elect Mitt Romney the next American President!

Let's give Mitt Romney a chance for five reasons:
1) Romney is an exceptional leader with "a stellar performance" as a businessman (Romney's Stellar Performance) and as a governor. He is a rare talent not only in America, but also in the world!
2) Romney is not a career politician. Romney knows who built America: the private sector!
3) Romney is not just a businessman like Ross Perot. Romney served in the public sector.
4) Romney is not a neo-con!

5) President Obama is just not good enough, at best.

Question 8: Is austerity a must?
Yes! Do not believe in any easy solutions - they are just more "feel good" lies!

We have screwed ourselves up so much and for so long that it's payback time! But the people should not sacrifice before the politicians do. The politicians will not sacrifice before the President does. So let's demand that the next President be a great President to set a great example.

Question 9: Can we invest and grow out of the Great Recession?
No! Our problems are structural. For example, there are now more takers than makers in America (Chapter 39: "America: from Public Schools to Government, What is Wrong?"). With the emerging economies joining the fray in the race for prosperity, how hard should, and can, American makers work to keep feeding more and more American takers? In other words, without fixing the structure first, the more we "invest" now by stealing from our future, the harder America will collapse later!

If the tick gets bigger than the dog, they both die!

"When Congress is in session, watch your wallet!" That was for the good old days! Today, when a politician utters the words "investment" or "affordable" (e.g. housing or healthcare), just say "no". Why? Because they are just euphemisms for giveaways in exchange for votes! What about "growth"? Again, do not be fooled! There is no way to grow America's economy at a real recovery pace of more than 2.5%, without first changing course and fixing the structure (Chapter 4)!

Question 10: Why is the structure so wrong?

It's the political system, stupid! The world has changed a lot, but we have not! We have been sleeping on the same political system for more than 200 years!

American politicians work for themselves first, their constituents a remote second, and their country dead last! They spend our money like it's theirs, for one purpose only: getting themselves re-elected! Still wondering why our national debt has already exceeded $16T? Wonder not! Our money has been used to buy votes for them!

Part 8: America and China

Chapter 49: Political & Economic Lessons from China
Chapter 50: Hello from China to America
Chapter 51: Warren Buffett and Chairman Mao: Something in Common?
Chapter 52: Freedom of the Press in America and in China
Chapter 53: Karl Marx and John Keynes
Chapter 54: America: Let The Rich Run The Country Like China Does!

"The political system does not matter, as long as it embraces capitalism."

--- Frank Li

Chapter 49: Political & Economic Lessons from China

China is becoming yesterday's America, while America is becoming yesterday's China!

China is a competitor, not an enemy, to America. The only way for America to have any chance to fend off the competition from China is to become better itself, which can't be done without a better understanding of China.

In Parts 4 and 6, I explained China to my fellow Americans in some depth already. In this chapter, I will provide an overview of China's recent history and list out five big political and economic lessons from China for America.

1. Overview of China's recent history (1949-1976)

Everything important in China is named "The People's". Three examples:
1) The name of the country: The People's Republic of China.
2) The name of the Army: The People's Liberation Army.
3) The name of the money: The People's money or Renminbi (or RMB for short).

It was not like that until 1949 …

1.1 What happened in 1949?

The CPC (Communist Party of China) led by Mao succeeded in the revolution. The proletarians (also known as "the People" or "the working class") became the masters, turning the country into a huge lab for an experiment called "socialism" (also known as "communism" in the West). The People purged the rich (i.e. shot them or sidelined them), named everything important theirs (i.e. "The People's"), and worshiped themselves: the workers, the peasants, and the soldiers!

1.2 What happened from 1949 to 1976?

A total disaster! Two examples:
1) A man-made famine as a result of the Great Leap Forward movement that killed some 20 million people around 1960 (think of North Korea today)!
2) The Great Proletarian Cultural Revolution (1966-1976), during which Mao purged his opponents within the CPC like he purged the rich after 1949.

By 1976, China became dirt poor, so poor and hopeless that a young man like me (born in 1959) thought of nothing but "getting the hell out of here" (think of the Cubans today)!

Why such a total disaster? Mao knew nothing about the economy and construction, nor did the People! What did they know? Robbing and killing the rich and destruction! In other words, once the proletarians were in charge, everybody in China became a proletarian!

1.3 What happened in 1976?

Mao died! Better yet, Mao did not have a son succeeding him! Mao's only (able) son Mao Anying was killed in the Korean War, thanks to the West ("Amen"), or today's China, under Mao Jr. or Mao III, could be as bad as today's North Korea!

Rumor has it that Mao never forgave Peng Dehuai, China's Command-in-Chief in the Korean War, for this "sin" and made up a reason to have him purged in the late 1950s. We may never know the real reason behind Peng's purge. What's known for sure is that Mao spent the rest of his life scrambling for a succession plan, without success.

1.4 What happened after 1976?
Deng Xiaoping became the leader in China. He reformed the country and set it on the right course.

2. What does China really look like today?
Everything important is still "the People's," but in name only. The economy belongs to the rich, while the autocrats, who are not elected by the People, own the government.

For a good understanding of today's China and today's CPC, read: <u>China's political anniversary: a long cycle nears its end</u>. Here are three excerpts:

1) *The party was established in 1921 in the name of people like him [a peddler]. But today it is widely seen as representing the entrenched interests of the wealthy elite – the kind of people who spend more on a single meal in Xintiandi than this peddler would make in an entire year.*

2) *With more than 80m members, it is the world's largest political organization. In spite of its insistence that it remains true to its Marxist-Leninist, Maoist heritage, though, it is perhaps better described as the world's largest chamber of commerce.*

3) *The first sentence of the manifesto of the CPC states that the party "is the vanguard of the Chinese working class". Yet today, fewer than 9% of its members are classified as "workers" while more than 70% are recruited from the ranks of government officials, businessmen, professionals, college graduates and military.*

What a huge difference from 1976!

Now, a big question: is today's Chinese system ideal? No, not at all! But it is infinitely better than yesterday's system under Mao! Furthermore, it appears to be, overall, slightly better than America's system. That is the key reason behind China's rise and America's fall. In a competitive world, all that a hiker needs to do, when chased by a hungry grizzle, is to run a bit faster than the other hiker!

3. Five big lessons from China
1) When the proletarians (or the working class) are in charge, we all become proletarians! Punishing success (i.e. the rich), you will end up without any success!
2) The system is everything! Between socialism and capitalism, choose the latter!
3) For prosperity, capitalism is a must, while democracy is merely an option. Sacrificing capitalism for democracy, you will end up with having neither!
4) Democracy could be an ideal form of government in theory. But no recipe to follow yet in practice. Here are two things known for sure though:
   - Democracy, as we know it today, does not work. Instead, the Chinese system (i.e. capitalism + autocracy) has fared far better than the other systems over the past two decades, with no end in sight.
   - For a third-world country like India, democracy is a liability for prosperity. As a matter of fact, there is not a single example of a third-world country achieving prosperity with democracy!
5) Time is often the best cure for many ills. Peace and trade, not war!

4. Closing

America, can't handle such big political and economic lessons from China yet? How about a lesson from Cicero in 55 BC? Here you go:

> "The budget should be balanced, the Treasury should be refilled, public debt should be reduced, the arrogance of officialdom should be tempered and controlled, and the assistance to foreign lands should be curtailed lest Rome become bankrupt. People must again learn to work, instead of living on public assistance."

What has the West learned over the past 2,067 years? Nothing, apparently!

Chapter 50: Hello from China to America

(Initially published at GEI on 11/4/2011)

"Knowing others is wisdom, knowing yourself is enlightenment."
--- Lao Tzu

As a Chinese-American who is enjoying the best of both countries, I have devoted a lot of efforts, through business as well as my writings, to the positive development of U.S.-China relations over the past decade. I believe with better understanding of each other, both countries will be much better off.

I am in China now, sitting comfortably in a teahouse with several college classmates to chat about anything and everything, from China's economy to Occupy Wall Street (which they found fascinating – it's like China, in its bad old days though). So there is no better time than now for me to write a small piece about China, the good, the bad, and the ugly, for my fellow Americans.

1. China: the good
Two examples:
1) Still remember the big earthquake in Haiti that happened in January 2008 and the bigger one in China that happened in May 2008? You may still hear about the former, as recovery has been very slow, but you have hardly heard about the latter for a long time, right? Recovered, totally! Thanks to the mighty power of China: the people as well as the government!
2) Read this: <u>10 years on, Afghan Americans see lost opportunities</u>. What a difference between Afghan-Americans and Chinese-Americans! As a latter, I

feel sorry for the former, as well as the Afghans in Afghanistan. I feel lucky for myself, as well as the Chinese in China. Far beyond that, I think this entire generation of the Chinese-Americans should feel the same way as I do for two main reasons:
- We are doing well in America in general.
- China, the dirt-poor country we left behind in the 1980s, has become so remarkably prosperous now that it has enabled us to enjoy the best of both.

2. China: the bad
Two examples:
1) Read this Time's cover story: <u>Be very afraid of the China bubble</u>! There are many bubbles in China. When any of them bursts, some people will get hurt. But there will be no financial crisis in China! Unlike the U.S. counterpart, the Chinese government has the power to pick and choose which bubble to deflate when it sees the necessity.
2) The top 2 problems in China are government corruption and environmental pollution. Despite all the efforts over the past decade, some problems have become ugly.

3. China: the ugly
Two examples:
1) Read this: <u>China's Railway Minister Loses Post in Corruption Inquiry</u>. Here is an excerpt: "*A total of 146,517 officials were punished for disciplinary violations in 2010 ... Of those, 5,098 were officials at the county level or above, and 804 of them were prosecuted.*" Need I say more about government corruption in China? The only good news in this aspect is that, despite corruption being endemic, at

least some of the bad people are being pursued and prosecuted.
2) Read this: <u>Foshan tragedy measures China's morality</u>. Here is an excerpt: *"Footage from a seven-minute video, in which a toddler in Foshan, a city in southern China, was hit twice by vehicles and ignored by 18 people walking by while she lay in her own blood, has stirred up fierce debate over China's moral crisis."* Can it get uglier than this? The Chinese are too busy making money to care about anything else - this is infinitely worse than the busy New Yorkers!

4. America vs. China

China, as a competitor, is well on its way to surpassing America as the largest economy on earth by 2030 (or by 2020 per IMF's formula). For this reason, every reasonably intelligent American should understand China, in order for America to have any chance in its head-on competition with China. What does your favorite sport team (e.g. Chicago Bears or Chicago Bills) do before a game? Study the opposing team!

Here is the simplest possible explanation of China to Americans: what's going on in China is raw capitalism plus a pro-business government that is of/by/for business (vs. people)! Nothing magical at all!

The issue of America vs. China can be simply explained as follows:
1) Capitalism: America is still way ahead of China.
2) Political system: China's system is, in my humble opinion, slightly better than America's, which apparently is more than enough to compensate for China's inferiority in capitalism.

Capitalism is not everything! Capitalism is the only thing!

5. America

If you think the current form of the American government is of/by/for the people, think again. Here are two perspectives:

1) Are our children and their children "people" too? If yes, do you still think it right that we spend their financial futures like there is no tomorrow?
2) If Congress is of/by/for the people, why is its disapproval rating at 87%?

Bottom line: the root cause of many American ills is its antiquated political system, nothing else! America's economic system (i.e. the free enterprise system) remains the best in the world, despite all its problems. China is winning the race with America in capitalism, while America has been self-destructing with democracy, as we know it today, destroying America, especially the capitalism part, faster and harsher than everything America's enemies have done, combined!

In short, America is ushering in her own demise!

6. Closing

As a Chinese-American, I am experiencing something extraordinary: My home country China, coming from nowhere, has become #2, while my adopted country, #1 America, has been declining so fast that #1 and #2 are about to switch positions. Is this good or bad? I am not sure - I am worried that a country like America can be very dangerous, when it becomes #2 in economy with a 1st-class military, especially with an example of the Iraq War.

It's good for the world for America to stay at #1 in economy! Most Chinese-Americans, and many Chinese, agree with me on this! But we, the Americans, must do it ourselves!

Chapter 51: Warren Buffett and Chairman Mao: Something in Common?

(Initially published at GEI on 12/30/2011)

Warren Buffett has been heavily in news recently. Here are two big stories:
1) Story 1: Warren Buffett on tax: He encouraged the government to raise taxes on the rich, namely, the billionaires, the millionaires, and even the 200-thousandaires.
2) Story 2: Warren Buffett on succession: He wants his son Howard to succeed him as *"a guardian"* of his mega company Berkshire Hathaway.

I was very shocked to hear story 1 and strongly disagreed with Mr. Buffett. However, it was not until I saw story 2 on "60 Minutes" that I intuitively and immediately linked him with Chairman Mao by asking myself this question: the old men are all the same, aren't they? Now, I have decided to publish my opinion about Mr. Buffett.

Here is my overall position on these two stories:
1) Tax: Mr. Beffett is entitled to his opinions about anything and everything, even if they are wrong. However, just because he is a financial guru does not mean he is wise.
2) Succession: As the largest shareholder of Berkshire Hathaway, Mr. Beffett certainly has the right to "recommend" his son as his successor to its Board of Directors. However, the Board owes it to all the shareholders to choose the most able, not the most connected, person to lead the company.

While I consider Mr. Buffett at the pinnacle of an American dream come true, I think he is very wrong on these two issues. Here is why:
1) Tax: Mr. Buffett could not have made it himself without being in the U.S., "the land of opportunity". Despite all the problems, we, the U.S., remain the best land on earth for anybody to make it, even as spectacularly as Mr. Buffett. Admittedly, America is deeply in trouble now. However, instead of identifying the root cause and fixing it, Mr. Buffett wants more taxes and hence more government spending. Worse yet, he wants to deprive the rest of us of the opportunity of success he himself enjoyed and used to his huge advantage! Would he be as successful as he is with the crushing taxes he now proposes? Maybe he is just too old to know what he is talking about – No disrespect and without political correctness, just business!
2) Succession: There is no success without succession (and *vice versa*)! Mr. Buffett had so many years to prepare his son for the top job at Berkshire Hathaway, but he was unable to do it. Now, after the departure of his long-time heir apparent, the 81-year-old Mr. Buffett seems to have no choice but to install his son at the helm, despite the fact that Howard is not qualified for the job by any normal standards! What is Mr. Buffett doing? Maybe he really is too old to know better. Once again, no disrespect and without political correctness, just business!

Here is the analogy between Mr. Buffett and Chairman Mao:
1) Both are/were highly successful in their early years. Mao was the first person to have unified

China over the past few hundred years, at least; Mr. Buffett made it by himself and is now one of the richest men on earth.
2) Mao made some grave mistakes in his late years, and Mr. Buffett appears to be making big mistakes now. Their traits on succession look particularly alike and troublesome. Here is what I wrote about Mao in Chapter 49 ("Political & Economic Lessons from China): *"Mao spent the rest of his life scrambling for a succession plan, without success."* Mr. Buffett is scrambling for a succession plan now! If the classic saying "there is no success without succession" holds true, Mr. Buffett is likely to fail ultimately, because there is no reason for Howard to be at this top job, except that he is Mr. Buffett's son. Howard is not very well prepared for the job, as he has acknowledged himself. Trial by fire often ends in flames – Time will tell.

Now, does it really make a good sense to compare Mr. Buffett, a businessman, with Mao, a revolution leader, in any way, be it in achievements or in mistakes? No, other than this general case in point: age matters! The more important you are, the more age matters. More specifically, when you are in an important position, you should be neither too young nor too old, especially when the well-being of your country (or company) is at stake! Puzzled? Hear me out ...

Look at what the Chinese did with the most important job in China: the Chinese Presidency. After suffering hugely from the rule of old men, epitomized by Mao, the Chinese set up an age range for the Chinese Presidency (Chapter 23) as follows:

1) In theory, the minimal age to serve is 45 and capped at 78 (i.e. done and gone).
2) In practice, a Chinese President typically takes office at about age 55 and finishes before age 70.

It has worked out remarkably well for China over the past two decades! Here is an excerpt from Chapter 23:

> *With this kind of top-down age limit, plus a bottom-up laddered system for career advancement (e.g. mayor, governor, VP, and President), a Chinese President is assured to have an optimal combination of experience (i.e. not too young) and judgment (i.e. not too old).*

Age matters! We, the U.S., should learn from China and do something similar with the American Presidency, such as raising the minimum age to 55 (Chapter 2).

Finally, two notes:
1) On succession, Mr. Buffett is actually more like North Korea's Kim II than China's Mao: Kim II passed his empire to his son; Mao did not! For more info on North Korea and its recent succession, read Chapter 59 ("America: what to do with North Korea?").
2) Sorry, Mr. Buffett, I am not picking on you. I am simply using you as an example to help expose the faults in the American political system! A noble cause at any cost!

Chapter 52: Freedom of the Press in America and in China

Is there freedom of the press in America? Yes! But it has not been realized until recently when the Internet finally made it possible. Before that, freedom of the press existed in America in theory only, but not in practice. Why? Because the press was not truly free!

Is there freedom of the press in China? No! But is it all that bad? No, not in my opinion! Why? Because freedom of the press in America, as we know it today, can sometimes be worse than the controlled media in China! Really? Yes, hear me out …

1. Conventional media and America

Conventional media (e.g. newspapers and TV) is not free. For-profit companies own them (mostly), for which ratings is everything: They give you what you want (e.g. Charlie Sheen or China bashing), and you give them what they want (e.g. putting up with the ads). Simply stated, it is all about "I help you feel good and you help me make some money." Little else matters, often not even the truth, especially in politics. Three net results:

1) The media and the politicians work in sync, because they both want the same thing: high ratings! The politicians need the media as their PR machines (e.g. Obama meets with left wing hacks Ed Schultz, Ezra Klein, Arianna Huffington and others at the White House), while the media craves the access to power (e.g. Diane Sawyer and Jake Tapper on the challenges of interviewing the President). Because of this kind of mutual reliance relationship, the media simply failed to question, let alone prevent, such a tragedy as the Iraq War.

Worse yet, the media tends to go to the extremes (e.g. MSNBC on the left and Fox on the right), often without balance, for the sake of making sensational news! Together, they help, consciously or not, to undermine America, with the extreme left (e.g. MSNBC) promoting democratic socialism and the extreme right (e.g. Fox) promoting democratic imperialism.

2) The media is powerful (e.g. 'Nightline' Nukes Newt), but not very trustworthy (e.g. Fox News Most Distrusted (And Trusted) Name In News: Poll). This is a terribly dangerous, even frightening, combination!

3) Americans, as compared with the Chinese, are not only generally under-informed, but also often misinformed, about many world affairs, especially on the Middle East and Asia, with the Iraq War and the situation leading up to it being the worst example. Bottom line: In my opinion, an average educated person in China today (e.g. a college graduate) knows a lot more about America than the other way around. More broadly, an average educated Chinese understands world affairs far better than an average educated American!

2. American media about the world

Still unconvinced about the deficiency of the American media covering world affairs? Here are three specific examples:

1) Watch the BBS series on "What the Chinese are doing globally?" Now, the question: Why can't we, as Americans, produce a quality program like that? Okay, it's BBC, the best in the world! But what about Al Jazeera?

2) <u>Hillary Clinton calls Al Jazeera 'Real News'</u>. Why is that? Can't we even compete against Al Jazeera out of a little Arab country called Qatar?
3) <u>China's crackdown on capitalism</u>. What a sensational title! The negative story is largely true and it's what an American typically wants to read (yes, China bashing). However, the sensational title alone has distorted the big picture: China, despite its pervasive endemic problems, is succeeding over the West because of capitalism and China will likely become more capitalistic than the U.S. soon, if the current trend persists. Want more evidence? Read: <u>A CEOs guide to innovation in China</u>.

No wonder the U.S. Middle East policy is a total failure (Chapter 60). No wonder many Americans still think China is a communist country. Thanks to the political-media complex for having brainwashed you! In fact, brainwashing is yet another similarity between democracy and communism, which I will discuss in-depth in Chapter 63.

3. Media in China

There is simply no freedom of the press in China. This is largely because of China's communist past, although solid progress has been made to open up the media over the past decade, with more to come.

No question, the Chinese government has much more direct control over the media than the American government. But is this all that bad? No, not in my opinion! Here is an example for a Chinese domestic issue: About two years ago, it was a news blitz about "another bad guy in China hurting some school children with knives." Do you know what happened afterward?

The Chinese government banned the media from reporting these kinds of stories in China, with the belief that many sick copycats were inspired by the stories. It worked - I agree with their assessment!

Internationally, the Chinese media is actually better than the American media: more objective, more even-handed, and less ideological. Why is that? Because the Chinese government policy is better than the American government policy! The Chinese government promotes peace and pursues a non-intervention approach that can be simply summarized as this: "let's do some business, without worrying much about ideology or politics." History proves, time and again, that this approach is the best, not only for China, but also for the world. Clearly, this is the opposite to America's approach of trying to be the world's policemen. (Yes, Ron Paul has got this one right!) As a result, the Chinese media's job is much easier than that of the American media. No example is more illustrative than this: In China, I saw both sides of the story on Syria (and Libya and Iran) on TV: the government side as well as the anti-government side. It was very refreshing for me, because the former is totally non-existent in America's mainstream media today!

4. Welcome to the Internet age!

The Internet has fundamentally changed the Middle East, though not necessarily for the better (for more, read Chapter 3). However, it will certainly fundamentally change America and China for the better!

4.1 The Internet and America

The Internet has already profoundly changed America, from the USPS to the established media. Yes, change is good – what's bad for the status quo is often good for America! As a result, Americans are now enjoying true freedom of the press for the first time ever. Today, we all can publish, instantly and worldwide! Even an electrical engineer like me can write and publish big time on politics!

Here is a simple comparison between my writing and the established media (Time magazine) on the same subject Warren Buffett:
1) Chapter 51: "Warren Buffett and Chairman Mao: Something in Common?"
2) Warren Buffett Is on a Radical Track.

On the same subject of Warren Buffett, can you see the differences between the two writings?

4.2 The Internet and China
The Internet has already profoundly changed China as well. Here is a must-read article for all open-minded Americans: Globalization 2.0: China's Parallel Internet.

The Internet will further change China for the better, with positive influence from America, hopefully …

5. Closing
As human beings, we all desire freedoms, including freedom of speech (a good thing) and freedom of excessive spending (a bad thing). Therefore, there needs to be a force out there to balance our unbounded desires. It may take the Wisdom of Solomon to determine where that boundary is for freedom of the press. Meanwhile, all of us, especially Americans, must avoid being overly simplistic, such as by dismissing China's media censorship as nothing but purely evil. To the contrary, given the dire economic condition of the West, I believe it's time for America to examine itself fundamentally

and thoroughly, starting with its antiquated political system.

Giordano Bruno was burned to death because of his Sun theory. I am still alive, thanks to freedom of speech and freedom of the press in America!

Chapter 53: Karl Marx and John Keynes

Human history of post-WWII can be simplified as the East vs. the West. The East collapsed in 1989 under the weight of communism, thanks to Marxism. The West is collapsing now as a result of reckless government spending, thanks to Keynesian economics, as we practice it today (i.e. only the part on spending, but not the part on savings). It is therefore important for us all to know more about Karl Marx and John Keynes, in order to fully appreciate my diagnosis (Chapter 1) and solution (Chapter 2) for America.

1. Karl Marx
Here is a description of Karl Marx per Wikipedia:

Karl Heinrich Marx (5 May 1818 – 14 March 1883) was a German philosopher, economist, sociologist, historian, journalist, and revolutionary socialist. His ideas played a significant role in the development of social science and the socialist movement. He published various books during his lifetime, with the most notable being *The Communist Manifesto* (1848) and *Capital* (1867–1894); some of his works were co-written with his friend and fellow German revolutionary socialist, Friedrich Engels.

Marx's theories about society, economics and politics—collectively known as Marxism—hold that all societies progress through the dialectic of class struggle: a conflict between an ownership class which controls production and a lower class which produces the labor for goods. Heavily critical of the current socio-economic form of society, capitalism, he called it the "dictatorship of the bourgeoisie", believing it to be run by the wealthy classes purely for their own benefit, and predicted that, like previous socioeconomic systems, it would inevitably produce internal tensions which would lead to its self-destruction and replacement by a new system, socialism. He argued that under socialism society would be governed by the working class in what he called the "dictatorship of the proletariat", the "workers state" or "workers' democracy". He believed that socialism would, in its turn, eventually be replaced by a stateless classless society called communism. Along with believing in the inevitability of socialism and communism, Marx actively fought for the former's implementation, arguing that both social theorists and underprivileged people should carry out organized revolutionary action to topple capitalism and bring about socio-economic change.

2. John Keynes

Here is a description of John Keynes per Wikipedia:

John Maynard Keynes, 1st Baron Keynes, CB FBA (5 June 1883–21 April 1946) was a British economist whose ideas have profoundly affected the theory and practice of modern macroeconomics, as well as the economic policies of governments. He greatly refined earlier work on the causes of business cycles, and advocated the use of fiscal and monetary measures to mitigate the adverse effects of economic recessions and depressions. Keynes is widely considered to be one of the founders of modern macroeconomics, and to be the most influential economist of the 20th century. His ideas are the basis for the school of thought known as Keynesian economics, as well as its various offshoots.

In the 1930s, Keynes spearheaded a revolution in economic thinking, overturning the older ideas of neoclassical economics that held that free markets would, in the short to medium term, automatically provide full employment, as long as workers were flexible in their wage demands. Keynes instead argued that aggregate demand determined the overall level of economic activity, and that inadequate aggregate demand could lead to prolonged periods of high unemployment. Following the outbreak of World War II, Keynes's ideas concerning economic policy were adopted by leading Western economies. During the 1950s and 1960s, the success of Keynesian economics resulted in almost all capitalist governments adopting its policy recommendations.

Keynes's influence waned in the 1970s, partly as a result of problems that began to afflict the Anglo-American economies from the start of the decade, and partly because of critiques from Milton Friedman and other economists who were pessimistic about the ability of governments to regulate the business cycle with fiscal policy. However, the advent of the global financial crisis in 2007 caused a resurgence in Keynesian thought. Keynesian economics provided the theoretical underpinning for economic policies undertaken in response to the crisis by Presidents George W. Bush and Barack Obama of the United States, Prime Minister Gordon Brown of the United Kingdom, and other heads of governments.

3. Discussion

Both Marx and Keynes were prolific in theory. Neither harmed society directly. It is their disciples, who used, and are still using, their works as the tools to effect changes that have caused severe damage to the world. Two examples:
1) Mao Zedong: It is apparent that Mao believed in nothing, other than himself. But he used Marx's

populist theories fully to his advantage, especially in support of his own theory of revolution and his brutal ruling of China (1949–1976). Mao also used Lenin and Stalin, only to turn on Stalin when Mao became "tired" of him, both ideologically and personally.

2) Franklin D. Roosevelt: FDR faced formidable challenges (e.g. The Great Depression) when he was elected to the American Presidency. He did everything possible to remain popular, including raiding the public treasury and introducing Social Security, thus ensuring his repeated re-elections (yes, three times)! Consequently, America was fundamentally changed from a society based on rugged individualism and unfettered capitalism to an entitlement society. It has only been progressively getting worse since then, with the government getting so big and fat now that its massive weight is crushing America. A key theory behind America's big government [spending] is Keynesian economics, which, together with the outdated American political system, has been severely damaging America's economy!

Worse yet for America, despite the fact that both Presidents Hoover and FDR admitted that it was WWII, not the massive government spending, that finally got America out of the Great Depression, many left-wing extremists (e.g. Paul Krugman and Robert Reich) still try to keep this biggest lie of the 20th century going by actively advocating deficit spending as the only way out of today's Great Recession. These folks have made their livings out of Keynesian economics. They blindly, irresponsibly, and shamelessly promote it, just like communists promoted Marxism a few decades ago, even in the face of mounting evidence that what they sell does not work, nor has it ever worked actually.

Now, the real truth about WWII and America ... Here is an excerpt from Chapter 57 ("Pyramid Theory II"):

It was WWII that finally got America out of the Great Depression, although Keynesians like to credit the massive government spending, which was the biggest lie of the 20th century. In other words, America did win WWII. But more significantly, America's competitors either destroyed themselves through the war (e.g. Germany and Japan) or screwed themselves up badly by adopting a fundamentally flawed system called "communism" after the war (e.g. China and the Soviet Union). As a result, America was left as the only game in town, making and inventing virtually everything and naming its own prices. This not only got America out of the Great Depression finally, but also created prosperity in America for the ensuing five decades.

In other words, from 1946 to 2000, America was the economic monopoly in the world: America simply could not screw up enough, because America could afford anything and everything. Three examples:
1) JFK: public-sector unions? No problem!
2) Jimmy Carter and Bill Clinton: The CRA (Community Reinvestment Act)? No problem!
3) The neo-cons: out-of-control spending on military? No problem!

Why are they big problems now? BRICS showed up - America is no longer the economic monopoly! Not only can we no longer afford the same screw-ups as before, but also it's payback time for the past screw-ups! What about a new screw-up like Obamacare? It's suicidal!

If you, as a Keynesian, insist on an analogy between the Great Depression and the Great Recession as the problem, do your solution with the analogy between WWII and WWIII (Chapter 48: "America: 10 Big Questions and 10 Honest Answers"), not massive government spending! Other than that, no solution from the past is applicable today! Why? Because the world today is very different from the past! America needs a new solution, which must begin with an accurate diagnosis (Chapter 1)!

Oh, Paul Krugman appears to possess great credibility after winning a Nobel Prize. Mikhail Gorbachev also won a Nobel Prize! But I called Gorbachev "brainless and reckless" for the way he dismantled the Soviet Union (read: Chapter 65: Kleptocracy). I have the same regard for Paul Krugman for the way he has been damaging America's economy, through relentless promotion of Keynesian economics!

4. Keynesian economics and entitlements

Once again, Keynesian economics is the driving theory behind the various entitlement programs in America, which started big time with the introduction of SS (Social Security). What, then, is SS, anyway?
1) SS is an entitlement program for those recipients who have not paid into it.
2) SS is not an entitlement program for those recipients who have paid into it. To those people, SS is like an insurance program: some get more out of it, while others less.

SS was a Ponzi scheme from its first day, and remains so today. It is therefore destined to fail. Worse yet, with the additional costs of ADC (Aid to Dependent Children), SSI (Supplemental Security Income), and free benefits for immigrants who have never contributed, SS funding is increasingly falling short, making its failure faster! In short, SS, as we know it today, will fail - the longer we keep resisting reforms, the harder it will fail us later!

Medicare is like SS in every way!

Medicaid is a total entitlement program from A to Z!

Feel free to go on and on, by yourself ...

5. Closing

Marxism is very bad. Keynesian economics, as we practice it today (i.e. only the part on spending, but not the part on savings) is also very bad! Both rely on the false premise of "something for nothing", which simply can't exist in the real world. We must recognize this and keep a watchful eye on the leaders espousing Marxism or Keynesian economics!

Chapter 54: America: Let The Rich Run The Country Like China Does!

(Initially published at GEI on 10/19/2012)

"Truth uttered before its time can be dangerous."
--- Meng Zhi, 300BC

Hello from China!

Here is a straightforward message to my fellow Americans: elect Mitt Romney the next American President and America will be much better off, guaranteed! Why? Two main reasons:
1) Mitt Romney is rich. That's a good thing in China. It once was and should continue to be a good thing in America, too!
2) Between Barack Obama and Mitt Romney, the Chinese would have chosen the latter in no time. So should, and must, America, too!

1. Why should Americans listen to the Chinese?
Three reasons:
1) The Chinese know that America is becoming more and more socialistic, which will be a total disaster - been there, done that! The Chinese just emerged from that hell! Socialism results in everybody being dirt poor, and being dirt poor is hell!
2) Although China is a competitor to America, the Chinese admire Americans in general. Most importantly, a troubled America means a troubled world, which the Chinese do not want to see, not yet at least.
3) We owe them more than $1T! Isn't that alone good enough for some respect?

2. Why is America so deeply in trouble today?
Two main reasons:
1) Democracy, as we know it today, has been progressively driving America deeper and deeper into socialism since 1933, at least. But no big problems showed up before 2000, because America was the economic monopoly from 1946 to 2000 - America could afford anything and everything, including democracy!
2) The bottom fell out at the turn of the 21st century, when BRICS began to show their strength. The rise of BRICS not only signaled the end of America's economic monopoly, but also revealed the naked truth about American democracy: It does not work! As a matter of fact, democracy is failing in America today for the same reason as it failed in "democratic" Rome (and Greece) more than 2,000 years ago: debts!

3. Why has China been rising so rapidly?
Change! Specifically,
1) Economically, China embraced capitalism after 1976.
2) Politically, China evolved into a system called "a dictatorship without a dictator." In this system, the rich people are in charge, and the government is, actually, of/by/for the rich. This is totally opposite to its communist past, which was led by the proletarians (i.e. "the working class"), resulting in everybody being a proletarian!

For more on the wealth of the Chinese leaders, read: China's Billionaire People's Congress Makes Capitol Hill Look Like Pauper. Here is an excerpt:

> *The richest 70 members of China's legislature added more to their wealth last year than the combined net worth of all 535 members of the U.S. Congress, the president and his Cabinet, and the nine Supreme Court justices.*
>
> *The net worth of the 70 richest delegates in China's National People's Congress, which opens its annual session on March 5, rose to 565.8 billion yuan ($89.8 billion) in 2011, a gain of $11.5 billion from 2010, according to figures from the Hurun Report, which tracks the country's wealthy. That compares to the $7.5 billion net worth of all 660 top officials in the three branches of the U.S. government.*

Obviously, we can debate all day whether the wealth in China is true or even legitimate (Chapter 65, "Kleptocracy"), but that is out of scope here. Suffice it to say that China's political system is far from being ideal. But it's still slightly better than America's (Chapter 16: "America: What is China's Political System, Anyway?"). For more, read Chapter 3.

Bottom line: China has been poor and China has been [relatively] rich. Being rich is a lot better than being poor! The Chinese have learned, finally, that when the rich are in charge, the country is far better off. On the contrary, when the working class was in charge (1949-1976), it pulled everybody down, all the way to hell!

4. Discussion

It's time to read this: The Truth about Tytler. Here is an excerpt:

A democracy cannot exist as a permanent form of government. It can only exist until the voters discover that they can vote themselves largesse from the public treasury. From that moment on, the majority always votes for the candidates promising the most benefits from the public treasury with the result that a democracy always collapses over loose fiscal policy, always followed by a dictatorship. The average age of the world's greatest civilizations has been 200 years.

Great nations rise and fall. The people go from bondage to spiritual truth, to great courage, from courage to liberty, from liberty to abundance, from abundance to selfishness, from selfishness to complacency, from complacency to apathy, from apathy to dependence, from dependence back again to bondage.

What do you think? Isn't this exactly what has been going on in America over the past decade, at least?

Two notes:
1) Jealousy of success (i.e. wealth) is the #1 root of communism!
2) Robbing and killing the rich is the #1 means of communists!

Two basics questions:
1) Why is there such a big outcry about Romney's wealth in America today? It's totally un-American! As Americans, we once cherished success, but now we condemn it!

2) Why wasn't John Kerry's wealth a big problem when he ran for President in 2003?

In case you do not know,
1) Romney earned his wealth, while Kerry married his!
2) The Chinese have far more respect for earned than for married! What about America?

Now, watch this short video: Romney's garbage man stars in new attack ad.

In a free society like ours with ample opportunities, the best these men and women in the video can do is to pick up trash. Yet, they want to help you pick the next American President? Give me a break! This is worse than communism! No wonder democracy, as we know it today, is dragging down America, like communism did with China a few decades ago!

Wake up, America!

The Chinese learned capitalism from America, mostly! It's time for America to learn from China about how to undo socialism!

5. How to undo socialism in America?
As the first step, elect Mitt Romney the next American President! Here are five reasons:
1) Romney is an exceptional leader with "a stellar performance" as a businessman (Romney's Stellar Performance) and as a governor. He is a rare talent not only in America, but also in the world!
2) Romney is not a career politician. Romney knows who built America: the private sector!

3) Romney is not just a businessman like Ross Perot. Romney served in the public sector.
4) Romney is not a neo-con!
5) President Obama is just not good enough, at best.

6. Closing

Romney may be exactly what America needs today. For more, read Chapter 29 ("Mitt Romney vs. Deng Xiaoping").

Part 9: America's Foreign Policy

Chapter 55: What's The Real Cost of The Iraq War?
Chapter 56: Emerging Economies: An Overview from 30,000 Feet
Chapter 57: Pyramid Theory II
Chapter 58: American Autumn vs. Arab Spring
Chapter 59: America: What to Do with North Korea?
Chapter 60: U.S. Middle East Policy: What Is Wrong?
Chapter 61: Top 10 American Misconceptions about the World

"Commerce with all nations, alliance with none, should be our motto. Money, not morality, is the principle commerce of civilized nations. Peace, commerce and honest friendship with all nations; entangling alliances with none."
--- Thomas Jefferson

Chapter 55: What's The Real Cost of The Iraq War?

(Initially published on 6/6/2010)

On March 20, 2003, the U.S. launched a war in Iraq. It has cost us dearly, not only in human lives and money, but also in our "international standing." The latter is not very well understood in America. So it's time for me to chip in my two cents ...

1. From a story on 60 Minutes

About six months ago, CBS's 60 Minutes aired an interview with a former CIA agent, who accompanied Saddam Hussein in his lonely days. Saddam confided in him that he never believed that the U.S. would have launched a war like that until it really happened. Upon hearing that, I knew Saddam was telling the truth and here is why: The U.S. system, viewed externally, was so perfect that it would just be impossible to see a questionable war like that launched. Saddam did not believe it, nor did many people in China. That perfect image of the U.S. system was completely shattered on that day of March 20, 2003!

In other words, the beacon went off on March 20, 2003!

2. Did the beacon really go off?

Yes! The U.S. would never be the same again! Now, which country benefited most from the Iraq War? Regionally, Iran, obviously! Globally, China! Not obvious? Here is why:

1) The U.S. defense industry is so well entrenched that it has to have enemies to survive. After the

Cold War, the obvious pick was China, with all kinds of accusations from communism to human rights. However, most of these accusations went away with the Iraq War. China rapidly moved forward (without much distraction from the U.S.) and has doubled its GDP since then.

2) It was a wake-up call for China: the U.S. system (i.e. capitalism + democracy) is not as good as it looked and the Chinese system (i.e. capitalism + autocracy) is not as bad as it was accused of. As a result, the push toward a U.S.-like democracy inside China before 2003 was largely gone!

What about the other emerging economies?

1) Russia: It adopted the U.S.-like democracy in a hurry after the Cold War, only to have everything ruined, especially the economy. Over the past few years, Russia has been closely watching and modeling after the Chinese system, with its ties to China being closer than ever.

2) Brazil: It has also looked at the Chinese system as a possible model, strengthening the already-tight bilateral relationship between the two countries even more.

3) India: Talk to the educated Indians, many have huge admiration for the modern China.

For more, read Chapter 56 ("Emerging Economies: An Overview from 30,000 Feet").

3. Are we winning in Iraq?

No, we are not - There are no winners in this kind of war! A more valid question is this: who could afford to lose more? It turned out that this is a war we could hardly afford to begin with. Besides, the Iraq War distracted us from our legitimate target: Osama Bin

Laden in Afghanistan. Now, regardless of the outcome of the war in Afghanistan, the cost will prove to be very high. Meanwhile, China is on par to double its GDP again in the next 7 to 8 years, well on its way to surpassing us as the largest economy on earth by 2030.

4. Can the beacon be back on again?

Yes, possibly, with the changes as I suggested (Chapter 2). But our time is running short.

As a young man growing up in China in the 1970s, I thought of nothing but "getting the hell out of here." Following the beacon, I left China in 1982 and came to the U.S. in 1985, becoming a U.S. citizen in 1997. However, China has fundamentally changed so much over the past two decades that I recently concluded that overall the Chinese system is slightly better than ours. Today, I devote myself to the positive development of U.S.-China relations. I focus on the U.S. side mostly, because that's where the danger is: a soon-to-be 2nd-class economy with a 1st-class military! In that sense alone, no Chinese-Americans want to see a declining America, let alone so rapidly and in a direction abandoned by China.

5. Closing

We, as a country, are deeply in trouble. The rise of China as a competitor was inevitable, but the Iraq War has helped China catch up with America much faster, both economically and politically. Unless we change soon, I believe March 20, 2003 will eventually be marked as the beginning of the end of democracy as we know it. That, my fellow Americans, is the real cost of the Iraq War!

Chapter 56: Emerging Economies: An Overview from 30,000 Feet

(Initially published at GEI on 7/7/2011)

BRIC (Brazil, Russia, India, and China) held its first annual meeting in Russia in 2009, and its second in Brazil in 2010. China hosted the third one this year (in April), when BRIC became BRICS ("S" for South Africa). The five BRICS countries are now known as the "emerging economies." But are they equal and how may you take advantage of them in business? My answers are very simple:

1) Pay special attention to China, as it is far ahead in the pack.
2) Pay good attention to Brazil and Russia, as they both are replete with vast amounts of natural resources.
3) Pay some attention to South Africa, as it's the most advanced country in Africa.
4) Pay a little bit of attention to India, as it has yet to get the basics right, although it has been trying very hard.

1. India

After becoming independent from the British in 1947, India took a noble standing internationally: non-alliance, neither to the East (i.e. the socialist block led by the Soviet Union) nor to the West (i.e. the capitalist block led by the U.S.). Unfortunately, India ended up with the worst of both. With "socialism," which destroys the basic work ethics in human beings, India got a bunch of non-performing state enterprises as the engine of its economy. With "capitalism," which seemed to go hand-in-hand with democracy (until China showed up recently), India embraced democracy early and quick, resulting in having so many individual human rights that you can't even acquire a piece of significant land today to build something big and serious (e.g. highways).

Obviously, India has changed a lot recently, but nothing fundamentally! The #1 challenge for India is to lift its massive population out of abject poverty (like China did one decade ago), for which India must understand two basics: (1) democracy is a nice-to-have after the must-have, namely, the [initial] success of capitalism, and (2) because democracy is already deeply rooted, India can't follow China (which lacks basic democracy) as an example of success. India must figure out its own way of success, which will take a long time. How long? 30 years at least!

2. Russia
The Soviet Union was a total disaster! Russia changed too quickly after the disintegration of the Soviet Union, adopting both a new political system and a new economic system overnight. The result has been chaos, to say the least. However, Russia does have a history of manufacturing (e.g. heavy machinery). More importantly, Russia is a country replete with vast amounts of natural resources, just like Canada and Australia. In that sense alone, nobody should ever underestimate Russia, the potential, if not the current ability.

The #1 challenge for Russia is to restore some "orders" before democracy gets way ahead of capitalism. Like India, Russia must understand that for prosperity, capitalism is a must, while democracy is merely an option. With this challenge met, Russia may become a major economic power soon. How soon? 10 years at least!

3. Brazil

Brazil, unlike Russia, does not have any advantage or disadvantage of "socialism" from the past. Like Russia, Brazil is rich in natural resources. So despite the fact that Brazil has no history of making anything (that you may know of), it will play an increasingly important role internationally, given its size and location. Yes, being in South America is a huge advantage today, such as winning the bid to host the 2016 Summer Olympics. Very importantly, while the French and the British were busy bombing Libya recently, Brazil surpassed both of them to becoming the 5th largest economy on earth (after the U.S., China, Japan, and Germany).

The #1 challenge for Brazil is to build a culture of creating products, which is very different from selling natural resources (like the Saudis)! This will take quite a while, 30 years at least.

4. South Africa

Like Brazil, South Africa is the most developed country in its continent and rich in natural resources. Unlike Brazil, South Africa is not likely to host a Summer Olympics within the next 20 years. Way to go!

5. China

China, like Russia, suffered a lot from "socialism" from 1949 to 1976. Unlike Russia, China did not change both the political system and the economic system overnight. Instead, China embraced capitalism quickly, while evolving its political system gradually into a better autocratic system over time. As a result, China today has the best of both "socialism" and "capitalism" (totally opposite to India). With "socialism," China re-built the infrastructure (e.g. airports, highways, and high-speed railways) quickly and it's world-class now. With "capitalism," China has become the world's epic center of manufacturing, with millions of factories, big and small, thriving.

The #1 challenge for China is to introduce democracy slowly but steadily, so as to avoid being dead-ended (China's political anniversary: a long cycle nears its end). Instead, China must evolve itself into a truly "harmonious" society built on top of a powerful economy. With that, China will become the largest economy on earth by 2030.

One big note: I believe the world would be a better place if we all adopted China's approach internationally: let's do some business together, regardless of the ideological differences. Why? Because today's ideological wrong could be tomorrow's right! Many human tragedies were the results of strong ideologies, be they religious or political. Here is an interesting article: Russian view of China's development.

In short, peace and trade, not war and debt!

6. Closing
This has been a simple overview of BRICS from 30,000 feet. Needless to say, all five countries face all kinds of big challenges of their own. However, the overall directions for all of them are very positive. Following the current trend, BRICS will become, by 2020, an axis comparable to G-8, with China playing a dominant role like the U.S. does at G-8.

Visit China and see her with your own eyes: the good, the bad, and the ugly!

Chapter 57: Pyramid Theory II

In Chapter 18, I presented Pyramid Theory I, which is primarily intended for America.

In this chapter, I will expand Pyramid Theory I into Pyramid Theory II, in the context of the world economy, and spell out its implication for America.

1. Human beings are earthly global by definition

Isn't it true that we human beings all originated in Africa many million years ago? Do you know of the existence of the Silk Road a few thousand years ago? What's the point? We human beings are earthly global by definition!

With the advancement of technologies (e.g. Internet and transportation), the globe has become flatter and smaller. For example, today, a U.S. customer may get his tech support phone call answered by someone in India, and the stuff you buy from Wal-Mart is often made in China. Is there anything wrong with this kind of globalization in general? No, absolutely not! America itself is a product of globalization, such as the Europeans coming to America in the first place and the import of slaves from Africa (which was very wrong). The challenge is to survive and thrive in this increasingly competitive globe. So here goes my Pyramid Theory II, which is somehow parallel to Pyramid Theory I.

2. Pyramid Theory II
   1) Wealth & power: There will always be a handful of countries sitting on the top, with more countries filling in the middle and the majority at the bottom.

2) Business: The big business must be global, not only for the resources, but also for the markets. The small business must have its own niche.
3) Jobs: Jobs of low skills (e.g. assembly work) will be further automated or migrated down the food chain from advanced countries to developing countries, where hundreds of millions of laborers will eagerly compete for these jobs.

3. What did Pyramid Theory II mean to China and America from 1820 to 1952?

Here are some simple stats from this book "How the west was lost" (page 15):
1) In 1820, China's world share of GDP was at an impressive 32.2%, while America's was a paltry 1.8% and Europe's was 26.6%.
2) By 1890, just 70 years later, China's world share of GDP was down to 13.8%, while America's was up to 13.8% and Europe's was up to 40%.
3) By 1952, China fell to 5.2%, while America and Europe were both 30%.

The exact numbers are not very important, but the trend is: China went from the heaven top to the hell bottom from 1820 to 1952, while America traveled the other way!

4. Pyramid Theory II for America and China

For more recent data on GDP and its share by country, click Data 360! Here is the message: The table is about to turn between China and America! Specifically, here is what's coming:
1) Wealth and power: China will surpass America in GDP by 2030, thus becoming the #1 power in the world, both politically and economically.

2) Business: Unless the American government becomes even more anti-business than today, American business will continue to do well, thanks to our deep capitalistic roots. The big companies (e.g. GE and Exxon) will become more global; the new companies (e.g. Apple and Facebook) will become bigger and better; and the small companies (e.g. National Scale Technology and W.E.I.) will become more nimble.

3) Jobs: The real unemployment rate in America will remain way above 10% for a long time. How long? One decade at least! Yes, America has forever changed in this sense - get used to the new reality! Note that it takes ~2.5% growth in GDP just to accommodate our population growth. The forecast is well below that (e.g. 2Q2011 GDP has been revised down to 1%), which means the real unemployment rate will only go up – simple math, no matter how many more speeches President Obama will give in the future. Actions speak louder than words! Now, what's beyond the next decade? It depends on what we do today, and we have three clear choices …

5. Three clear choices for America

5.1 Choice #1: 30% poor

30% of Americans will live "poor", but 70% of Americans will live fine. This is the best scenario if we become better by metamorphosing now (Chapter 2). Specifically, we must change the political system, and restore America as the "land of opportunity". Alarmed by this number of 30%? Read: more than 1 in 5 children in the U.S. live in poverty or altogether, there are now almost 46 million in the U.S. on food stamps, roughly 15% of the population. That is an increase of 74% since

<u>2007</u>. Still think we are okay without the big changes? Pull your head out of the sand and think again! More profoundly, we may have to largely undo the 2nd half of the 20th century, from Social Security, to Medicare & Medicaid, to public-sector unions! Is this impossible? China largely undid its 2nd half of the 20th century! Why can't we?

5.2 Choice #2: 100% poor

100% of Americans will live "poor". This will happen if we continue on the current path of out-of-control government spending. In that sense, democracy, as we know it today, looks more and more like *de facto* communism (e.g. China under Mao and the former Soviet Union), which destroyed capitalism first, and ultimately the country, for the sake of "the people". The result will be communism too: being dirt poor – Been there, done that!

5.2 Choice #3: WWIII

After all, it was WWII that finally got America out of the Great Depression, although Keynesians like to credit massive government spending. In other words, America did win WWII. But more significantly, America's competitors either destroyed themselves through the war (e.g. Germany and Japan) or screwed themselves up badly after the war (e.g. China and the Soviet Union) by adopting a fundamentally flawed system called "communism". As a result, America was left as the only game in town, making and inventing virtually everything and naming its own prices. This not only got America out of the Great Depression finally, but also created unprecedented prosperity in America for the ensuing five decades. Analogously, it may well take WWIII to get America out of the Great Recession. The only difference this time is America may be the culprit, as America has both the capability and incentive to provoke WWIII, especially if the neo-cons get their way! In fact, the seeds for WWIII might have already been sowed with the Iraq War.

6. Closing

Life is a series of choices, which applies not only to individuals, but also to countries. America has been fortunate with the best political and economic systems over the past 200+ years. But America's political system is no longer the best, and that is the real reason behind America's steep decline now. Yes, it's the political system, stupid!

Here is a quote: *"Remember, democracy never lasts long. It soon wastes, exhausts, and murders itself. There never was a democracy yet that did not commit suicide."*

Who said it? **John Adams**!

Is America on a suicidal path now? Yes!

Can America still save itself? Maybe, maybe not …

Chapter 58: American Autumn vs. Arab Spring

(Initially published at GEI on 10/7/2011)

"If you are not a Liberal at 20, you have no heart. If you are not a Conservative at 40, you have no brain."

--- Winston Churchill

Ever heard of the term "American Autumn", which is also known as "Occupy Wall Street"? It started on September 17, 2011, when a few college students camped out, occupying Wall Street. Since then, not only has the crowd been getting bigger, it has also become a national movement, spreading to the big cities from Boston to Los Angeles. Although this movement does not look very serious at this time, some people are worried, comparing it to the Arab Spring that has already toppled several regimes in the Middle East and North Africa.

I, too, am worried. Here is my position on this movement:
1) Americans have many reasons to be frustrated. I especially have sympathy for the students, who are "$100K in college debt, but no jobs."
2) They are protesting in a wrong place: Wall Street! They should be in Washington D.C., where the real problem is, so is the real solution!

Now, let me replay from Chapter 18 ("Pyramid Theory I"): the rumored dialog between China's Mao and Richard Nixon in 1972:

1) Mao: "Aren't you worried about a revolution, as guns are so widely available over there?"
2) Nixon: "No. Revolutions are not caused by guns, but by the smart people at the bottom. The American system allows the smart people to move up. So there will be no revolution in America."

Nixon was right, at that time!

America has changed quite a lot since then. Here are two main reasons we all should be worried about the American Autumn:
1) High unemployment: More than 14 million Americans have been out of work for more than two years, with no relief in sight! Although the official unemployment rate is at 9.1%, the real number is much higher, perhaps above 15%. Worse yet, the unemployment rate for the young people (e.g. recent college graduates) is even higher, definitely above 20%!
2) America is no longer the "land of opportunity" as it was in 1972 when Nixon met with Mao. In fact, America has moved decisively *"from a nation of makers to a nation of takers, with more Americans working for the government than working in construction, farming, fishing, manufacturing, mining, and utilities combined."*

Why is America in such a bad shape? It's the political system, stupid! America's antiquated political system is the #1 reason behind America's decline but we have yet to recognize it! Instead, we keep trying to fix some symptoms without addressing the root cause, making a bad situation much worse. Unconvinced? Think about this: On September 8, 2001, President Obama gave a big

speech on his jobs bill to Congress. Here are two big problems with that speech:
1) President Obama called for a class warfare against the rich in that speech and his jobs bill was filled with new taxes, especially on the rich.
2) It was a big campaign speech in disguise. This not only was a new low in the American Presidency, but also means that President Obama will carry the class warfare throughout his remaining time in office until the 2012 election.

10 days after that speech, the American Autumn started on Wall Street. Was it a coincidence? I do not think so! President Obama provoked it! Will it end soon? No, because President Obama has both the incentive and the means to keeping it going throughout his re-election campaign until November 2012!

The American Autumn could turn into a proletarian revolution, led by President Obama! If that happens, it would be much more significant than the Arab Spring in human history, because it would end America, as we know it!

Shouldn't more Americans be worried about the American Autumn?

Chapter 59: America: What to Do with North Korea?

(Initially published at GEI on 12/23/2011)

North Korea's dear leader, Kim II, died a few days ago. His 3rd son is now in charge, as Kim III. There is no better time to talk about North Korea than now, as evidenced by some timely expert opinions. So it's time for me to chip in my two cents. I will briefly but succinctly answer five pertinent questions as follows:
1) What's North Korea?
2) Will North Korea under Kim III be as crazy as before?
3) What should America's Korea policy be?
4) What went wrong for the U.S. on Korea policy?
5) What will the Korean peninsula look like in 20 years?

1. What's North Korea?

It's one of the two communist regimes left on earth (the other is Cuba). It's living hell over there: politically repressive and economically miserable, just like China under Mao – been there, done that! Oh, what about those crying faces and tears in the news? They are fakes, mostly! The Chinese know it, as they shed a lot more tears, also mostly fakes, in 1976 when Mao died. Mao's death turned out to be the best thing for China over the past few decades, if not centuries!

2. Will North Korea under Kim III be as crazy as before?

No! North Korea under Kim III is unlikely to be as crazy as it was under Kim II. By "crazy," I mean causing various "incidents" over there, such as attacking South

Korea with <u>some artillery shells</u> in November 2010, killing four people and destroying a few buildings.

2.1 Why was North Korea under Kim II so crazy?
There were three main reasons:
1) North Korea was deeply in trouble, both economically and politically, particularly with a shaky succession plan. Was there a better way to fool your own people than by showing a strong hand to an obvious external enemy?
2) We, the U.S., gave it good reasons to be troublesome! We stationed troops in South Korea for about 20 years too long – remember: the Cold War ended in 1989! Most problematically, we held military exercises over there, including at the Yellow Sea, which was provocative not only to North Korea, but also to China.
3) Who benefited most from these "crazy" incidents?
    - China: Every time an incident happened, China got the calls from the U.S., "begging" for help.
    - The U.S.: Every incident helped justify the continued U.S. military presence over there (as many U.S. war hawks want).

2.2 Why is Kim III unlikely to be as crazy as Kim II?
Here are three main reasons:
1) His priority will ostensibly be to consolidate his power at home first.
2) He is hopefully too young and too inexperienced to do anything "crazy," plus the China factor, to be discussed later.
3) A new ruler tends to more moderate to begin with. I think the fact that he was educated in the West (Switzerland) should help him act more sanely, too.

3. What should America's Korea policy be?

Just get out of there! We are no longer needed over there and we can no longer afford to be over there, even if South Korea projects that it needs us.

China has diplomatic relations with both Koreas, and is fully capable of keeping the North in check, if China really wanted to do so. But what's the incentive for China to do that when the U.S. keeps having huge military presence in the region and, worse yet, keeps having military exercises at the Yellow Sea?

What about our continued military presence over there to contain China? What a big joke! China is competing with us economically, not militarily. The Cold War ended in 1989!

4. What went wrong for the U.S. on its Korea policy?

More specifically, why can't we simply get out of there more than 20 years after the Cold War ended in 1989? Or more broadly, why can't we cut our out-of-control military spending drastically? It's the political system, stupid! For more, read Chapter 40.

Today, our defense spending is by far the largest in the world. In fact, it's more than the next 16 biggest spending countries combined! That's way beyond the need for defense by any definition! That's for offense. That's for naked aggression as the Iraq War! Can we, Americans, be as easily fooled by our politicians as the folks in North Korea by Kim II?

The biggest threat to our national security today is nothing but a bankrupting U.S. economy, to which out-of-control military spending has been contributing! The biggest enemy to the survival of the United States is also here at home: the systematically corrupted U.S. political system – the mind-nothing-but-reelection-only career politicians have been destroying America by emptying her public treasury! When can we, Americans, recognize these problems and fix them before it's really too late?

5. What will the Korean peninsula look like in 20 years?

The two Koreas will become one (just like the two Germans before) within two decades, with the South coming out on the top. Meanwhile, everything is going to be fine, with or without the U.S., because of the China factor, which can be highlighted as follows:

1) The political system in the North is doomed. The Chinese know it better than anybody else. China favors the South, not only economically but also politically.
2) If anything bad happens in the Korean peninsula (e.g. famine in the North), China will be negatively impacted most (e.g. millions of refugees from the North crossing the border to China). The same applies to the nuclear weapons in the North! Why should we, the U.S., worry more about them than China? Can we, Americans, still think straight, basically and logically?
3) China knows the history (and so does Japan): the Koreans can never be conquered!

What about China's concern over the continued U.S. military presence over there? Not much! Remember: China is a country with extra-ordinary history and patience. The U.S. has been there for more than 60 years already. What difference does it make for another 10 or 20?

On top of everything, the Chinese are too busy making money everywhere, including Africa, South America, and Southeast Asia.

For a comprehensive Chinese view of China vs. the U.S. in this 21st century, read this: "Globalization 2.0: A Century for Sale, Any Taker?"

6. Closing

It's time for America to wise up! For example, we, as a country, have simply failed to adapt adequately after the Cold War ended in 1989, which is one reason behind America's steep decline today. Overall, we have been fooled by our politicians for way too long! Remember this: in theory our politicians work for us. But in practice, they serve themselves and special interest groups (e.g. the defense industry) far better than us! Once again, it's the political system, stupid!

As for the Korean peninsula (and Taiwan), no American intervention, no problem!

Chapter 60: U.S. Middle East Policy: What Is Wrong?

(Initially published at GEI on 1/13/2012)

The answer is "almost everything!" Here are three latest news stories that triggered this writing:
1) Afghan leader Karzai condemns 'US Marines body desecration' video.
2) Iranian nuclear chemist killed by motorbike assassins.
3) Geithner prods China, Japan on Iran oil imports.

Let's discuss these three issues one by one.

1. Afghanistan
This story, once again, proves this historical perspective: little good comes out of a war, any war! In case you are unaware, nobody has ever "won" in Afghanistan, either the British in the mid 1800s or the Soviets in the 1980s. Why should it be different this time for Americans?

2. Iran
Why are we, Americans, so worried about Iran, especially its nuclear program? Just like we should let the Chinese worry about North Korea, we should let the people in the Middle East (e.g. Israelis) worry about Iran! Yes, Israel is our friend, but we must not do her job! Two questions:
1) Isn't this assassination an act of terror? Condemn it publicly, which we already did, and help stop it, both publicly and privately, which we are unlikely to do!
2) Which country has helped Iran most to become a dominant force in that region today? The U.S.!

How? Read Chapter 55 ("What's the real cost of the Iraq War?")!

3. Geithner in China

What is Mr. Geithner doing in China about Iran? China will always act according to its own interest, not the U.S. interest! Very importantly, didn't we just refocus our military on Asia (i.e. China)? What a laughing stock Mr. Geithner must have been in China right now!

4. Summary

Because these three stories are all linked to the Middle East, it's time for us to go back to a root point: 9/11/2001. All Americans with an open mind should read this: Ron Paul on 9/11: Ask the right questions and face the truth.

Bottom line: It's time to review our foreign policy holistically, as part of the discussion of this profound subject: towards an ideal form of government (Chapter 3).

One case in point: militarily, we are the only superpower on earth. Economically, we are much closer to Europe (i.e. bankruptcy) than to China, a rising star.

5. Closing

The 21st century belongs to either China or America for sure. But which one is going to come out on top? It depends on who can adapt and change as quickly as needed.

Change means, in no small part, which country will undermine itself less. Unfortunately, we keep screwing ourselves up, both domestically and internationally, while China seems to be finally on the right track, after badly hurting herself for more than 200 years!

Here is a quote:

"Commerce with all nations, alliance with none, should be our motto. Money, not morality, is the principle commerce of civilized nations. Peace, commerce and honest friendship with all nations; entangling alliances with none."

Who said it? **Thomas Jefferson**!

Peace, not war! Let's just trade with everyone, like the Chinese do!

Chapter 61: Top 10 American Misconceptions about the World

America is deeply in trouble (Chapter 1), and Americans are confused - who the hell would have thought that twenty short years after America won the Cold War in 1989, an immigrant from China would come out and say, to our face, that "democracy does not work and the totalitarian government in China (which he calls 'autocracy' or 'a dictatorship without a dictator') is, overall, slightly better than the American political system"? Worse yet, he seems to back himself up with history, a lot of facts, and some new theories, such as Pyramid Theory I (Chapter 18), Pyramid Theory II (Chapter 57), and The Loop Theory: Capitalism vs. Socialism (Chapter 19) ...

In Chapter 8 (Top 10 American Misconceptions about China), I tried to help my fellow Americans understand China better. Now, it is time for me to try to help my fellow Americans understand the world better.

Top line: This is really about America's foreign policy, on which I largely agree with Ron Paul, especially the non-intervention part! Furthermore, I personally hold two groups accountable for the total failure of our foreign policy:
1) The neo-cons for the wars of choice (e.g. Iraq).
2) The politicians for pandering to the defense industry, which is totally out of control now.

Misconception 1: America is the greatest nation in the history of the earth

When I heard Mitt Romney say it (America is the greatest nation in the history of the earth) repeatedly on

TV, I was incredulous, despite the fact that some Americans have stated it similarly before (e.g. Is America still the greatest nation on earth). To me, naming America the greatest nation in the history of the earth is presumptuous. It is like naming Michael Jordan the greatest basketball player ever. It's nice for a Chicago Bulls fan like me to hear that, but it's not true. The greatest basketball player ever is, arguably, Wilt Chamberlain. By the same token, China deserves the honor as the greatest nation in the history of the earth for one simple reason: *"Among all human civilizations of the past 5,000 years, China led more time than any other nation"* (Chapter 7: "America: What is China, Anyway?). China is easily more than 10 times longer than America in leadership! On top of that, China is poised to again be the largest economy on earth by 2030!

There is little consequence in naming Michael Jordan, or anybody, the greatest basketball player ever. However, there are consequences in naming America the greatest nation in the history of the earth: it's misleading and it's brainwashing (Chapter 63)! Worse yet, it does not help America recognize its current problems and find solutions. Worst of all, we are running out of time while succumbing to brainwashing!

Misconception 2: American troops are needed all over the world

Currently, American troops are present in about 150 countries (How many countries have US troops in them), but why? Should we continue to be the world's policemen even as we bankrupt ourselves at home?

The Cold War ended in 1989 and the world changed dramatically after that! But we, America, have failed to

adapt adequately, resulting in a total failure of our foreign policy. Two examples:
1) Chapter 59: "America: What to Do with North Korea?"
2) Chapter 60: "U.S. Middle East Policy: What Is Wrong?"

Misconception 3: 9/11 changed everything
America did change fundamentally after 9/11, but mostly in the wrong direction!

The 9/11 attack was an attack on America! We responded decisively and correctly by going after the culprit, Osama bin Laden, in Afghanistan. But almost everything else went wrong, especially the Iraq War (Chapter 55) and the Patriot Act. How could we have gone so far astray? Two reasons:
1) Incompetence: Our leaders were either too dull to know the real reason behind the 9/11 attack or too cowardly to face the truth. It's time to listen to Ron Paul (Ron Paul on 9/11: Ask the right questions and face the truth)!
2) Politics: I believe President George W. Bush launched the Iraq War, at least partially, for the sake of his re-election. For more, read Chapter 36 ("Blogojevich and Pearl Harbor: They Are Related!").

Misconception 4: The Iraq War was correct
The Iraq War was wrong, dead wrong! It was a naked aggression against a sovereign nation! It was totally un-American, because America had previously never launched a massive pre-emptive war like that! Whether Saddam was evil or not is totally irrelevant!

Here is a quote:

"Allow the president to invade a neighboring nation, whenever he shall deem it necessary to repel an invasion, and you allow him to do so whenever he may choose to say he deems it necessary for such a purpose - and you allow him to make war at pleasure."

Who said it? **Abraham Lincoln!**

Misconception 5: We are winning in Afghanistan

Wrong! As a matter of fact, no foreigner has ever won in Afghanistan, either the British in the mid-1800s or the Soviets in the 1980s. They were just the latest two before us after more than one thousand years of strife over there!

Americans are finally awake. Read: Americans to Obama: Get out of Afghanistan!

It's time for President Obama to wake up with two strong messages:
1) Stop listening to the generals! History has repeatedly shown that "the wars are too important to be left to the generals" (per Georges Clemenceau).
2) The Afghan War, any war, must not be part of consideration for the re-election!

Misconception 6: The war on terror makes sense

The war on terror is a *non sequitur*, both in name and in content! It's ill defined; it lasts forever; and it is failing, like most wars of choice (e.g. the war on drugs)!

A key difference between America and China today can be easily experienced at the airports: In China, airport security is largely a formality. But in America, it's almost unbearable (e.g. scanners and pat down). With that alone, I am afraid Osama bin Laden succeeded in disrupting a big part of America's economy.

Is America safer today than yesterday? No! America has far more enemies today than yesterday!

Misconception 7: Democracy is the best form of government

Democracy is so good that President George W. Bush launched the Iraq War to "spread" it. This argument is only valid in America, thanks to brainwashing (Chapter 63)!

Democracy is so good that the American government has been actively involved in subverting legitimate governments all over the world, especially in the Middle East. As a result, the people in the Middle East are suffering more, a lot more! Any doubt? Iraq is much worse off today than in Saddam's days, with no end in sight (e.g. Iraq militia stone youths death "emo" style). Egypt is much worse off today than in Mubarak's days, with no end in sight (e.g. "The Egyptian Revolution: A Year later")! Now imagine: what if America had decided to bomb China on June 4, 1989, to "protect" the pro-democracy students?

Democracy must come from within! The notion that America should support any rebellion against any government in the name of supporting and spreading democracy is simply stupid and wrong! The #1 problem in the Middle East is abject poverty, for which the only solution is capitalism, not democracy! As a matter of fact, there is not a single example of a third-world country achieving prosperity via democracy! For more, read Chapter 3 ("Towards an ideal form of government").

Above all, democracy, as we know it today, does not even work in the West (any more)! The entire West is now on the verge of bankruptcy. Several European countries are already there, with more to follow, including America!

Why did democracy stop working? Because of the rise of China and the incompetence of the American political system, or more generally, of the entire western system of democracy! Any doubt? Just look at this simple fact: China, a non-democracy, is the largest foreign creditor of both America and Europe!

Misconception 8: Russia's Putin is a bad man
Did Putin win the election recently? Yes! Was the election issue-free? No! How long did it take America to develop its current election system? More than 200 years! Yet, it's still imperfect!

After the Cold War ended in 1989, Russia made a huge mistake by embracing democracy and capitalism overnight, resulting in the destruction of their economy and untold human suffering. The Russians must solve these complex problems by themselves, over time. Meanwhile, leave the judgment of Putin to the Russians and history. No American intervention, no problem, at least for us!

Misconception 9: Need a UN resolution on Syria or Iran
Russia will not support it! Worse yet, here is the latest news: Russia Anti-Terror Troops Arrive in Syria.

In principle, let the folks over there work out their problems, over time! After all, they have lived their own lives there for thousands of years before American intervention. Are we going to change anything with our involvement? Yes, most likely for the worse only!

For a totally new perspective, read: Nuclear Armed Iran is a Road to Middle East Peace

Misconception 10: We are the only super power on earth

This claim is arguably still correct. But our days are clearly numbered if we stay the course (Chapter 1). To know what the Chinese have been building at home while we have been busily bombing and nation-building around the world, watch this slide show: China's amazing bridges.

Always remember this: peace & prosperity, not war and debt!

Part 10: Six Democracy-Communism Similarities

Chapter 62: Democracy-Communism Similarity #1: Destruction of Capitalism
Chapter 63: Democracy-Communism Similarity #2: Brainwashing
Chapter 64: Democracy-Communism Similarity #3: Ideology
Chapter 65: Democracy-Communism Similarity #4: Kleptocracy
Chapter 66: Democracy-Communism Similarity #5: 'You didn't built that'
Chapter 67: Democracy-Communism Similarity #6: Stupidity

"Democracy is the road to socialism."

--- Karl Marx

Chapter 62: Democracy-Communism Similarity #1: Destruction of Capitalism

Democracy, as we know it today, is akin to communism in one critical aspect: destruction of capitalism! Here is the subtle difference between them: communism violently destroyed capitalism overnight, while democracy has been peacefully destroying capitalism over time.

Democratic destruction becomes from both sides, the left (more) and the right (less). Here are two examples:
1) From the left: <u>Al Sharpton: Please tell Romney, we're not envious, we are fed up</u>.
2) From the right: <u>The GOP's weird war on wealth</u>.

I have already touched upon this subject extensively. In this chapter, I will explicitly draw a link between democracy and communism. It is built heavily on two previous chapters: Chapter 18 ("Pyramid Theory I") and Chapter 19 ("Loop Theory - Capitalism vs. Socialism").

1. Definitions
1) Communism: Per Wikipedia, communism is *"a social, political and economic ideology that aims at the establishment of a classless, moneyless, stateless and revolutionary socialist society structured upon common ownership of the means of production."* Two real-world examples: Cuba and North Korea.
2) Democracy: Per Wikipedia, democracy is *"generally defined as a form of government in which all adult citizens have an equal say in the decisions that affect their lives."* One real-world

example: the U.S. (call it a "Republic," if you like, which is too academic for me).

2. Communism

No serious discussion of communism can start without mentioning Karl Marx, who was well known for his theory of societal development, as shown in Figure 1: that society advances in phases from some early forms (e.g. tribalism and slavery) to feudalism, to capitalism, to socialism, and finally to communism.

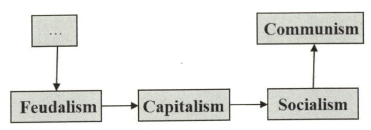

Figure 1: Marx's theory of societal development

At a very high level, Marx's theory is correct. In practice, two individuals capitalized on this theory more than anyone else: Lenin and Mao. Both of them eventually failed for the same reason: They jumped from feudalism to socialism via a violent revolution that first destroyed capitalism (in its primitive stage in their respective countries). No doubt, the Soviet Union was a total disaster, as was China under Mao (1949-1976). As a matter of fact, Mao was China's last *de facto* emperor, an epitomized symbol of feudalism!

Today, there exist only two communist countries: Cuba and North Korea. They are the worst on earth! All others have painfully failed and changed.

3. The Loop Theory: capitalism vs. socialism

Figure 2 shows the Loop Theory (Chapter 19). It extends and truncates Marx's theory as follows:
1) Capitalism and socialism are in a loop, requiring balancing from time to time. Capitalism is a must for prosperity. Socialism, if poorly managed, may set us back to feudalism (or even further back)!
2) Communism is so remote that we all should ignore it.

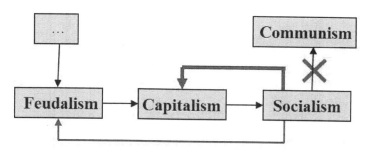

Figure 2: The loop theory

4. Pyramid Theory I

Pyramid Theory I, as presented in Chapter 18, is premised on one simple assumption: everything substantive in our society is pyramidal, with the "winners" sitting on the top and the majority below them. Three examples:
1) Wealth: Bill Gates and Warren Buffett are on the pinnacle. The rest of us fill in the middle and bottom.
2) Jobs: There are always more low-pay jobs than high-pay jobs (relatively). If you are good, get a high-pay one.
3) Business: There are always more workers than owners. If you are really good, be an owner!

The pyramidal shape not only follows physics (e.g. gravity), but also is the result of our capitalism at its best: You can make it if you work hard and if you are good (and lucky), even all the way to the 1% club! I am a modern-day example of an American dream come true (Chapter 74: "My American Dream Has Come True").

However, no matter how much our society advances (e.g. computers and the Internet), there are always the needs of having garbage collected and lawns mowed. In other words, while we are the best on earth to give anybody and everybody opportunities to move up (i.e. success), the majority of us will end up in the middle or bottom, as it should be. But democracy changes that …

5. Democracy

American democracy, as we know it today, is all about obtaining votes. Because of the lack of term-limits, most, if not all, of the politicians work for one supreme purpose only: getting re-elected *ad nauseam*. So they will do anything and everything to win your votes, including emptying the public treasury and creating various socialistic schemes in defiance of Pyramid Theory I. Two examples:

1) Home ownership: If you want a bigger and better home than you can actually afford, no problem - we will have Fannie Mae or Freddie Mac help you out.
2) Job creation: We are willing to spend on such wasteful things as a bridge to nowhere and Marine One, all in the name of job creation (or preservation), so that some of you can pretend to be working while the government can pretend to be paying you.

Here is a big problem: the government has little money of its own (other than money printing). Instead, it subsidizes the "losers" by taxing the "winners". In other words, it punishes success! As a result, the pool of winners will become smaller and, at this pace, will be dried out or chased away soon. Still wondering about my statement "America is becoming yesterday's China"? Wonder not! Democracy, as we know it today, looks more and more like communism (i.e. China under Mao or the former Soviet Union), and it is destroying America faster than most Americans realize! Yes, punishing success, you will end up without any success!

To make the point even more explicit, let me say this: the left-most Democrats today sound and act like the communists in China I was used to when I was growing up, from the class warfare (i.e. "the class struggle between the proletarians and the bourgeois" in communist terms) to the fake notion of "serving the people" by the career politicians (i.e. "serving the people with heart and soul," as per Chairman Mao).

6. Capitalism 101

For a quick lesson on capitalism 101, watch this short video: USA falls short on capitalism; true capitalism India style.

7. Democracy -> socialism -> bankruptcy

Two points:
1) There is not a single precedent of a third world country achieving prosperity via democracy. The key to prosperity is capitalism, not democracy!
2) Democracy was successful in the West largely because it was a luxury built on the strength of capitalism. The West could afford it until now, but not any longer!

Democracy, by definition, leads to socialism, which, *"if poorly managed, may set us back to feudalism,"* according to the Loop Theory (Chapter 19). Unfortunately, socialism has yet to be proven manageable: Most democratic counties have so overspent their future for the present and have gone so deeply into destructive socialism that the West, as a whole, is now on the verge of bankruptcy. Several European countries are already there, with more to follow, including the U.S.!

8. Where is the U.S. today, really?
We are in a steep decline! Our national debt was $9T in 2009 when President Obama took office. It has now exceeded $16T, which is more than our annual GDP! President Obama has, without question, proven to be the biggest spender, by far, in U.S. history! What's the consequence? Read: Debt slavery: why it destroyed Rome, why it will destroy us unless it's stopped.

We are in a crisis! We are much worse off today than in 2009 when President Obama took office. Any doubt? Read this (Meet the Jobless in Iowa), or this (College Graduates Face Record High Debt in the Age of Record High Unemployment), or this (The Hidden America), or this (Santa finds kids giving shorter lists in recession). Need you read more?

We are in a total mess! Read this: "Ron Paul on 9/11: Ask the right questions and face the truth", and this: 10 reasons the US is no longer the land of the free.

What's the way out of this total mess? "No way" (like Europe), according to Randy Wray! Or dictatorship, according to history! Again, here is the teaching from John Adams:

"Remember, democracy never lasts long. It soon wastes, exhausts, and murders itself. There never was a democracy yet that did not commit suicide."

9. Democracy vs. communism

Here is a simple comparison between communism and democracy: Millions gather at North Korea Kim II's funeral and thousands gather to remember Chicago firefighter.

Kim II was a king in North Korea. A firefighter in the U.S. is a public servant. Does the number of people attending a public funeral have any significance to proportionally demonstrate the importance of the dead person? If yes, adding all the public servants together, how many thousands of "kings" do we end up having in the U.S.?

Public-sector unions must go (Chapter 43)! They are communistic and they are anti-America!

10. Closing

Fortunately, democratic socialism has not destroyed capitalism in the U.S., yet. Better still, I believe I have the most accurate diagnosis for America (Chapter 1), as well as the best solution (Chapter 2). The question is: Can we change before it's really too late?

If we can't, then democracy will definitely match up with communism in destruction: democracy will destroy the West as spectacularly as communism destroyed the East, by the same means: destruction of capitalism!

Chapter 63: Democracy-Communism Similarity #2: Brainwashing

"I never gave anybody hell! I just told the truth and they thought it was hell."

--- Harry Truman

I am teaming up with Derryl Hermanutz, an enthusiastic observer of media and democracy, on this one!

1. What is brainwashing?
According to Wikipedia, brainwashing, or "mind control," *refers to a process in which a group or individual systematically uses unethically manipulative methods to persuade others to conform to the wishes of the manipulator(s), often to the detriment of the person being manipulated.*

2. Brainwashing in communism
Brainwashing and communism are almost synonymous, because communism would have died long ago without brainwashing; brainwashing developed to its peak under communism.

The two biggest communist countries were the Soviet Union and China (1949-1976). In communism, the euphemism for brainwashing is "propaganda". For an overview of how it worked in the Soviet Union, click: Propaganda in the Soviet Union. For a highlight of how it worked in Communist China, click: Propaganda in Communist China.

I grew up in Communist China. So I know firsthand how brainwashing worked over there. Let me give you my personal perspective with two key points:
1) There are two departments with highest priority in the CPC (Communist Party of China): Propaganda Department (or PR in the West) and Organization Department (or HR in the West). The former had complete control of the media. Because everything belonged to the public, it then belonged to the CPC, giving these two departments complete control of virtually everything in China.
2) Because communism was *de facto* feudalism in mask in China, everything was built on falsehoods, from the notion of leaders "serving the people" (vs. self-serving) to the practice of calling the people at the bottom (i.e. the workers, peasants, and the soldiers) the "masters".

How was it possible to perpetuate such massive falsehoods necessary for communism to survive? Propaganda! Here is a big example: in 1958, Mao launched the Great Leap Forward campaign. It was a total disaster! As a result, tens of millions of people starved to death from around 1960. But the communist propaganda machine spun it as a "3-year natural disaster".

"Tell a lie 1,000 times and it will become the truth." Unfortunately, you can fool some people all of the time, or all the people some of the time. But fortunately, you can't fool all the people all of the time. Today, there exist only two communist countries: Cuba and North Korea. They are the worst on earth! All others have painfully failed and changed.

China is no longer a communist country *per se* (Chapter 8)! China embraced capitalism big time after Mao died in 1976 and found her own way of success, such as without blindly embracing democracy as Russia did. As a result, China is now well on her way to becoming the largest economy on earth by 2030, while Russia lags far behind. For more, read Chapter 56 ("Emerging Economies: An Overview from 30,000 feet").

3. Brainwashing in democracy

Brainwashing in democracy is not as obvious as in communism. So it's time to have a serious discussion about it.

3.1 Crystallizing public opinion

In 1922, Walter Lippmann published his book "Public Opinion", which offered an incisive psychological and sociological examination of the emotional, irrational, herd-conformity factors that contribute to people's opinions.

In 1923, Edward Bernays published his book "Crystallizing Public Opinion", in which he argues that "crystallizing public opinion" is essential to a democratic government of large-scale nations: to "govern" a vastly disparate people, you have to unify their minds. Bernays criticized Lippmann for knowing the public mind so well, but failing to use that knowledge to manipulate the mind. Bernays spent a long career creating the opinion-making machinery, which would provide the "news" that would become the "history" of the 20th century. The engineered perceptions, not reality, provide the carefully crafted contents of people's "public opinions".

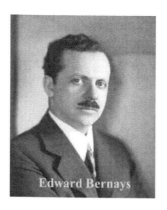
Edward Bernays

"Creating a media event," Bernays counsels his clients, "is something that disrupts the normal flow of public attention. I will show you how to craft that event to direct public opinion along the channels that serve your purposes."

America's media reports on a stage-managed theater, which they believe to be "events". The events are carefully crafted by PR counsels, like Bernays, to generate exactly the media "take" that results. The media buys the illusion, and then does the work of selling it to the public. When interviewed in 1990, Bernays, then nearly 100 years old, told Stuart Ewen (who wrote the introduction to a recent reprinting of "Crystallizing Public Opinion"), "We, PR counsels, have had no direct contact with the mass media for about 50 years. The job of a PR counsel is to instruct a client on how to take actions that just interrupt the continuity of life in some way to bring about the desired media response."

It is the media whose opinions are manipulated in the first place. They believe they are reporting and editorializing on "news". But "news" is the creation of media events that induce the desired public opinions, first in the media, then in the masses.

To the delight of the reigning power structure, most people assume the Enlightenment ideal that people form their opinions from evidence and hold those opinions "rationally", subject to alteration when contrary evidence comes to light. In fact, almost all people are selectively fed their opinions by "authorities", or the media, and they cling to their "opinions" with blind devotion rather than base them tentatively on rational evidence. Ask them to justify their opinions and you will get a defensive rant, simply regurgitating the "opinion" that has been fed to them; they will often act not unlike an angry monkey jumping around threateningly. You'll likely not get a cool rational explanation of the evidence and logic that supports belief in one conclusion and weakens belief in alternate conclusions.

Beliefs are held as "opinions", not "hard knowledge", though people usually believe that they "know" things rather than recognizing that they merely "believe" them. Most individual's opinions, and all public herd opinions, are held emotionally, not intellectually or analytically, so public opinion is created by manipulating people's emotions and instincts, not their rational minds.

In his 1928 book, Propaganda, Bernays writes of Lippmann's predecessors Wilfred Trotter and Gustave Le Bon:

> *"Trotter and Le Bon concluded that the group mind does not think in the strict sense of the word. In place of thought it has impulses, habits and emotions. In making up its mind, its first impulse is to follow the example of a trusted leader. This is one of the most firmly established principles of mass psychology."*

As Ewen writes, Bernays correctly gathered from Le Bon, Trotter, Lippmann etc. that, "Without a thorough comprehension of the unconscious and instinctual triggers that stimulate human behavior, the work of the PR counsel would be impossible."

Insofar as the masses have "reasons" for believing what they believe, they arrive at those reasons after the fact, to justify their beliefs; often they don't think up the reasons! Talk radio and other professional partisans think up and sell prepackaged "reasons". The masses' beliefs are not built up deductively from careful examination and coherent compilation of evidence. Often, the reasons they give have nothing to do with the real reason they have the beliefs they have. They were told what to believe, showed what to believe, and they form their "opinions" in that way.

3.2 Public opinion creation in America
Three examples: Iraq, Libya, and Iran & Syria.

3.2.1 Iraq
Iraq's WMD ("weapons of mass destruction") was uniformly presented, by the media-political complex, as the "reason" behind the Iraq War. How about Alan Greenspan's claim that it was "largely about oil"? How about the assertion that President George W. Bush launched the Iraq War for the sake of his re-election?

WMD was the media event. The subsequent media coverage and public opinion on the Iraq War universally focused on this engineered diversion of WMD. Did any American mass media outlet do in-depth investigative reporting of alternate American motives for the Iraq War? No! They all fell for the bait, and sold it to the American public.

3.2.2 Libya

Why did NATO wage war on Libya? The sales job for the media-political complex was that NATO was supporting the Arab Spring against Gaddafi's "brutal" regime. By all credible accounts, Libyans' support for Gaddafi's regime was far higher than Americans' support for "Obama's regime" (e.g. Congress disapproval rating at 87%). Therefore, should NATO support an Occupy Wall Street military takedown of the "massively unpopular" Obama regime in the protection of the 99%?

Or, if you like, should NATO support a Tea Party military takedown of the "tyrannically oppressive" Obama regime in the defense of America's Constitution and founding principles?

Is there any logic behind NATO's thinking, and action, at all?

3.2.3 Iran and Syria

Is Iran's nuclear program, not weapons, really such a big threat to anybody, more so than the nuclear weapons extant in Pakistan or India?

Many Americans have swallowed whole the media event, the illusion, that America's current preparations to invade and engineer regime change in Iran and Syria is about nuclear threats and democratic revolution. Some manipulative students of Bernays dreamed up these plausible but unproven scenarios; some political mouthpiece announced them in a "media event"; and these fabrications become the subject of American media attention and then morph the "opinions" of many Americans. "Should America permit a nuclear Iran?" "Should America support the freedom fighters in Syria?" The other possible motives for American action against these nations never see the light of media coverage or American herd opinion. It's all about "patriotism" and "making the world safe for democracy."

In short, it looks like Iraq, all over again!

3.3 Brainwashing in America

Any time a credible but politically unpalatable explanation for real world events is expressed in the American public sphere, it is often denounced as "conspiracy theory", then dismissed and studiously ignored by the mass media. Public opinion, the public herd mind, obediently follows suit and closes itself to any such crazy conspiracy talk.

Today, many of the American "news and opinion leaders" start with a basic proposition and then report on what they can find in the events of the day, which can spin to support their thesis. Examples are people like Rush Limbaugh and Ed Schultz. These people are not looking to expand their minds but simply to confirm what they have locked firmly in their beliefs. Unfortunately, some of their viewers may feel they are learning something about the news but most are simply engaging in the same belief confirmations.

Now, let's get to the basics: What is news? <u>N</u>orth, <u>E</u>ast, <u>W</u>est, and <u>S</u>outh! It simply means news comes from all directions, especially for the international news! Why, then, can't the American mainstream media match with the Chinese to show both sides of the stories on Iran and Syria? Why, then, can't the American mainstream media match with Al Jazeera for <u>"real news"</u>? They can, but they won't! Why? Because the American media is not truly "free", either spiritually ("free" as in freedom) or monetarily ("free" as in free food)! For more, read

Chapter 52 ("Freedom of the press in America and in China").

Welcome to the Internet age! Today, we all can publish, instantly and worldwide. Real freedom, at last!

3.4 Back to Edward Bernays

Bernays died in 1995, before the Internet and the blogosphere really got going. But he surely would have recognized the free flow of unmanaged information as an existential threat to his profession of molding public opinion to serve powerful moneyed interests. While we thoughtfully observe (Chapter 52) that the American mass media misinforms Americans, Bernays explains that the media itself is being systematically misled, and merely passing along the illusions as "news".

Change the political system (Chapter 2) and stop listening to Edward Bernays!

4. To whom should we listen?

Here is a quote:

"Commerce with all nations, alliance with none, should be our motto. Money, not morality, is the principle commerce of civilized nations. Peace, commerce and honest friendship with all nations; entangling alliances with none."

Who said it? **Thomas Jefferson**!

Here is another quote:

"Allow the president to invade a neighboring nation, whenever he shall deem it necessary to repel an invasion, and you allow him to do so whenever he may

choose to say he deems it necessary for such a purpose - and you allow him to make war at pleasure."

Who said it? **Abraham Lincoln**!

Apparently, the Chinese have been listening to Thomas Jefferson and Abraham Lincoln a lot more than we Americans have! For example, the Chinese trade with everybody; the Chinese promote peace, without a single war over the past few decades; and the Chinese value capitalism dearly, after a near-death experience with communistic socialism.

Still wondering why China has been rising so rapidly while America has been declining so steeply over the past decade? Wonder not! It's the political system, stupid!

5. Closing
Has the case been sufficiently made that brainwashing is yet another similarity between democracy and communism, in addition to "destroying capitalism"? You be the judge!

Unfortunately, while we debate these things, more wars are likely in the Middle East and more deeply America digs itself into a troubled hole, not only economically, but also politically and morally ...

Chapter 64: Democracy-Communism Similarity #3: Ideology

1. What is ideology?

According to Wikipedia, *"an **ideology** is a set of ideas that constitute one's goals, expectations, and actions. An ideology can be thought of as a comprehensive vision, as a way of looking at things (compare worldview), as in several philosophical tendencies (see Political ideologies), or a set of ideas proposed by the dominant class of a society to all members of this society (a "received consciousness" or product of socialization). The main purpose behind an ideology is to offer either change in society, or adherence to a set of ideals where conformity already exists, through a normative thought process. Ideologies are systems of abstract thought applied to public matters and thus make this concept central to politics. Implicitly every political or economic tendency entails an ideology whether or not it is propounded as an explicit system of thought. It is how society sees things."*

The two biggest opposing ideologies throughout the 20th century were communism and democracy. Democracy won decisively in 1989, when the Cold War ended.

The 21st century has been very different so far, with two world-shaking phenomena:
1) The rise of China.
2) The decline of America (and the West).

So let's examine the two phenomena from an ideology perspective …

2. Ideology in communism

The two biggest communist countries were the Soviet Union and China under Mao (1949-1976). For an overview of how the communist ideology worked in the Soviet Union, click here: State Ideology of the Soviet Union. For a highlight of how it worked in Communist China, click here: Communist Ideology in China. Both countries failed miserably and engendered untold human misery and deprivation.

I grew up in Communist China, whose communist ideology had two core ideas:
  1) Domestically: Communism is the best form of government, as it is for the people, with everything belonging to the people.
  2) Internationally: The proletarians in China, or in any other country, will not be truly liberated until the entire human race is liberated. So wherever there was a communist movement (e.g. North Korea, Vietnam, or even Albania), China offered support.

What a tragedy! Communism eventually collapsed due to the economic devastation it caused! In short, when the proletarians were in charge, everybody became a proletarian!

3. Ideology in democracy

Here are two core ideas in the democratic ideology in America today (corresponding to the two core ideas in the communist ideology):
  1) Domestically: Democracy is the best form of government, as it is of/by/for the people. So let's do everything possible for the people (= votes), such as creating all kinds of socialistic entitlement programs, growing the government to add a

massive number of government employees to the middle class, waging a class warfare against the rich (Class Warfare: Government Workers vs. The Taxpayers), and worst of all, initiating a naked assault on capitalism (Watch: Obama campaign's new ad paints Romney as a job-killing economic "vampire")!

2) Internationally: Democracy is so good that President George W. Bush turned off the beacon to launch the Iraq War to "spread" it. Democracy is so necessary that the American government has been actively involved in subverting legitimate governments all over the world, especially in the Middle East. For more, read Chapter 61 ("Top 10 American Misconceptions about The World").

Meanwhile, America's economy is collapsing at home. As a matter of fact, today's America looks more and more like yesterday's China! Why and how? Because democracy is yielding the same results in America today as communism did in China a few decades ago!

4. The U.S. vs. China

History has provided two important lessons:
1) The political system does not matter, as long as it embraces capitalism!
2) Capitalism is not everything; Capitalism is the only thing! Because capitalism has proved to be the only way to prosperity, a political system without capitalism will fail, be it communism or democracy!
   - China failed before (1949-1976) and the U.S. is failing now, both for the same reason: destruction of capitalism!

- The U.S. thrived before because of unfettered capitalism (and rugged individualism), and China is thriving now by practically incorporating capitalism into communism (also known as "state capitalism").

Is it coincidental the democratic U.S. is declining as "communist" China rises?

5. The West vs. China
The entire West is on the verge of bankruptcy. Several European countries are already there, with more to follow, including America!

In contrast, China, a non-democracy (but "state capitalism"), has been advancing so fast and so well over the past three decades that it is now the largest foreign creditor of both Europe and America! Furthermore, China is well on her way to becoming the largest economy on earth by 2030, dethroning America!

6. A moment of truth
It's time to face the truth: Democracy, as we know it today, does not work. It has failed in Europe and it is failing in America now (Chapter 1)!

America's problems are big and structural! Three examples:
1) Gridlock has paralyzed our government for years.
2) When the two parties finally manage to get something done together, it's often a wrong thing (Bipartisanship Is Behind Government's Worst Programs)!
3) The launch of the Iraq War showed that there were neither checks nor balances within our government. Instead, it was, and still is, corrupted

to its core. For more on U.S. government corruption, go back to Chapter 36 ("Blagojevich and Pearl Harbor: They Are Related!").

7. The outlook of the West

The recent election results in Europe (e.g. France and Greece) made one thing clear: Europe is already too deeply into socialism to save itself! Electing socialists to fix the problems caused by socialism meets Einstein's definition of insanity: Doing the same thing over and over again and expecting different results.

Italy is even worse: They abandoned democracy recently, as Mario Monti *"was invited by President Giorgio Napolitano to form a new technocratic government,"* without an election! Two basic questions and answers:
1) Did the sky fall over Italy without democracy? No!
2) Will Italy get better with Mr. Monti being the Prime Minister? Yes, most likely!

America must find our own way out of the trouble. Here is what's certain:
1) We must not follow Greece or France, as many left-wing extremists are hoping (The loser In European Election Results? Austerity")!
2) We can't follow Italy, as we do not have a President who can appoint a Prime Minister (but a bunch of useless czars).
3) It's time for America to change the course by, minimally, imposing some serious austerity (i.e. spending cuts) before it's really too late!

More profoundly, America should subscribe to my diagnosis (Chapter 1) and solution (Chapter 2).

8. Closing

Like communism, democracy, as an ideology, has many merits in theory. But in practice, it looks more and more like communism. Consequently, unless it can adapt to the changing times, like the Chinese did with communism, democracy, as we know it today, will destroy the West as spectacularly and painfully as communism destroyed the East!

Chapter 65: Democracy-Communism Similarity #4: Kleptocracy

"Good people do not need laws to tell them to act responsibly, while bad people will find a way around the laws."
--- Plato, 400 BC

1. What is kleptocracy?

According to Wikipedia, "***Kleptocracy**, alternatively cleptocracy or kleptarchy, (from Greek: κλέπτης - kleptēs, "thief" and κράτος - kratos, "power, rule", hence "rule by thieves") is a form of political and government corruption where the government exists to increase the personal wealth and political power of its officials and the ruling class at the expense of the wider population, often without pretense of honest service. This type of government corruption is often achieved by the embezzlement of state funds.*"

In short, kleptocracy means stealing and government corruption.

2. Kleptocracy in communism

Communism is kleptocracy by definition! In fact, it's too generous to call communism (i.e. robbery) "kleptocracy" (i.e. stealing). "Armed robbery" is more apropos!

The two biggest communist countries were the Soviet Union and China under Mao (1949-1976). Both failed and then changed in their own ways highlighted as follows:
1) The Soviet Union: It was dissolved, became Russia, and changed to a sort of stilted democracy overnight, thanks to Mikhail Gorbachev (i.e.

brainless and reckless) and Boris Yeltsin (i.e. heartless and reckless), resulting in untold human misery, a few billionaires (e.g. Mikhail Prokhorov), and a doubtful future.
2) China: It changed for the better over time, thanks to the wisdom of one individual: Deng Xiaoping, resulting in China's extraordinary success today and a new political system that appears to be slightly better than democracy, as we know it (Chapter 7: "America: What is China, Anyway?").

Bottom line:
1) It was a positive change from armed robbery (i.e. communism) to stealing (i.e. kleptocracy) for both Russia and China.
2) The West must not dismiss China's system (i.e. "state capitalism") lightly just because stealing is prevalent there (China's Macroeconomic Miracle: Kleptocracy). It's the direction and the rate of change that matter most, and it is a long and tortuous journey to transition from communism to an ideal form of government (Chapter 3).
3) Democracy, as we know it today, has become totally kleptocractic and bankrupting!

3. Kleptocracy in democracy
Three readings:
1) Chapter 2: "American Democracy: Massive Falsehoods at the Top!"
2) Chapter 36: "Blagojevich and Pearl Harbor: They Are Related!"
3) Insider Trading in Congress.

Overall, American politicians have long been openly and proudly "spreading the wealth" of the nation to special interest groups (e.g. public-sector unions) in exchange for votes! America's national debt already exceeds $16T. How much more should we allow them to steal from the public treasury and from our future generations before saying "enough is enough"?

4. The U.S. vs. China

It's easy to steal in China, as money is everywhere! But it can be restless. Here is a rumored story about Wang Lijun, the man who brought down Bo Xilai, and Wen Qiang, Wang's predecessor: Before his execution, Wen shared his prophesy with Wang: "you will be like me in a few years!" Apparently, Wang took Wen's advice seriously: He was well prepared for his doomsday and escaped to the American Consulate in Chengdu before Bo could have settled with him "locally" by taking him into custody, possibly with a speedy trial followed by a speedy execution. By running into the American Consulate, Wang saved his life with two major results: (1) Beijing took custody of him shortly afterwards and (2) he had a chance to confess his own crimes together with Bo's.

Like China, stealing is widespread and systematic in the U.S. Unlike China, stealing can be open and restful in the U.S. Three examples:
1) For many American politicians, stealing from the public treasury and from the future generations is a way of life – nobody is losing sleep because of it!
2) What about Insider Trading in Congress? Nancy Pelosi is certainly not losing sleep because of it (Confronting Pelosi on Insider Trading)!
3) Although the launch of the Iraq War has been widely regarded as the biggest mistake ever in American foreign policy, nobody has been held accountable for it! Tens of thousands of Iraqis

died. What about the U.S. casualties? 4,486 deaths and over 100,000 wounded! It was a crime against humanity! Yet President George W. Bush appears to be resting well in retirement. Where is the basic justice? For a perspective from Africa, read: Tutu: Bush, Blair, should face trial at the Hague.

Here is the latest article on China's corruption: "The family fortunes of Beijing's new few". Very bad, isn't it? But between that and the Iraq War, I would pick the former every time! Besides, we have our "royal" families too: the Kennedys, the Bushes, or even the Clintons.

5. Discussion

It's easy for America to pick on China (and *vice versa*), and debate forever about whose system is better, while losing valuable time solving our own problems. So let's keep the debate simple by focusing on the results (vs. processes) and the political systems (vs. individuals):

1) Results: China is well on her way to becoming the largest economy on earth by 2030, while the entire West is on the verge of bankruptcy. Several European countries are already there, with more to follow, including America. Wondering about America's tomorrow? Look at Europe today (Europe's Problems Put Another 4.5 Million Jobs at Risk)! Wondering about America's next generation? Look at this generation in Europe (Class 2012: 5 Europe grads face rocky future)!

2) Political systems: Forget about China's Bo or America's Pelosi, or even President Obama. Let's think about the political system, holistically: towards an ideal form of government (Chapter 3). Here is the bottom line:

- *"The political system does not matter, as long as it embraces capitalism!"* (Chapter 64: "Ideology").
- Today's Chinese government is more pro-business (i.e. pro-capitalism) than today's American government, even per Steve Wynn. That is the most important difference between China and the U.S. today! That is the key reason behind China's rise and America's decline!

What, then, is the solution for America? Bet on Mitt Romney by demanding that he be a great President as I suggested (Chapter 26: "An Open Letter to Mitt Romney")!

6. Closing

Like communism, democracy, both as an ideology and as a form of government, has many merits in theory. But in practice and effect, democracy looks more and more like communism. Consequently, unless it can be adapted to the changing times, like the Chinese did with communism, democracy, as we know it today, will destroy the West as spectacularly and painfully as communism destroyed the East!

Chapter 66: Democracy-Communism Similarity #5: 'You didn't build that'

1. What is 'you didn't build that'?
In a recent <u>campaign speech</u>, President Obama stated: "If you've got a business - you didn't build that."

There has been a lot of discussion about this. None is better than this video discussion from the Wall Street Journal: <u>Ad Watch: What Does 'You Didn't Build That' Really Mean</u>? This video provides some context from which you can form your own opinions.

In this chapter, I will share mine.

2. How do I feel about 'you didn't build that'?
As the founder and owner of a business, I was deeply offended by that statement, and would like to simply reply like this: "Yes, I built that!" Additionally, here are two basic questions for President Obama:
1) Did not all the unsuccessful business people in the U.S. have the same (if not more) "help" from the government but fail anyway (e.g. Solyndra)?
2) Don't the successful business people pay, through confiscatory taxes, for all the government "help" they receive?

As someone who grew up in communist China (1949-1976), I found President Obama's statement distressing and sounding eerily familiar ...

3. 'You didn't build that' in communism
One core idea of communism is the denial of the ownership of private property - all in the name of "you didn't build that". The people (or proletarians) did! So the communists in China did two things:

1) They confiscated the property of the "rich" (e.g. factory owners and landlords), making them government property.
2) They took all your rights away, and then gave some back to you - while demanding that you be grateful to them.

What was the result? China became dirt poor! Why and how? It turned out that the proletarians were proletarians for a good reason: they did not know how to build! In other words, "when the proletarians were in charge, everybody became a proletarian" (Chapter 64: "Ideology")!

4. 'You didn't build that' in democracy
A few years ago, someone conducted a worldwide survey based on one single question: "what do you think of Bill Gates?" Here are some results:
1) America: "He is great. I wish my child will be like him."
2) Spain: "He is good, but he should pay more taxes."
3) France: "He is evil. Let's burn down his house and confiscate all his property."

The details of the survey are not important - you get the point, hopefully.

There should be no place in America for such an outrageous statement as "you didn't build that"! I have already written a lot about America (e.g. Chapters 7 and 8). Here are two key points:
1) America thrived previously due to rugged individualism and unfettered capitalism. America is in decline now because of its slide towards socialism.

2) No public servant in America, including the President, must be allowed to say to a master "you didn't build that"! It's insulting; it's un-American; and it's communistic!

Unfortunately, President Obama said just that! It is totally unacceptable and it is utterly indefensible, despite all the efforts by the White House and the Obama campaign!

Was it a gaffe? Yes, if gaffe means "when a politician tells the truth" (per Wikipedia). I believe it was an accurate reflection of President Obama's ideology for three reasons:
1) He previously loudly professed "spreading the wealth", and he recently initiated a naked assault on capitalism (Obama: Bain attacks 'not a distraction'),
2) His policy over the past four years speaks amply about his ideology. As a result, we are now more deeply in debt and more deeply into socialism than ever, with no easy way back!
3) He has never owned or led a business. Instead, he has mostly been a public servant, but frequently spoke over his masters!

5. The U.S. vs. China
In China, there are no real democratic elections, yet. But some experiments have been conducted at the low levels. For example, at the village level, people often elect the richest person to be the village leader. Why? Because we all want to be like him (or her)!

In the U.S., we now face a critical choice: who should be our next President? Should we give Mitt Romney, a successful businessman, a chance, or continue with

Barack Obama, a community organizer, a career politician, and a "not-good-enough" President at best? For the Chinese, the answer is a no-brainer. But for Americans, who knows …

China has come a long way to leave communism behind and embrace capitalism, while the U.S. is rapidly moving the other way! Thomas Sowell said it the best: we are "moving in the direction of the kind of economy that China has been forced to move away from" (The Limits of Power).

6. Discussion

Like communism, democracy has many merits in theory. But in practice and effect, democracy looks more and more like communism. I have, so far, identified five similarities between them, with this latest one, "you didn't build that", being the most obvious (I think). Democracy has resulted in a communistic person being the American President! What more evidence do you still need to be convinced that democracy, as we know it today, is moving toward communism? Do you need an open communist as the American President?

Now, two basic questions for you:
1) Romney's tax returns: Are you supposed to be angrier about what Mitt Romney does with his own money than about what President Obama does with your money (Who is Barack Obama)?
2) Obama's grades in college: Everybody knows Barack Obama was inexperienced before becoming the President. But many think he is smart. If that's true, why is it so hard for him to reveal his grades in college (Obama campaign makes case for releasing his college transcripts)?

President George W. Bush did (a C student at Yale)!

All signs indicate that Barack Obama received a lot of "help" from the government throughout his life – good for him! But it's simply unacceptable for him to insult the successful business people, the heart and soul of America, by saying "you didn't build that"!

Something is profoundly wrong here: President Obama does not seem to understand America, its essence, at all! No wonder America is so deeply in trouble ...

7. Closing

America, where do you go from here?

Chapter 67: Democracy-Communism Similarity #6: Stupidity

1. What is stupidity?

According to Wikipedia, "*Stupidity* is a lack of intelligence, understanding, reason, wit, or sense. It may be innate, assumed, or reactive - "being 'stupid with grief' as a defense against psychological trauma", a state marked with "grief and despair, making even simple daily tasks a hardship.*"*

Stupidity was obviously needed in communism. It is becoming increasingly clear that stupidity is also needed in democracy.

2. Stupidity in communism

Stupidity is deeply rooted in communism, because communism relies on stupidity to win power first and then to rule.

2.1 Stupidity was needed for China's communists to win

After WWII, two parties ruled China: Kuomintang, which headed the Nationalist Government, and the CPC (Communist Party of China), which controlled a good portion of the countryside. The world powers (i.e. the U.S. and the former Soviet Union) were in favor of some kind of settlement between the two parties, such as adopting a parliamentary system to share power or even dividing China into two parts like the two Germanys or two Koreas. But Mao wanted neither – he wanted to rule all China!

The People's Liberation War ensued. Mao prevailed in three short years, forcing the Nationalist Government to retreat to Taiwan.

How could the CPC have won so quickly? Chen Cheng, a leader of the Nationalist Government, said it the best: "We fought for an ideal, but they fought for the people".
1) What was the ideal? Some type of parliamentary democracy modeled after the West!
2) How did the CPC fight for the people? It promised a good life for them all, including immediate largess by robbing and killing the rich thereby repossessing their property. Proletarians no more, overnight – What a deal! The people fought hard for the CPC and the CPC delivered: the People's Republic of China was born in 1949!

2.2 Stupidity was needed for China's communists to rule

Grabbing power by force is one thing. Actual governing is another. It turned out that communism brought absolute poverty and a total lack of real freedoms to China (other than the initial free robbing and free killing of the rich). Why and how? The redistributed wealth was quickly consumed and "the people" (i.e. workers, peasants, and soldiers) did not know how to make anything!

It was hard for Mao to rule (1949-1976). On top of brainwashing (Chapter 63), Mao managed, again and again, to crush his opponents (e.g. all kinds of bourgeois and the intellectuals) by mass movements, relying on "the people", who continued to support him in hope for a better tomorrow, which never came. Finally, Mao started the Cultural Revolution by mobilizing hundreds of thousands of know-nothing students.

3. Stupidity in democracy

Democracy, as we know it today, means more and more poverty (e.g. Poverty In The U.S. By The Numbers) and less and less freedom (e.g. economic freedom). Neither is as bad in America as in Communist China, but the worst is yet to come.

It is apparent that one key reason behind the demise of democracy is stupidity. It's now endemic and becoming self-perpetuating.

3.1 Bottom-up

1) Nobody is too stupid to run for the President. Read this: So you want to run for president? Just sign here. It asks *"far fewer questions than a McDonald's job application"*!
2) Nobody is too stupid to vote. No ID, no problem. Even the deceased are often still registered to vote, as well as Mickey Mouse and Goofy!
3) Americans want their President to be one of them (so that they can figuratively have a beer together), and get what they want – an average Joe being the President! Both George W. Bush and Barack Obama turned out to be the worst Presidents in history!

3.2 Top-down

1) If I give you food stamps, will you vote for me (again)? For more, read: Obama is the 'food stamp President'.
2) If you are gullible enough to believe, I give you everything you want in the form of "affordable" housing, healthcare, or student loans, will you vote for me (again)?

3.3 From the left

Many social problems in America now are caused by stupidity, both personal stupidity and system stupidity. Two examples:
1) Some 15% U.S. Uses Food Stamps.
2) Single Moms Obama's X-factor?

First off, let's agree that both are problems in general to our society. Secondly, let's accept the cold fact that the bigger the food-stamp crowd is and the bigger the single-mom crowd is, the better for President Obama's re-election, his main impetus throughout his first term! So President Obama has both the incentive and the means to being the food stamp President, or more broadly, to expand socialism, especially the "government dependence" part, for the sake of re-election, his utmost priority. Finally, let me point out that President Obama's war on the rich and his naked assault on capitalism (e.g. Ad Watch: What Does 'You Didn't Build That' Really Mean?) are surely Marxist.

3.4 From the right

1) Religious right: One of the many things our founding fathers did right is the separation of church and state (or religion and politics). Unfortunately, the religious right betrayed it, resulting in the abortion issue getting into the GOP platform more than 20 years ago, and it has been there ever since. In a close election, it could be the difference, especially when it is now portrayed as the politics of rape and abortion.
2) Neo-cons: They are largely responsible for the disastrous American foreign policy, especially the Iraq War. It has been damaging America from the right just as badly as socialism has from the left! On foreign policy, it's time to listen to Ron Paul

([Ron Paul on 9/11: Ask the right questions and face the truth](#))!

3.5 By "the people"
Did you notice that the Chicago Teachers Union was on striker in September 2012? What was the issue? Pure greed and stupidity!

Now, why the big mess and whom to blame, ultimately?

JFK! Here is an excerpt from Chapter 30 ("American Presidents: Three Best and Three Worst"):

> *"President Kennedy might well be recognized as the worst American President twenty years from now, as America finally realizes the magnitude of the damage he caused by allowing public-sector unions in 1961."*

Are you now one step closer to that realization than when you started reading this book?

3.6 On China bashing
On this subject, the left and the right often concur. Two examples:
1) From the left: [Death by China](#). This one blames China for everything. It tries to fool Americans in a way similar to what Mao did in China many decades ago!
2) From the right: [Why Are Media Ignoring Rising Threat of China?](#) This one simply tries to make something out of nothing by exaggeration, in order to support the out-of-control spending on military (Chapter 40).

Why is this happening? Three main reasons:
1) The authors (e.g. Professor Peter Navarro) are just trying to make a living.
2) There is nothing to lose, but everything to gain, in doing what they do.
3) They rely on misinformed Americans, and are trying to make them stupid via brainwashing (Chapter 63)!

Here are three simple questions and answers with regard to the general subject of the U.S. vs. China:
1) What's the reason beyond China's rise? Capitalism!
2) What the reason behind America's decline? Socialism!
3) What's the key difference between the U.S. and China? It's the political system, stupid! Overall, China's political system appears to be slightly better than America's!

3.7 Back to the top

Here is a recent development: <u>Obama warns Egypt: Are you ally or enemy?</u> What a dumb question and a stupid posture! Of course, Egypt will be an enemy, if not already! The way we conduct ourselves internationally, especially in the Middle East, will only result in more and more enemies for America!

Now, how have we been conducting ourselves in the Middle East, specifically?
1) We recklessly turned off the beacon to launch the Iraq War.
2) We have been recklessly spreading something called "democracy", which does not even work at home!

For more, read Chapter 60 ("U.S. Middle East policy: what is wrong?").

In sharp contrast, the Chinese do not have these kinds of international headaches at all. Instead, they have been busily making money, internationally and peacefully. Again, are you still wondering about the secrets behind China's rise? Peace and capitalism! What about the reasons behind America's decline? War and socialism!

4. Discussion

People are different. Like intelligence, stupidity is a way of life - you can't prevent people from being stupid, especially in a free society like ours. In other words, being stupid is a right, just like being obese (Chapter 45: "Obese: to be or not to be")!

However, when our political system becomes stupid, we all suffer, tremendously! Worse yet, the reasons are obvious why our system has become so stupid, but we are unable to fix it!
1) Why has our political system become so stupid? We are lazy and stupid – We have been sleeping on it for more than 200 years, resisting changes!
2) How to fix our political system? My solution (Chapter 2) is the best on the table!

5. Closing

Stupidity appears to be playing an increasingly significant role in democracy just as it did in communism. As a result, unless democracy can be adapted to the changing times, like the Chinese did with communism, it will destroy the West, as spectacularly and painfully as communism destroyed the East!

Part 11: Famous Quotes and Interpretations

Chapter 68: America: What Did Winston Churchill Mean?
Chapter 69: What Did Ronald Reagan Mean
Chapter 70: What Did Abraham Lincoln Mean?
Chapter 71: What Did Thomas Jefferson Mean?
Chapter 72: What did George Washington?

Chapter 68: America: What Did Winston Churchill Mean?

(Initially published at GEI on 9/2/2011)

1) *Democracy is the worst form of government except all the others that have been tried.*
   - He meant: When you see China catch up with America with a new form of government, study it and adapt!

2) *To build may have to be the slow and laborious task of years. To destroy can be the thoughtless act of a single day.*
   - He meant: President George W. Bush, it was reckless for you to launch the Iraq War in 2003! It will eventually prove to be the beginning of the end of democracy, as we know it. Or more bluntly, it will eventually be marked as the beginning of the end of America, as we know it.

3) *Never, never, never believe any war will be smooth and easy, or that anyone who embarks on the strange voyage can measure the tides and hurricanes he will encounter. The statesman who yields to war fever must realize that once the signal is given, he is no longer the master of policy but the slave of unforeseeable and uncontrollable events.*
   - He meant the Iraq War, obviously! Any questions?

4) *One day President Roosevelt told me that he was asking publicly for suggestions about what the war should be called. I said at once 'The Unnecessary War'.*

- He meant: President Obama, end the war in Afghanistan, now – it's no longer necessary, nor worthwhile.

5) *The price of greatness is responsibility.*
    - He meant: President Obama, stop blaming others - take responsibility for the disastrous status of the American economy today and have it fixed!

6) *It's not enough that we do our best; sometimes we have to do what's required.*
    - He meant: President Obama, if you are incapable of fixing the economy, let someone who is capable do it.

7) *A love of tradition has never weakened a nation, indeed it has strengthened nations in their hour of peril; but the new view must come, the world must roll forward.*
    - He meant: Read Frank Li's writings on American politics!

8) *The British nation is unique in this respect. They are the only people who like to be told how bad things are, who like to be told the worst.*
    - He meant: America, Frank Li has the most accurate diagnosis for America (Chapter 1), as well we the best solution (Chapter 2).

9) *If you are not a Liberal at 20, you have no heart. If you are not a Conservative at 40, you have no brain.*
    - He meant: In addition to raising the minimum age of the American Presidency to 55, raise the voting age to a minimum of 21, so that voting is at least as important as drinking, or perhaps even to 40 when you are wise enough to do so.

10) *It is a good thing for an uneducated man to read books of quotations.*
   - He meant: You must be bloody thrilled to be able to read Dr. Frank Li's mind when he writes like this!

Chapter 69: What Did Ronald Reagan Mean?

(Initially published at GEI on 10/28/2011)

1) *A people free to choose will always choose peace.*
   - He meant: President George W. Bush, it was reckless for you to launch the Iraq War in 2003!

2) *It's silly talking about how many years we will have to spend in the jungles of Vietnam when we could pave the whole country and put parking stripes on it and still be home by Christmas.*
   - He meant: President Obama, end the war in Afghanistan, and all wars, now!

3) *How do you tell a communist? Well, it's someone who reads Marx and Lenin. And how do you tell an anti-Communist? It's someone who understands Marx and Lenin.*
   - He meant: Read Chapter 19 ("Loop Theory – Capitalism vs. Socialism")

4) *Mr. Gorbachev, tear down this wall!*
   - He meant: Times have changed. The challenge is on the American side now! The Berlin Wall came down in 1989, but America has failed to adapt to the changing world by adequately changing itself, from foreign policies to domestic policies. As a result, by 2000, America had not only more economic competitors than ever, but also more political enemies (e.g. Islamic extremists) than ever. Worse yet, the incompetence of America's political system in general, and specifically of the American Presidency, have finally become more evident than ever. After two disastrous Presidents in

George W. Bush and Barack Obama, today, America has not only even more economic competitors and political enemies than in 2000, but also much stronger duals than in 2000!

5) *How can a president not be an actor?*
   - He meant: Democracy is a showbiz by definition (Chapter 24: "From NBA, to American Idol, to American Presidency"). But, President Obama, you went too far on September 8, 2011, when you gave a speech on your jobs bill to Congress. It was a campaign speech in disguise!

6) *The best minds are not in government. If any were, business would steal them away.*
   - He meant: Public-sector workers should serve, truly serve, not profit!

7) *Government always finds a need for whatever money it gets.*
   - He meant: President Obama, stop the class warfare! America does not have a revenue problem; America has a spending problem.

8) *I am not worried about the deficit. It is big enough to take care of itself.*
   - He meant: A deficit is acceptable when the economy is projected to grow. President Obama, where will the growth come from for America in the next decade? If you can't answer this question honestly, succinctly, and convincingly, then control the deficit and reduce the debts! Spending for the purpose of your own re-election? That's totally unacceptable! Printing money is not a real solution – It's irresponsible!

9) *They say the world has become too complex for simple answers. They are wrong.*
   - He meant: The solution for many American ills today is to reform the political system and run the country like a business, simple and straightforward!

10) *It has been said that politics is the second oldest profession. I have learned that it bears a striking resemblance to the first.*
    - He meant: It does not have to be that way, especially at the President level. America is desperately in need of a great President to turn things around now. Bet on a Republican this time, because the odds are much better than the Democrats!

Chapter 70: What Abraham Lincoln Mean?

(Initially published at GEI on 1/27/2012)

1) *Allow the president to invade a neighboring nation, whenever he shall deem it necessary to repel an invasion, and you allow him to do so whenever he may choose to say he deems it necessary for such a purpose - and you allow him to make war at pleasure.*
   - He meant: President George W. Bush, it was reckless for you to launch the Iraq War in 2003!

2) *America will never be destroyed from the outside. If we falter and lose our freedoms, it will be because we destroyed ourselves.*
   - He meant: Presidents George W. Bush and Barack Obama, your policies have done more damage to America than all of America's enemies have done, combined! The biggest threat to America is its faltering economy, as it is now!

3) *Government of the people, by the people, for the people, shall not perish from the Earth.*
   - He meant: If you think the current American government is of/by/for the people, think again! Two perspectives:
     - Are our children and their children people too? If yes, do you still think it right that we spend their financial futures like there is no tomorrow?
     - If Congress is of/by/for the people, why is its disapproval rating at 87%?

4) *I destroy my enemies when I make them my friends.*

- He meant: America, we have too many enemies already (Chapter 40: "It's The Out-Of-Control Spending on Military, Stupid!"). Change the foreign policy fundamentally and change the Cold War mentality, starting with changing the political system!

5) *I don't like that man. I must get to know him better.*
   - He meant: Seek to understand before being understood. This applies not only to individuals, but also to countries. China is a competitor, not an enemy! For more, read Chapter 49 ("Political & Economic Lessons from China").

6) *Marriage is neither heaven nor hell, it is simply purgatory.*
   - He meant: Work out your differences as a couple. Nothing is more important than the family - it's the core and fiber of our society built to last (Chapter 4). When that core is broken, you will have nothing but trouble, everywhere and all the time.

7) *Let not him who is houseless pull down the house of another, but let him work diligently and build one for himself, thus by example assuring that his own shall be safe from violence when built.*
   - He meant: America has been the "land of opportunity" and must remain so: you can make it if you work hard and you are good (and lucky). No class warfare must be allowed! Redistribution of wealth is wrong and is un-American - earn it or go without!

8) *The people will save their government, if the government itself will allow them.*

- He meant: Have you seen anything better than this diagnosis (Chapter 1) and this solution (Chapter 2)?

9) <u>Economic principles of Abraham Lincoln</u>:
   - You cannot bring about prosperity by discouraging thrift.
   - You cannot strengthen the weak by weakening the strong.
   - You cannot help small men by tearing down big men.
   - You cannot help the poor by destroying the rich.
   - You cannot lift the wage earner by pulling down the wage payer.
   - You cannot keep out of trouble by spending more than your income.
   - You cannot establish sound security on borrowed money.
   - You cannot build character and courage by taking away a man's initiative and independence.
   - You cannot help men permanently by doing for them what they could and should do for themselves.

10) *Republicans are for both the man and the dollar, but in case of conflict the man before the dollar.*
    - He meant: America is desperately in need of a great President to turn things around now. Bet on a Republican this time, because the odds are much better than the Democrats!

Chapter 71: What Did Thomas Jefferson Mean?

(Initially published at GEI on 3/30/2012)

1) *I abhor war and view it as the greatest scourge of mankind. The most successful war seldom pays for its losses.*
   - He meant: President George W. Bush, it was reckless for you to launch the Iraq War in 2003! President Obama, end the war in Afghanistan now! Stop listening to the generals, as "the wars are too important to be left to the generals". The Afghan War, any war, must not be part of consideration for your re-election!

2) *My reading of history convinces me that most bad government results from too much government.*
   - He meant: President Obama, the government is way too big!

3) *Commerce with all nations, alliance with none, should be our motto. Money, not morality, is the principle commerce of civilized nations. Peace, commerce and honest friendship with all nations; entangling alliances with none.*
   - He meant: Trade with everybody, like the Chinese do, especially over the past two decades. Trade helps politics, not the other way around!

4) *I have no ambition to govern men; it is a painful and thankless office.*
   - He meant: Read Chapter 25 ("Let's Redefine the American Presidency, Now")!

5) *Never spend your money before you have earned it.*
   - He meant: Balance the budget!

6) *It is incumbent on every generation to pay its own debts as it goes. A principle which if acted on would save one-half the wars of the world.*
   - He meant: President Obama, stop spending like there is no tomorrow! The national was $9T when you took office in 2009, and it is now over $16T. You are by far the biggest spender in U.S. history! Pay off the debts!

7) *Nothing gives one person so much advantage over another as to remain always cool and unruffled under all circumstances.*
   - He meant: For all the problems America has today, have you seen anything better than this diagnosis (Chapter 1) and this solution (Chapter 2)?

8) *The man who reads nothing at all is better educated than the man who reads nothing but newspapers.*
   - He meant: Read Chapter 63 ("Brainwashing")!

9) *The spirit of this country is totally adverse to a large military force. We did not raise armies for glory or for conquest.*
   - He meant: Read Chapter 40 ("It's The Out-Of-Control Spending on Military, Stupid!").

10) *I propose that the Constitution, and each one following it, expire after 19 or 20 years.*
    - He meant: It's time to significantly amend the Constitution as follows:
      ➢ Limiting the American Presidency to one-term (e.g. six years).

- ➤ Raising the statutory requirements for the American Presidency, such as the minimum age to 55 (from 35) and only after having served as a state governor for one full-term, at least.
- ➤ Introducing strict term-limits for Congress, preferably one-term (e.g. six years) as well.

Chapter 72: What Did George Washington Mean?

(Initially published at GEI on 11/23/2012)

1) *My first wish is to see this plague of mankind, war, banished from the earth.*
   - He meant: President George W. Bush, it was reckless for you to launch the Iraq War in 2003! President Obama, end the war in Afghanistan now! Stop listening to the generals, including General David Petraeus, because "the wars are too important to be left to the generals". The Afghan War, any war, should not have been part of consideration for re-election!

2) *Observe good faith and justice toward all nations. Cultivate peace and harmony with all.*
   - He meant: Peace and prosperity. For more, read Chapter 61 ("Top 10 American Misconceptions about The World").

3) *The constitution vests the power of declaring war in Congress; therefore no offensive expedition of importance can be undertaken until after they shall have deliberated upon the subject and authorized such a measure.*
   - He meant: How many undeclared wars have we had after WWII?

4) *Government is not reason; it is not eloquent; it is force. Like fire, it is a dangerous servant and a fearful master.*
   - He meant: Limited government is the way to go!

5) *Over grown military establishments are under any form of government inauspicious to liberty, and are to be regarded as particularly hostile to republican liberty.*
   - He meant: Read Chapter 40 ("It's The Out-Of-Control Spending on Military, Stupid!").

6) *Labor to keep alive in your breast that little spark of celestial fire, called conscience.*
   - He meant: Read Chapter 4 ("Built to Last: Structure and Conscience").

7) *The basis of our political system is the right of the people to make and to alter their constitutions of government.*
   - He meant: For all the problems America has today, have you seen anything better than this diagnosis (Chapter 1) and this solution (Chapter 2)?

8) *The time is near at hand which must determine whether Americans are to be free men or slaves.*
   - He meant: Pay off the debts, or it will lead us all to slavery - debt slavery!

9) *We should not look back unless it is to derive useful lessons from past errors, and for the purpose of profiting by dearly bought experience.*
   - He meant: Peace and prosperity, not war and debt!

10) *Truth will ultimately prevail where there is pain to bring it to light.*
    - He meant: Democracy, as we know it today, no longer works. It's time to significantly amend the Constitution as suggested in Chapter 2!

Part 12: My Personal Life

Chapter 73: The Battle Hymn of the Tiger Dad
Chapter 74: My American Dream Has Come True
Chapter 75: My Father Li Dexin
Chapter 76: Parenting in America: 25 Years back and 25 Years Ahead
Chapter 77: My 30-Year College Graduation Reunion
Chapter 78: Swimming, Olympics, and More
Chapter 79: Olympics and Economies
Chapter 80: October 6, 1982

Chapter 73: The Battle Hymn of the Tiger Dad

(Initially published at GEI on 7/22/2011)

In her book Battle Hymn of the Tiger Mother, Amy Chua espoused one type of strict Asian-American parenting philosophy. The Time magazine made it a media sensation when it published an article entitled "Tiger Moms".

Here is an excerpt from the Bookmarks Magazine review:

> *Most critics agreed that Battle Hymn of the Tiger Mother is an entertaining read – Lively and humorous, written with the intent to shock. More controversial is Chua's stereotyping of Chinese and Western cultures, not to mention her authoritarian parenting methods. Critics judged the book largely by asking the following questions: Should self-esteem come before accomplishment, or accomplishment before self-esteem?*
>
> *If the latter, should it be achieved by threats and constant monitoring? Chua's teenage daughters are undeniably accomplished, but at what emotional cost? While some reviewers found that Chua's technique borders on abuse and her writing was, at best, self-serving, others were impressed by her parenting results and opined that the West could learn a few things from this remarkably driven Chinese American mother.*

Now, as a Tiger Dad, I feel obligated to speak out as follows: It is an interesting book, followed by many interesting articles in the media. While many points in the book are valid, the book effect for sensation is everywhere, inevitably and understandably.

Although I believe the Chinese way of "tough parenting" has many merits, the American way is better overall, and I have proven it!

1. Am I qualified to be a Tiger Dad?
Yes! In fact, I think I am more qualified to talk about the subject of "parenting in America the Chinese way" than Amy Chua for three main reasons as follows:
1) I was born in China, but Amy was not. I grew up in China, but Amy did not.
2) My wife was also born in China and grew up in China, but Amy's husband is a white man, thus nothing Chinese at all.
3) I have more complete results to show than Amy does! My two sons (ages 24 and 22) are beyond college, while Amy's two daughters have yet to go to college.

2. America vs. China in education
While the students in China are obviously better in math, the students in America are better overall (e.g. leadership, critical thinking, and social interaction) after high school. I mean those at the top brackets, such as the top 20% students in the top 20% schools.

3. My Chinese way in America
When in Rome, do it the Roman way! I was determined to raise my two sons the American way, which simply means this: Be good at some sports. After having them try several sports, I decided on swimming

for them in 1997. Both of them eventually became Illinois state champions and the rest is history. Along the way, they gave up many Chinese things, such as piano playing and the Saturday Chinese school. No, neither of them speaks Chinese today.

What about the schoolwork (through high school)? It's mostly in the genes! Additionally, I did set up a positive environment for them, such as scattering many good books around them when they were very young. Two things for sure though: (1) my wife and I never really helped them with any schoolwork, and (2) neither of them studied for the college exams. Strangely, they both ended up with the same ACT score (34) and almost identical SAT scores (~1500, math and verbal combined). These scores were hardly impressive by the Chinese standards. But swimming got my elder son into Yale (Economics) in 2005 (and he is now a successful trader on Wall Street), while overall quality led my younger son into GE (the leadership program) in January 2011, after three and a half years at Michigan (Business).

4. Closing

There are many ways to do the same thing. In parenting, between the Chinese way and the American way, I chose the latter and I am very happy about it! For more, read Chapter 76 ("Parenting in America").

Chapter 74: My American Dream Has Come True

(Initially published at GEI on 8/12/2011)

Despite all its problems, America remains the best land on earth, with many people, Americans or not, hoping to realize "my American dream."

There are many American dreams. Just to name a few: hitting a mega-lottery, owning a big house (the bigger, the better), having your own business, or just for freedom. Here is my American dream: to achieve modest financial independence and then do whatever I want, such as Writing about politics (e.g. this book) and on the scale industry.

Today, I have realized my own American dream, on top of being a proud "Tiger Dad" (Chapter 73)!

1. Growing up in China (1959 - 1982)
I was born in China in 1959 and grew up in the horrible days of the Cultural Revolution (1966-1976). I graduated from high school in 1976 without knowing what to do, as there was no college, nor jobs - much worse than an Egyptian teenager on the street today! Then good fortune came in 1977: China re-opened its universities after closing them for more than a decade, and I made into Zhejiang University, a top university in China! Moreover, as China continued to open up, I learned a lot more about the West – I was determined to see it, and the only way possible for me, or anybody in China then, to do it was to earn a scholarship.

I studied very hard in college. After scoring the top in a national exam for graduate studies abroad, I earned a

Chinese government scholarship and was sent to the University of Tokyo, the best university in Japan, in 1982. For more, read Chapter 80 ("October 6, 1982").

2. Studying in Japan (1982 - 1985)

I did well in Japan. Aside from the regular work toward my M.E. degree, I studied Japan in depth. Something memorable worth mentioning: I participated in a speech competition entitled "How should we contribute to the world peace?" I won, as shown by the photo below!

In hindsight, given the title of the speech, my instinct for politics was there – I just never had a chance to develop it until recently …

Okay, Japan was good. But it was only my first stop to see the West. In 1985, I gave up everything in Japan (e.g. the scholarship and Ph.D. in progress) and moved to America, as a Ph.D. student at Vanderbilt University.

3. Doing Ph.D. at Vanderbilt (1985 - 1988)

Upon landing in Nashville, I encountered two big problems right away: (1) my stipend of $10,000 a year was hardly enough to support the two of us (yes, I was just married), and (2) my English was gravely inadequate: I could hardly understand the people around me, let alone have any dialog! Fortunately, my job as a research assistant did not require much verbal communication up-front - just hacking out a lot of computer code with some good ideas and writing some research papers. I spent most of my time, often up to 14 hours a day, in front of a computer, while picking up English as fast as I could, with one simple goal in mind: finish here as soon as possible so as to start a "real life" anew!

Guess what? I finished my Ph.D. in a (then) record time of three short years! I was not the smartest around, but I was the most focused. Most importantly, I got the job done! Additionally, in 1987, my wife gave birth to our first child, who turned out to be a future Yale material (Chapter 76). Not bad for the first three years in America: a Ph.D. degree and a child!

4. Working in Europe (1988 - 1991)

I started my "real life" by joining a European company and moved to Brussels in 1988. It was my third big stop to see the West. I lived in Brussels for two and half years and traveled throughout Europe for both business and pleasure. Europe was good, but America was the best, especially for raising my family (Oh, my wife gave birth, in 1989, to our second child, who turned out to be a future leader at GE). With that conclusion, I joined NEC America and moved to Dallas in 1991. I finally settled down in America!

5. Working in Corporate America (1991 - 2004)

With a complete set of global experiences under my belt, I was ready to work my way up in Corporate America. However, a big problem soon became clear: I was a foreigner with a lot of deficiencies (e.g. English and cultural holes). To climb up the corporate ladder, I must overcome these deficiencies, fast. I tried, to the best of my ability, and I did move up steadily, but not fast enough for the ambitious me. Finally, after some 16 years in Corporate America (and Europe) with many ups and downs, including being fired a few times, I came to the conclusion that the only way for me to be happy was to run my own show, for which I had to start my own business.

6. Starting and running my own business (2005 - present)

I founded West-East International, an import-export company, on July 1, 2005. The first line of business was to sell "Made in China" transducers (which are the key components in electronic scales) in America. What a fun run since then! I wish I could have struck out on my own a lot earlier, such as in 1996 when I had the first opportunity. But I was too obsessed with Corporate America then to realize the opportunity.

Like all self-starters, I had to decide, as a first thing, how to position myself in the marketplace: a low-key also-ran or a high-profile game changer. The latter, of course! For example, it was not a fashionable thing to openly sell the transducers "Made in China" then, but I did it anyway. On top of everything, I went out of my way in marketing. For example, I managed to appear on the cover of "the Weighing and Measurement magazine in June 2007" (after being in that industry for barely two years) with an interview article (page 6), in which I clearly and boldly defined the industry for years to come, including the China factor. Controversial as it was at the time, that article remains a blueprint of the scale industry to date, time-tested!

Seven years and counting, we have succeeded wildly in the scale industry, because of our superior business model, a sharp vision, perfect execution, and a unique way of doing business (more on this later). As a result, we have expanded into multiple lines of business in multiple industries, including helping some American companies invest and do business in China.

7. Writing about politics (2008 - present)

With the success in business, I ventured into a new arena: Writing about politics. It all started in April 2008, after a sports writer at the Chicago Tribune wrote a nasty article about China's preparation for the Beijing Olympics. It was so unfair and irresponsible that "he is not going to get away with it without hearing from me." So I wrote him an email, and heated email exchanges ensued. When it was all said and done, I realized that the entire chain of emails could be a good material for customer education. So I emailed it to my customers and prospects. To my surprise, far more of them than I expected were sympathetic to my cause. More importantly, they found my writings interesting and educational. So I just followed with more writings and more emails. It is totally "out of control" now, as I publish weekly at Global Economic Intersection.

8. My way of doing business

One advantage of having your own business is that you can do whatever you want (and bear the consequence, of course). Here are three things I have done very differently from others in the scale industry:

1) I use email as a big marketing tool. Today, my at-least-twice-a-week email newsletters are very popular in the scale industry.
2) I found a way to fill my email newsletters with good contents. The Wednesday funnies are quality

jokes contributed by the scale men (and women) all over the world. My weekly publications at GEI fill up the Friday serious. According to the conventional wisdom, a businessman like me is not supposed to openly mix politics with business. Talking about politics in front of customers is a big no-no. But I did it anyway, with the calculation that I would win over, in the long run, a lot more loyal and better-educated customers (i.e. the winners). This strategy has worked out remarkably well for me.

3) I pay little attention to political correctness. I write uniquely not only because of my unique life experience, but also because I do not have a boss and I do not write for a living!

No guts, no glory! As my business becomes bigger and more successful, I will try a lot more new and big ideas, toward achieving my full potential!

9. Closing

My American dream has come true! To thank America maximally in my own way, I want to save it with my pen (or keyboard, to be more precise). I believe I have the most accurate diagnosis for America (Chapter 1), as well as the best solution (Chapter 2). What I need to do is to sell them – Is there a bigger challenge than that?

My writings are now widely enjoyed by many, to the point that I have been called "a modern-day Thomas Jefferson"! Can you believe this has actually happened, today in America, to an immigrant who grew up in China in the 1970s as a hopeless teenager?

Chapter 75: My Father Li Dexin

(Initially published at GEI on 4/27/2012)

My father Li Dexin passed away on April 17, 2012, at age 88.

His last significant job was the CPC (Communist Party of China) Secretary in the city of Hangzhou in the 1980s. So he was somebody in China, as evidenced by the following news:
1) My father's death as TV news in China.
2) My father's death as newspaper news in China.

Here is an excerpt from the news above: "Chinese Vice President Xi Jinping and former Premier Zhu Rongji sent their condolences and best wishes to the family." This was above and beyond the regular CPC protocol. So my father was not just somebody in China - he was special ...

1. Overview of my father's life

1.1 1924-1949
My father was born in 1924 into a family of a "rich peasant" (better than a landlord, but worse than a

peasant, in communist terms). He left home in 1942 to fight against the Japanese and joined the CPC in 1943. After Japan was defeated in 1945, he fought against the Nationalists, who retreated to Taiwan in 1949.

1.2 1949-1966

In 1949, as part of the CPC takeover, my father settled down in Zhejiang province. He rose steadily along the CPC ranks until 1966 (i.e. the beginning of the Cultural Revolution), when he was purged, together with tens of thousands of other CPC cadres.

From 1949 to 1966, he did not really know what he was doing, other than following Chairman Mao, a brilliant man proven to him throughout his life by then. He obviously did not know that Mao's talent was limited to military strategies.

Dad was a good writer and wrote quite a few significant articles for the CPC, especially for its leaders in Zhejiang. Some of them were really good (e.g. "turning Hangzhou into Geneva of the East"), but others were totally wrong, in my view today, of course.

1.3 1966-1976

This was the period of the Cultural Revolution. He spent the bulk of this period in a re-education camp and did hard labor. His faith in Mao was totally shaken and he started thinking in a new direction. As a result, he became a better man, older and wiser.

1.4 1977-1988

Mao died in 1976 and China changed. Many of the purged CPC cadres were called back, including Deng Xiaoping at the top and my father in the middle.

Dad got his first big career break to be an executive of some kind: He was named the CPC Secretary in Jinhua District. He led the economic reforms in the countryside big time. It was so big, bold, and controversial that it got the attention of Wan Li, China's First Vice Premier and a top reformer at the time. Wan not only supported him, but also spread his countryside reform model widely in China.

In 1983, Dad was promoted to be the CPC Secretary in Hangzhou. This gave him a big chance to carry out his economic reforms in a big city, especially for realizing his early dream of "turning Hangzhou into Geneva of the East". Again, it was big, bold, and controversial. Again, he had the support from the top guns like Wan.

Dad served out his first 5-year term hugely successfully, but he was ineligible for "re-election" for a second 5-year term because of the age limit (i.e. finishing the term at that level before age 65). He retired into a ceremonial role in 1988.

1.5 1989-1994

After the Tiananmen Square thing on June 4, 1989 (Chapter 13: "Tiananmen Square"), China swung to the left. Zhao Ziyang was purged and Dad was "investigated". The left-wing politicians who hated his reforms finally got a chance to get him. Luckily, he got away with a reprimand only (vs. jail), largely because he stayed clean economically, which has been the graveyard for many Chinese politicians.

Dad officially retired in 1994, when he reached 70 (again, because of the age limit).

1.6 1994-2012

Dad stayed active for the remainder of his life. He published many articles and books. His most significant contribution was the proposal of an "ocean economy", which laid the foundation for the development of Ningbo, Zhoushan, and the <u>longest sea-crossing bridge</u>.

2. My father and me

I was born in 1959. Life was generally good for me from 1959 to 1966, as both my parents were CPC cadres. However, everything turned bad after 1966: we were forced to move from a nice 5-room cottage to a 2-room dorm and lived there, without the parents around (as they were sent to different re-education camps), until late 1971. Worse yet, I was badly bullied not only in school, but also by the neighborhood kids. Miserable, totally!

Both my parents were fully back at work in 1977. By then I was a grown man. I was determined to leave China, and I did, in 1982. For more, read: Chapter 74 ("My American Dream Has Come True").

In 1994, I invited my parents to America. They spent six months with us and saw a lot of America, as I took them everywhere (e.g. Niagara Falls, Yellowstone, Disney World, Washington D.C., and NY City). Dad kept a diary throughout this period and published it in China after he went back, helping many Chinese understand America better.

Among all my siblings, I lived the least amount of time with my parents. To make up the lost time, I have been visiting China twice a year since 2005, spending some quality times with them.

As I get older, I find myself more and more resembling to my father. Two examples:
1) The interest in world politics.
2) The passion for writing.

Thanks, Dad, for the good genes!

3. Good-bye

On April 11, 2012, I flew from Chicago to Shanghai and arrived at home in Hangzhou on the evening of April 12. As always, I rushed to the hospital to see my parents, who have been there for the past few years. Although physically weak, mentally, Dad was as sharp as he was 30 years ago. We had a good talk for more than one hour and parted happily, with the agreement to talk again "tomorrow". However, about six hours later, we got an emergency call from the hospital, saying my father was in coma. We rushed to the hospital, only to learn that Dad had a massive internal brain bleeding. He never regained consciousness and passed away on April 17.

4. Closing

In the end, Dad cared about two things:
1) As a parent, he cared about the well-being of his five children. He was happy about it way before his end.
2) As a politician, he cared about how he would be remembered in history. He wasn't sure about it in the end.

Now, with the condolences from Xi Jinping, the next Chinese President, and Zhu Rongji, the top reformer in China in the 1990s, Dad should be all set.

Dad, rest in peace …

Chapter 76: Parenting in America: 25 Years Back and 25 Years Ahead

(Initially published at GEI on 5/4/2012)

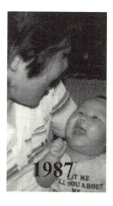 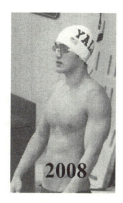

Twenty-five years ago today, I became a father: my first child was born on May 4, 1987. Happy birthday, Dan!

As parents, we all want to see our children do well. If they do, we are happy parents. If they don't, our hearts get broken. This is human nature, universally!

For a child to do well, all three elements must be right: parenting, self-effort, and the environment.

There has been no better environment than America anywhere in the world over the past 25 years! But will that still be true 25 years from now? I'm worried, deeply …

1. Some flashback

Twenty-five years ago, I was a Ph.D. student at Vanderbilt University, living on a research assistantship of $1,000 a month. Life was tough. Two examples:

1) In order to prepare for our first child to arrive, my wife and I moved from a 1-room studio to a 1-bedroom suite, an expensive, but absolutely necessary, upgrade!
2) After Dan was born, I moonlighted as a front-desk man downstairs in our on-campus dorm. It was a graveyard shift (12am-4am), at $5/hour, but good enough to buy a lot of diapers! Better yet, the job was basically duty-free, allowing me to do a lot of reading, writing, and thinking about my day-job (i.e. the Ph.D. work).

Most importantly, I was hopeful and determined: "I shall finish my Ph.D. as soon as possible, so as to start a real life anew." After all, a key reason for me to come to America in 1985 was to pursue a better life not only for myself, but also for my children ...

2. America, the beautiful!
Twenty-five years later, I am happy to say that I have made it! For more, read Chapter 74 ("My American Dream Has Come True").

What about Dan? He is on his way to making it too! In 2005, he became an Illinois state champion in swimming. More significantly, he was the only male high school graduate that year, in the entire state of Illinois, who made both IHSA's All-State Academic Team (13 males and 13 females) and the Chicago Tribune's Scholar-Athlete Team (10 males and 10 females). He graduated from Yale in 2009, and is now a successful trader on Wall Street. I am so proud of you, Dan!

Oh, my younger son is just as outstanding as his elder brother. I will write about him in two years, when he reaches 25.

America, what a beautiful country to live in!

America, what a great place to raise kids! For more, read Chapter 73 ("The Battle Hymn of The Tiger Dad")!

I love America!

3. Where is America today?
Unfortunately, America is deeply in trouble today! Here are two perspectives:
1) Debt slavery: why it destroyed Rome, why it will destroy us unless it's stopped.
2) Today's Reckless Spenders Enslave Future Generations.

Is the future referred to by these perspectives too far away for you? Read this: 53% of all young college graduates in America are either unemployed or underemployed!

Just as a parent has the duty to provide the best for his children, even if it means a lot of self-sacrificing, a country has the duty to provide the best for its next generation. America is ignoring this obligation and doing the exact opposite: our politicians are spending the financial futures of our children for political capital today! Watch this video: Spenditol - YouTube.

Why is that? Getting re-elected *ad nauseam* (Chapter 1)!

America needs to be saved!

4. Saving America

I believe I have the most accurate diagnosis for America (Chapter 1), as well as the best solution (Chapter 2).

Now, why should I, an electrical engineer by training and a businessman by practice, be so passionate about Writing about politics? It is my way of giving back to America!

America must be saved!

5. Closing

Unless we change soon, America will be finished, in far less than 25 years! What, then, will you say to your children or grandchildren 25 years from now?

Chapter 77: My 30-Year College Graduation Reunion

(Initially published at GEI on 6/1/2012)

On April 13-14, 2012, I attended a class reunion: the 30-year college graduation reunion of Class 77 - Industrial Automation, Electrical Engineering, Zhejiang University, China (note: "Class 77" in China equates to "Class 81" in the U.S.). It was an exciting event for me for three main reasons:
1) It was the first time ever for me to attend a reunion of this class.
2) It was by far the biggest reunion for this class: 43 out of the 48 people showed up.
3) It was the first time for me to meet with more than half of the former classmates over the past 30 years!

1. Class 77

This class was unique in two ways, at least:
1) We were admitted, in 1977, as the "first class" of "real" college students since 1966! Why the "first class"? Because the colleges were closed from 1966 to 1975 (thanks to Chairman Mao and the Cultural Revolution). Why "real"? Because although some colleges were re-opened in 1975, the students were admitted only by the recommendations of the working class (i.e. workers, peasants, and soldiers), with neither academic qualifications nor formal entrance exams. In contrast, we were admitted via a national exam, just like those before 1966 and after 1977.
2) Because of this 10-year gap in China's culture, my classmates varied hugely in age, from born in 1950

to born in 1961, an 11-year gap! It was quite an interesting class of people, with some dedicating themselves to chasing girls (or boys), while others barely reaching puberty ...

46 of us (40 men and six women) managed to graduate on time in January 1982, with the other two graduating in June 1982.

We then moved on in different directions, with some of the "better" students heading overseas (e.g. Japan, Germany, the U.K., and the U.S.). Today, we reside in two countries only: 37 in China and 11 in the U.S.

2. The U.S. vs. China

How do I compare the lives of those living in the U.S. with those living in China? Here is my assessment:
1) Education: Most of us living in the U.S. have Ph.D. degrees in engineering (from MIT to the University of Toledo), whereas the folks in China "wasted" less time as students. **Edge**: the U.S.
2) Career: Most of us living in the U.S. are engineers, whereas the folks in China may be doing better professionally: They are professors, high-ranking government officials, company owners, or high-level managers. **Edge**: China.
3) Family: Most of us living in the U.S. have more than one child, whereas the folks in China have only one (some do have two, but that is the result of two marriages). **Edge**: the U.S.
4) Retirement: Most of us living in the U.S. must work for a long time before being eligible for Social Security at age 65 (or possibly even later), whereas most of the folks in China are looking forward to retirement now (men at age 60 and women 55), if not retired already. **Edge**: China.

5) Standards of living: This is a no-brainer. **Edge**: the U.S.

Overall, the folks in the U.S. are better off, 3:2. So think I, at least. This becomes even more apparent when we ask our next generation in America: they are very happy to be Americans, today!

Here is what I learned recently from a second generation Chinese-American (not my children): "There is only one reason you don't like America - you are not very good!" Can it be expressed any better?

3. Class 77, again
Overall, we are perhaps the luckiest generation in Chinese history for two main reasons:
1) We were lucky to have made it into Class 77, right place and right time!
2) We have witnessed the spectacular changes in China over the past three decades (and counting), which is totally unprecedented in human history! For example, thirty years ago, a Chinese was lucky to have a new bicycle. Today, many of them have new cars! More importantly, the Chinese are now standing tall internationally, from the lowest thirty years ago!

4. Closing
We will have the next reunion in 10 years ...

Chapter 78: Swimming, Olympics, and More

(Initially published at GEI on 7/27/2012)

Olympics 2012 opens today in London.

On the USA Men's Swimming Team, there are three "special" Olympians from Illinois: Conor Dwyer, Matt Grevers, and Tyler McGill. Why are they so special to me? You will understand it by looking at the table below.

Memory	Month, Year	Meet	Event	Illinois State Champion	2nd Place	Comment
1	August, 1998	IL Swimming State Championships (Age Group 9-10)	200m free	Conor Dwyer	Ben Li	Ben is my younger son
2	February, 2002	IL High School Swimming State Championships	Total team score	NCHS - Naperville Central High School (Dan Li)	Lake Forest High School (Matt Grevers)	NCHS won by 1.5 points!
3	March, 2002	IL Swimming State Championships (Age Group 13-14)	50y free	Tyler McGill	Dan Li	Dan is my elder son

Congratulations to Conor, Matt, and Tyler! I have been watching you for more than a decade, from age groups, to high school, to NCAA, and all the way through the recent Olympic trials! Swim fast in London!

Like many sports parents, I dreamed about being an Olympian parent too. But that dream was soon dashed as I became more insightful into the sport(s):
1) It's all about height in the end! As they say in sports, there is only one thing that cannot be learned (or taught): height!
2) Height is mostly determined in genes! With two Asian parents, my two sons were limited in their potential in most sports for one simple reason: not tall enough!

So for my two sons, swimming was not an end in itself, but a means to excellence in life. Luckily, it has worked out well for them: They both became Illinois state champions and moved on with their lives beyond swimming (Chapter 73: "The Battle Hymn of The Tiger Dad").

Now, on Olympic swimming ... will Team USA do well in London? Yes! Will it achieve its full potential? No! Why? It's "tapering", stupid!

According to Wikipedia, tapering *"refers to the practice of reducing exercise in the days just before an important competition"*. USA Swimming holds its Olympic trials a few weeks before the Olympics. Most of the swimmers taper for, and peak at, the trials, without enough time to re-adjust for the Olympics (except for the overwhelmingly good swimmers like Michael Phelps and Ryan Lockte)! The Australian Team pointed this out to USA Swimming a few years ago when it revealed its secret of success: the Australian Olympic Team is formed around March, with enough time to train and taper for the Olympics! But for some reason, USA Swimming has yet to make this adjustment. Maybe it will do so after losing a few more times to the Australians ...

Next, you surely have heard about this story: U.S. Olympic Uniforms Spark Fury in Congress. Chicago Tribune's Philip Hersh has five words for Congress: "Put up or shut up." For more, read his article: On Olympics uniform issue, Congress wears the emperor's new clothes. I enjoyed reading it!

Now, on Philip Hersh - he got me into Writing about politics four years ago! Here is an excerpt from Chapter 74 ("My American Dream Has Come True"):

> "It all started in April 2008, after a sports writer at the Chicago Tribune wrote a nasty article about China's preparation for the Beijing Olympics. It was so unfair and irresponsible that 'he is not going to get away with it without hearing from me.' So I wrote him an email, and heated email exchanges ensued ..."

That sports writer was Philip Hersh! Was that article of his "nasty" in hindsight? Yes! Beijing Olympics 2008 was a spectacular success and will remain one of the best Olympics, ever!

Finally, on the Olympics beyond swimming ... here are five big questions for you to ponder:
1) Why do you have to be black to run fast and jump long?
2) Why do Africans dominate long distance running?
3) Why are the whites so dominant in the high jump.
4) Why are Asians so hopeless in almost all sports other than their "own" (e.g. ping pong and badminton)?
5) Why is there an age limit (i.e. 16) in women's gymnastics, but not in other sports (e.g. swimming)?

Hint: the answers lie in race, genes, and politics! I will discuss them in future writings. Meanwhile, let's just enjoy Olympics 2012: swimming, track & field, gymnastics, and much more, while keeping this subject in mind: U.S. Versus China in Olympic Medal Count.

Chapter 79: Olympics and Economies

(Initially published at GEI on 8/17/2012)

London Olympics 2012 closed on August 12.

I spent numerous hours watching it, and enjoyed it more than any of the previous Olympics, thanks largely to the "Illinois Three" (Chapter 78: "Swimming, Olympics, and More"). Better yet, they all won gold medals! So special congratulations to Conor Dwyer, Matt Grevers, and Tyler McGill! Great jobs in London! You made Illinois swimmers and parents proud!

Congratulations to Team USA for the outstanding performances and wonderful results, especially for winning the medal race against China!

1. The Olympics

The Olympics are great! Despite all the problems, from the past (e.g. 2002 Winter Olympic bid scandal) to the present (e.g. Olympics shot put champ stripped of gold for doping), the Olympics remain one of the best venues for world peace. This is particularly important today, when there are so many [armed] conflicts all over the world.

As a worldly person, you should have watched Olympics 2012. As an American, you should have paid attention to the medal table, which in itself was an Olympic race between the U.S. and China, not only this time, bus also over the past decade.

2. The U.S. vs. China at the Olympics

Here is a recent article in the Chicago Tribune (8/13/2012): Team USA back on top in gold, overall medals counts. Additionally, there was a full page to graphically depict "how U.S. topped China" at Olympics 2012.

A win is a win is a win. Congratulations to Team USA! However, after celebrating the win "battle", we must face the reality that the U.S. may be losing the "war" ...

3. The U.S.- China race on overall medal count

Table 1 below shows the race over the past seven Olympics, from 1988 to 2012.

Overall medals won	1988	1992	1996	2000	2004	2008	2012
The U.S.	94	108	112	94	102	110	104
China	28	54	54	58	63	100	88
Total medals awarded	739	815	842	928	929	958	962

The graph below visualizes Table 1 "horizontally".

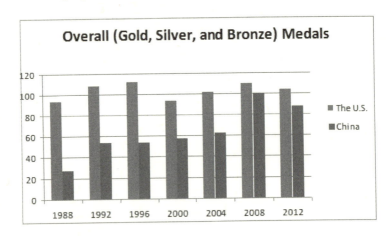

Two notes:
1) The U.S. has been steady, with its overall medal count being around 100.
2) China has been rising rapidly, from 28 in 1988 to 88 in 2012.

Two pie charts below visualize Table 1 "vertically" for 1988 and 2012, respectively.

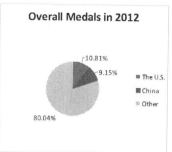

Three notes:
1) The size of the pie increased from 739 in 1988 to 962 in 2012.
2) China's share increased significantly from 3.79% in 1988 to 9.15% in 2012, an increase of more than 240%!
3) America's share actually decreased from 12.72% in 1988 to 10.71% in 2012.

4. Why has America's share decreased?
Three main reasons:
1) The rise of China.
2) The rise of the rest (vs. the West). For example, the athletes from the Caribbean countries (e.g. Jamaica) now dominate the sprinting events on the track (e.g. 100 and 200-meter dashes), while African athletes dominate in distance running (e.g. 800 meters and up). They are gaining their shares, mostly at America's expense.
3) America's stagnation.

5. Is it a big deal to lose shares?
No, it's not a big deal, if you think the Olympic medal count is merely a bragging right for a country.

Yes, it's a big deal, if it mirrors the economies as follows:
1) Not only is the U.S. dominance over, the U.S. has actually been in a decline, with its share getting smaller over time.
2) China is rising rapidly, with no end in sight.
3) For the U.S., this time it's different: the Chinese are not like the East Germans or the Soviets a few decades ago. Specifically,
    - The Chinese are for real. Behind China's Olympic medal count is the strength of its economy and a big wallet, stuffed with more than a trillion US dollars (and growing) as the U.S. debt to China.
    - China's rise is sustainable, because China's system, overall, appears to be slightly better than America's system.

Consequentially, unless there is a change in the system on the U.S. side, the same trend will continue.

6. Understanding China better

It's not easy for Americans to acknowledge the unwelcome trend and understand the real reasons behind it, thanks to brainwashing in America (e.g. China's Gold Standard and Medals come at a cost). For example, China's Project 119 is often depicted as evil in the U.S. media (e.g. While China is busy winning, its athletes might be losing), but it is actually an open secret behind China's success! Here is a description of Project 119 per Wikipedia:

With the awarding of the Games of the XXIX Olympiad of 2008 to Beijing in 2001, the government of China embarked on a program to increase its medal load. Project 119 was established to gain medals in the sports of Track and Field, Swimming, Rowing & Canoe/Kayak and Sailing. These sports had a total gold medal count of 119 in the 2000 Summer Olympics. At those Games, China had only won one medal in all these sports. China wished to finish on top of the medal count and gold medal total at its own games

To me, Project 119 was brilliant. After all, I did a similar "project" for my two sons: I carefully studied several sports in the sports frantic America, and strategically chose swimming as their sport (before they became obnoxiously rebellious), which worked out very well (Chapter 73: "The Battle Hymn of The Tiger Dad").

Now, for those Americans who still don't feel a sense of urgency, let's look at the race for the gold medals ...

7. The U.S.- China race on gold medal count

Table 2 below shows the race for the gold medals between the U.S. and China:

Gold medals won	1988	1992	1996	2000	2004	2008	2012
The U.S.	36	37	44	37	36	36	46
China	5	16	16	28	32	51	38
Total medals awarded	241	260	271	300	301	302	302

The graph below visualizes Table 2 horizontally. As you can see, the race for the gold is even closer than that for the overall, with China being on the top once already in 2008!

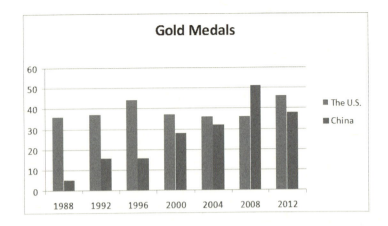

China's share increase in gold becomes even more striking than in overall when Table 2 is visualized vertically with two pie charts below for 1988 and 2012, respectively.

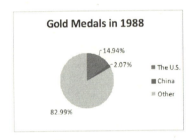 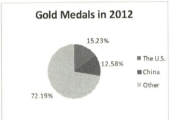

Three notes:
1) The size of the pie increased from 241 in 1988 to 302 in 2012.
2) China's share significantly increased from 2.07% in 1988 to 12.58% in 2012, an increase of more than 600%!
3) The U.S.'s share increased slightly from 14.94% in 1988 to 15.23% in 2012.

8. Discussion

Sports are a big deal in the U.S., and it's a good thing (Chapter 76: "Parenting in America: 25 Years Back and 25 Years Ahead"), although commercial sports are becoming more and more questionable nowadays (e.g. Penn State Hit with $60 Million Fine).

China may never surpass the U.S. as the kingdom of sports. But China is destined to win more medals than the U.S. in the coming Summer Olympics, in both the gold and overall. Why? It's the system, stupid! There is a system in China for winning more and more Olympic medals. But there is no such system in the U.S., only the massive talent and a lot of potential for personal gains, which eventually will prove inadequate against the Chinese system and the Chinese "machines" (e.g. diving).

I predict China will win more medals than the U.S. in the Summer Olympics by 2030, when China's economy will surpass the U.S. economy. I can even predict where the biggest difference will be made between now and 2030: swimming! Three reasons:
1) There are a lot of medals in swimming!
2) Unlike track & field, swimming is a sport for which the Chinese can be hopeful. I reached this conclusion in 1997 when I enrolled my two sons in competitive swimming (Chapter 73), and I stand by this conclusion today.
3) China already has its super-stars in Sun Yang and Ye Shiwen. Just need a few more! America, you have been forewarned …

9. Closing

The Olympic medal count is a big deal, but the economies are far bigger deals. Amazingly, they seem to go hand in hand …

Chapter 80: October 6, 1982

(Initially published at GEI on 10/6/2012)

Do you remember what you were doing on October 6, 1982? Perhaps not, as it was 30 years ago! But I do, because it was a special day for me – I left China, finally, on that day, for Japan!

No, I did not leave China in a boat. Nor did I sneak out of China in darkness. Rather, together with other 149 "special" Chinese students, I left China with a huge honor: we were chosen by the government to pursue graduate degrees in Japan! We were warmly sent off by some Chinese officials, in anticipation that we would all come back home, upon completion of our studies, for the modernization of China.

1. How were we chosen?

Via the exams for graduate schools before we finished college in early 1982! Yes, we were part of Class 77 (Chapter 77: "My 30-Year College Graduation Reunion").

My graduate school exam consisted of five parts as follows:
1) English (a national exam)
2) Political Science (a national exam)
3) Advanced Math (Zhejiang Univ.'s exam)
4) Advanced Electrical Engineering (Zhejiang Univ.'s exam)
5) Advanced Electronics (Zhejiang Univ.'s exam)

I scored the best in my major and earned a slot to Japan. The other 149 folks went through a similar process in the top universities all over China.

Here was a big problem: many of us, including me, did not know a single word of Japanese ... No problem – the government planned it way ahead already!

2. How were we prepared for Japan?

In March 1982, all 150 of us were gathered in two places in Northeast China (100 in Dalian and 50, including me, in Changchun) to study Japanese. It was a crash course in Japanese: 10 hours a day, five days a week, for six months, with all the teachers being Japanese! What a great way to quickly learn a difficult foreign language!

Ready or not, all 150 of us boarded a giant chartered plane to Tokyo on October 6, 1982.

3. To which universities did we go?

Because we were absolutely the best and brightest students from China, and the first large group of graduate students ever sent out by the People's Republic of China to Japan, we were entitled to attend the best universities in Japan. Otherwise, it would have been an intolerable insult to China, would it not?

No problem – the Chinese government worked it out with the Japanese government way ahead: We were assigned to the seven "Imperial Universities" (i.e. Tokyo, Kyoto, Osaka, Nagoya, Tohoku, Hokkaido, and Kyushu), plus Tokyo Institute of Technology (a.k.a. Japan's MIT) and The University of Tsukuba (Japan's new all-tech university).

I was assigned to the University of Tokyo (a.k.a. Japan's Harvard), and was very happy about it - it must have been the exam score! See, "*just do well in school, good life will follow*," as a Chinese proverb says ...

The photo below shows the author in 1982, shortly after arriving in Japan.

4. Where are we now?

In 1985, I was the first, out of the original 150, to leave Japan, on my own, for a better place called "the United States of America". About 10 folks followed me to the U.S. in their own ways later. Most of the rest completed their degrees (mostly Ph.D.) in Japan and went back to China. Many have since become VIPs in China, as they helped China fundamentally change itself for the better over the past two decades.

As for me personally, read Chapter 74 ("My American Dream Has Come True"). Over the past decade, I have devoted a lot of effort to the positive development of the U.S.-China relations, and will continue to do so for the rest of my life.

5. Closing

Someday, we will have a re-union. I am sure all of us will have different stories to tell. But one thing in common is that we all shall remember October 6, 1982. It was what we all worked hard for throughout college and it was the date that profoundly changed us all …

Epilogue

The 2012 U.S. election is over. As a staunch supporter of Mitt Romney, I was deeply disappointed by Romney's loss! But was I surprised by it? No, not at all! As a matter of fact, in my open letter to Mitt Romney dated 5/18/2012 (Chapter 26), not only did I predict the eventual outcome, I also spelled out a virtually guaranteed path to success for Romney. Unfortunately, he did not listen.

Where will America go from here? I am not optimistic. Two predictions:
1) President Obama will compete with President Kennedy for the title of the worst American President ever.
2) It's time for the GOP to seriously adjust, if it hopes to win another presidential race within the next decade. One way to do it is to endorse this book.

Coincidentally, less than 10 days after the 2012 U.S. election, China changed its leadership too. Will the new Chinese leaders meet their challenges? Let's wait and see. Oh, what is the biggest challenge ahead for the Chinese leaders? *"The smooth ride set out by Deng will be over soon. A new greatness must appear for the next China"* (Chapter 3).

Now, do you still remember the image below?

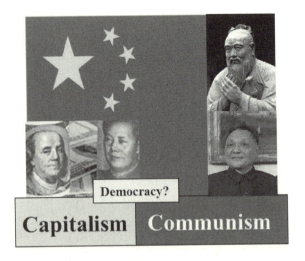

It is the caption picture for Part 6 ("China: in Some Depth"). But I have yet to explain it in any way. Why not? It's a puzzle for you and the Chinese leaders to solve!

Meanwhile, the race between the U.S. and China will continue. Which one will come out on top? China! Why and how? Capitalism and adaptability!

America must be saved, now!

Once America is saved, I will write a companion book entitled "Saving China, American Style". But will that day ever come? Will that ever be necessary? Let's wait and see …

About the Author

Frank (Xiaofeng) Li (厉晓峰) is the Founder and President of W.E.I. (West-East International), a Chicago-based import & export company.

Frank was born in Hangzhou, China, in 1959, and grew up in the horrible days of the Cultural Revolution. He was a hopeless teenager when China re-opened its universities in 1977, after closing them for more than a decade! He was lucky enough to have made into Class 77.

Frank received his B.E. degree from Zhejiang University (China) in 1982, M.E. from the University of Tokyo in 1985, and Ph.D. from Vanderbilt University in 1988, all in Electrical Engineering. He worked for several companies all over the world until 2005, when he founded his own company W.E.I. Today, W.E.I. is a leader in the scale industry not only in products & services, but also in thought & action.

Frank started writing about business and politics in 2008. Since May 2011, he has been a weekly columnist at Global Economic Intersection. He writes extensively and uniquely about American politics, for which he has been called a "modern-day Thomas Jefferson."

Z240_037_50

6x9

PAPERBACK

CREAM_60LB

207-412

Due Date